Governance and Public Management

Series Editors
Robert Fouchet
Universite Aix Marseille
Marseille, France

Juraj Nemec
Faculty of Economics and Administration
Masaryk University
Brno, Czech Republic

IIAS
International Institute
of Administrative Sciences

IIAS Series: Governance and Public Management
International Institute of Administrative Sciences (IIAS) –
Improving Administrative Sciences Worldwide

To cover the diversity of its members, the IIAS has set up four sub-entities:– The EGPA (European Group for Public Administration)– The IASIA (International Association of Schools and Institutes of Administration)– The LAGPA (Latin American Group for Public Administration)– The AGPA (Asian Group for Public Administration) Website: http://www.iias-iisa.org *Governance and Public Management Series* The *Governance and Public Management* series, published in conjunction with the International Institute of Administrative Sciences (IIAS), brings the best research in public administration and management to a global audience. Encouraging a diversity of approach and perspective, the series reflects the Institute's conviction for a neutral and objective voice, grounded in the exigency of fact. How is governance conducted now? How could it be done better? What defines the law of administration and the management of public affairs, and can their implementation be enhanced? Such questions lie behind the Institute's core value of *accountability*: those who exercise authority must account for its use to those on whose behalf they act. All books in the series are subject to Palgrave's rigorous peer review process: https://www.palgrave.com/gb/demystifying-peer-review/792492.

More information about this series at
http://www.palgrave.com/gp/series/15021

Michiel S. de Vries · Juraj Nemec
David Špaček
Editors

Performance-Based Budgeting in the Public Sector

palgrave
macmillan

Editors
Michiel S. de Vries
Department of Public Administration and Institute of Management Research
Radboud University Nijmegen
Nijmegen, The Netherlands

Juraj Nemec
Department of Public Economics, Faculty of Economics and Administration
Masaryk University
Brno, Czech Republic

David Špaček
Department of Public Economics, Faculty of Economics and Administration
Masaryk University
Brno, Czech Republic

ISSN 2524-728X ISSN 2524-7298 (electronic)
Governance and Public Management
ISBN 978-3-030-02076-7 ISBN 978-3-030-02077-4 (eBook)
https://doi.org/10.1007/978-3-030-02077-4

Library of Congress Control Number: 2018959241

This Palgrave Macmillan imprint is published by the registered company Springer Nature Switzerland AG
The registered company address is: Gewerbestrasse 11, 6330 Cham, Switzerland

Preface

This book is the result of a collaboration of scholars of many different countries. They were all asked by the editors to describe and analyze if there was any performance-based budgeting in their countries, how this had developed through time, and where the country stands now in that regard. Performance-based budgeting as such is seen as a welcome development as it seeks to improve expenditure efficiency by systematically linking funding to results making use of performance information to achieve that linkage. It is an instrument to get value for money when taxpayer's money is involved and that value is found in the performance of the agency receiving funding out of collective resources.

Nonetheless, many dilemmas are involved. The introduction of performance-based budgeting suffers from all kinds of side-effects, notably its perversity effect—e.g., manipulation of performance outputs and the gaming involved; its futility effect—e.g., the non-use of the performance information; and its jeopardy effects—e.g., the costs involved in juggling statistics that could better have been invested elsewhere. These three effects are visible in all countries incorporated in this book. Seemingly, this could result in the conclusion that it is better to refrain from such budgeting. That is, however, not the conclusion drawn here. Seen in the practices in different countries is also that the appearance of such effects is temporary as the performance measurement, the indicators, the controls et cetera through time evolve and close the system in such a way that the nasty side-effects are minimized. The way performance-based budgeting develops shows that the actors responsible for performance-based budgeting increasingly recognize the effects and over time deal with these effects. Thus such systems tend to improve, although do not always have become optimal.

The different chapters in this book describe how those developments are ongoing in different countries, how governments 'learn' how to improve on this type of budgeting, and how such developments can be explained. The chapters provide information on the way this evolved in countries not often incorporated in comparative research in Public Administration and Management, such as South Africa, the Ukraine, and Russia.

All this results in the hypothesis formulated at the end of this book that the introduction of performance-based budgeting is perhaps in need of the initial 'bolt holes' enabling stakeholders to abuse the system as this reduces potential resistance to its implementation. Once a performance-based budgeting system is introduced, the recognition and visualization of the opportunistic behavior being the result of the imperfections in the performance base, might result in a shared view about these imperfections and in a consensus that the system should and could improve. Seen in all the countries investigated in this book is that this does indeed result in adaptations meant to reduce the possibilities for manipulation of performance outputs, the non-use of the performance information, and the costs involved in juggling statistics.

This book would not have been possible if it were not for the existence of international organizations like NISPAcee, IIAS, EGPA and IASIA, and the international conferences they organize. It is during such conferences that scholars conducting research into the same issues of the public sector meet, discuss, and start to collaborate. This book is the result of such collaboration (especially of the work of the IASIA Working Group VI: Public Sector Governance, Leadership and Management and the NISPAcee Working Group on Public Finance and Public Financial Management). The preparation of this book was possible also thanks to the direct support from the Czech Research Agency GACR, the research project "Performance Management in Public Administration: Theory and Practice in the Czech Republic and Other CEE Countries", ID (CEP) GA16-13119S.

Special thanks to Diya Elizabeth Abraham—without her help during the editing process this publication would not be possible.

Brno, Czech Republic — Juraj Nemec
Brno, Czech Republic — David Špaček
Nijmegen, The Netherlands — Michiel S. de Vries

Acknowledgements

Preparation of this book was supported from the project of the Czech Science Foundation GA16-13119S and from the project of the Grant agency of Masaryk Uuniversity MUNI/A/1223/2018.

Contents

Notes on Contributors

Nadezhda Bobcheva serves her second term as a municipal councilor at the Municipal Council of Silistra (Bulgaria). At present, she is the Deputy Chairperson of the Municipal Council of Silistra and chairs the Standing committee on Regional and International co-operation, Projects and Programmes. Her professional experience also encompasses work as a civil servant in both local and regional governments. She has been a team member, coordinator and consultant in projects focused on local development. Her main fields of interest include public finance, public service provision, and inter-municipal cooperation.

Tjerk Budding is program director of the postgraduate program for Certified Public Controller at the Vrije Universiteit Amsterdam, The Netherlands. His research interests include performance management, cost accounting, and financial accounting. He published in leading accounting journals such as *Management Accounting Research* and *Financial Accountability & Management.* He is co-author of the book *Public Sector Accounting.*

Michiel S. de Vries is full professor of the Department of Public Administration and of the Institute of Management Research at Radboud University of Nijmegen (The Netherlands) and distinguished professor at Kaunas Technological University (Lithuania). His research concentrates on local government, policy evaluation, policy change and comparative public administration. He recently published the monograph *Understanding Public Administration* (Palgrave).

Joseph Drew is a Senior Research Fellow in the Institute for Public Policy and Governance at the University of Technology Sydney. His research interests focus on expenditure and revenue structures for local government, performance measurement and corporate governance. Previously Joseph worked in senior management positions in performance monitoring within the retail banking sector. Joseph is the author of over 40 scholarly works and has consulted with numerous Victorian and New South Wales councils on municipal reform, accounting, finance and economic matters.

Bram Faber is Ph.D. student at the Zijlstra Center for Public Control, Governance & Leadership of the Vrije Universiteit Amsterdam. His research interests include innovations in public accountability, and uses of ICT in public sector reporting and service delivery.

Nirmala Govender is the Head: Performance Monitoring and Evaluation at eThekwini Municipality in South Africa. She is a Certified Internal Auditor (CIA), has a Bachelor of Accountancy Degree, a Post Graduate Diploma in Business Administration and a Masters in Business Administration (MBA). She is currently a doctoral student.

Nataliia Grynchuk is Associate professor, Ph.D. in Economics, Associate Professor of the Regional Administration, Local Self-Government and Urban Management Department, National Academy of Public Administration under the President of Ukraine, Kyiv, Ukraine. She is the author of more than 100 publications on regional and local development, public policies, and governance. She has participated in many national and international research projects, in particular with the Network of Institutes and Schools of Public Administration in Central and Eastern Europe.

Štefan Hronec focuses on public sector, public services, public sector funding, budgeting, and public service planning within his pedagogical and scientific research activities. He is the author of 5 scientific monographs, co-author of 1 university textbook, 3 textbooks and more than 90 scientific articles. He regularly performs at relevant domestic and foreign conferences. It has outputs registered in the Scopus database and in the WoS database. Within the framework of scientific and research activities he cooperated on projects of international and national importance (APVV, VEGA, GACR, NISPAcee, etc.).

Robert Jahoda lectures Public Finance at Masaryk University. He is a member of the Czech Expert Committee for Family Policy and a member of the European Social Policy Network, which aims to provide independent expertise in the Czech social policy to the European Commission. He publishes in both local and foreign journals.

Andrey Klimenko is director of the Institute for Public Administration and Governance and Head of School of Public Administration of National Research University Higher School of Economics. He took an active part in research and the development of the concept of administrative reform in Russia, as well as in elaboration of strategic proposals on the modernization of Russian civil service, performance management and budgeting. He also contributes to the development of bachelors and masters programs in Public Administration.

Maja Klun is Professor of Economics in Public Sector at Faculty of Administration, University of Ljubljana. Her main fields of research are public finance and economics of public sector. She publishes in different journals and conference papers and is co-author and co-editor of scientific monographs.

Nicole Küchler-Stahn is Professor for Public and Nonprofit Management at Frankfurt University of Applied Sciences. Her research deals with performance budgeting and performance management in the public and nonprofit sector.

Sara Giovanna Mauro is Research Fellow at the Institute of Management, Scuola Superiore Sant'Anna of Pisa. She holds a Ph.D. in Management. Her primary research interests are in public sector accounting and management, with a focus on performance budgeting, performance management, participatory budgeting and co-production.

Juraj Nemec is Professor of Public Finance and Public Management at Masaryk University in Brno, Czech Republic and at Matej Bel University Banska Bystrica, Slovakia, with 36 years of experience in teaching in public finance, public sector management, health economics and policy. He published over 400 books, book chapters and scientific articles. He holds several positions in international organizations in the public administration area.

Peter Pisár is Associate Professor at the Faculty of Economics, Matej Bel University in Banska Bystrica. Since 2003 he has been working at the Department of Finance and Accounting. The focus of his research is public finance, financial management in the public sector and innovation policies, with emphasis on public budgets management, public support policies and innovation public support. In this area, he also actively works in private sector non-profit institutions. He is supervisor of doctoral students in the field of public finance and public policy.

Purshottama S. Reddy is a Senior Professor at the University of Kwazulu Natal in South Africa. He is currently the Vice President of the International Association of Schools and Institutes of Administration (IASIA): Programmes, the Project Director of the Working Group on Subnational Governance and Development of the IASIA. He is a rated researcher and the editor/coeditor of ten books.

Christoph Reichard is Professor Emeritus of Public Management and a member of the Potsdam Center for Policy and Management at the University of Potsdam. Some of his recent research topics deal e.g., with budgeting, accounting reforms in Europe, performance management, organization of public service delivery, public sector education.

Roberta Ryan is a leading social researcher and policy, program evaluation and stakeholder engagement practitioner with over 30 years' experience in both the public and private sectors. Roberta is the Director of the Institute for Public Policy and Governance and the Centre for Local Government at the University of Technology Sydney. Roberta has completed over 300 social research and evaluation projects, including major national reviews and evaluations, methodologically complex projects using outcome and process evaluation approaches, program logic and many service reviews and evaluations.

Miroslav Šipikal is Associate Professor at the University of Economics in Bratislava. Since 2005 he has been teaching at the Department of Public Administration and Regional Development, Faculty of National Economy of University of Economics in Bratislava. His main research interest has been regional policy, education, evaluation of regional policy measures.

David Špaček is Associate Professor at the Department of Public Economics, Faculty of Economics and Administration, Masaryk University, Brno. His primary research interests are in public administration and management, with a focus on performance management, quality management, strategic management, e-government/e-governance and human resources management.

Ed Vosselman is Professor of Accounting at Radboud University. His research interests particularly concern the accounting-control-trust nexus in both private and public organizations. He is a member of the Editorial Board of *Qualitative Research in Accounting and Management* and *Maandblad voor Accountancy en Bedrijfseconomie*. Currently, he is strongly engaged with issues of controllership and performance management, particularly in public sector organizations. During eight years, under the umbrella of the Dutch Association of Controllers, he chaired a Quality Assurance Committee in which program managers of all postgraduate courses in Controlling at Dutch universities participated. In the context of the 'Dutch Association of Supervisors in Health Care Organizations' he chairs a Committee Innovations in Supervisory Boards.

Aziza Zemrani is Associate Professor at the University of Texas Rio Grande Valley. The author has a long history of academic and public service both in the United States and abroad. She has worked for the government of Morocco as well as numerous American institutions. Her area of interest is budgeting, and finance, both national and international, and cultural competency.

List of Figures

List of Tables

PART I

Introduction

CHAPTER 1

Dilemmas in Performance-Based Budgeting

Michiel S. de Vries and Juraj Nemec

1.1 Introduction

The central theme of this book are the many dilemmas and paradoxes of performance-based budgeting. In itself performance-based budgeting is laudable, as tax-payers' money should be invested in such a way that government is able to function, and the concept is central to measuring *what the public sector is accomplishing with the resources provided*, as distinct from the narrower focus on how much money is being spent in any area (cf. World Bank 2010, p. 15). However, as a recent OECD report stated "Performance budgeting frameworks are abundant in the OECD but are generally flexible and not linked with allocation decisions" (OECD 2014, p. 76). Further—"In general it appears that line ministries in 2011 use performance information less than in 2007 and more countries

M. S. de Vries (✉)
Department of Public Administration and Institute of Management Research, Radboud University Nijmegen, Nijmegen, The Netherlands
e-mail: m.devries@fm.ru.nl

J. Nemec
Department of Public Economics, Faculty of Economics and Administration, Masaryk University, Brno, Czech Republic
e-mail: juraj.nemec@umb.sk

M. S. de Vries et al. (eds.), *Performance-Based Budgeting in the Public Sector*, Governance and Public Management,
https://doi.org/10.1007/978-3-030-02077-4_1

report that performance information is 'not used' in budget negotiations. When performance targets are not met, there are oftentimes 'no consequences'" (ibid.).

At a scholarly level, Breul (2007, p. 330) states that "systematic integration of performance into budget decision making has yet to occur." His explanation is that "Notwithstanding the effort to date, it continues to be difficult to assess systematically either the effectiveness of programs or their relative efficiency when compared with similar activities in other areas of government and the private sector." Schick (2014) asked in a recent paper "Why doesn't results information weigh more heavily in budget work? Given large investments in measuring performance and collecting relevant data, why hasn't the expectation that better-informed governments will make more effective use of public money been realized?" (p. 10) and "Can governments perform if budgets do not?" (p. 28). In the same vein, Willoughby and Benson (2011, p. 1) conclude, "Unfortunately, establishing a direct link between and among performance measurement, program evaluation and final appropriations remains elusive." Moynihan and Beazley (2016, p. 12) claim "Information about inputs is still perceived as the most vital data in annual budget decisions" and regarding performance budgeting, "A sober look at their experience makes it hard to avoid the conclusion that it is time to rethink what purposes it serves and how to customize approaches to each unique country context." Furthermore, Tarschys (2002, p. 99) tells us that "Public institutions and public policy programs have developed impressive survival skills, sometimes in spite of very modest results. Integrating performance evaluation into the budgetary process has proved to be difficult."

These introductory remarks result in the provocative question whether the concept of performance-based budgeting is ready for retirement. This question is asked, because many American scholars argue that performance budgeting started in 1950. If this is true, it implies that the concept is by now almost 70 years old and this poses the question, whether its life cycle (and limited results achieved) provides indications that it is time for the pensioning off of this concept which once was intended to modernize government. This book will argue that the opposite is the case. Whereas performance budgeting has been criticized in theory for its limitations, it is simultaneously increasingly popular among some governments. The OECD (2014) mentions the Netherlands and New Zealand as front-runners in performance budgeting, but as different authors in this book show, many developing countries are rapidly catching up, if not outpacing these two countries—especially in their quantity of performance schemes. Major international organizations, especially the World Bank, recommend the introduction of performance budgeting as the core element of public finance reforms—and provide financial and advisory resources for this. However, the impact of new schemes remains rather limited, as some of the chapters in this book clearly document.

In order to understand what is going on, we first analyze the development of performance-based budgeting through the years. This introductory chapter embeds the contents of this book within existing theories of performance-based budgeting and structures the subsequent chapters. First, we address the meaning of performance-based budgeting, how it compares to previous patterns of budgeting, how it first came onto the agenda, and its subsequent development. Like all concepts in Public Administration there were several phases to its development. This raises the question of whether the time has come to adopt a new approach, or whether we should stick with a concept that many countries still think is very relevant?

1.2 Performance-Based Budgeting

Although many definitions of performance-based budgeting exist, the original idea was to relate budgets for programs to their performance, at least to a certain level. In the most direct case performance-based budgeting relates to the following—if a program could show it performs, then it is entitled to more money, and if it doesn't, its funding is to be decreased or even ended. For example, Behn (1994, p. 70) argues that performance budgeting aims to: "Measure the performance of different agencies, and then adjust agency budgets accordingly. Agencies that do a good job should have their budgets increased. Agencies that do a poor job should have their budgets cut." In less direct cases performance-based budgeting is a budgeting system where the input costs are related to the performance.

In all its forms, performance-based budgeting seeks to improve expenditure efficiency by systematically linking funding to results, making use of performance information to achieve that linkage (Robinson 2002). Robinson and Brumby (2005, p. 5) define performance budgeting in a somewhat more modest way, as "procedures or mechanisms intended to strengthen links between the funds provided to public sector entities and their outcomes and/or outputs through the use of formal performance information in resource allocation decision-making." Its main object is to attain "greater rationality in expenditure planning, with the aim of allocating limited funds more effectively to the areas where they will be of greatest social benefit" (Robinson and Brumby 2005, p. 15).

In order to understand the implications of performance-based budgeting it is necessary to discuss its constituent terms, that is budgeting and performance.

Formally, a budget is a financial statement prepared preferably before the beginning of the year (but in some countries delayed), in order to forecast the expenditures and revenues for that year (Brusca et al. 2018, p. 171). Another way of putting it, is that "it is a document, or a collection of documents that define(s) the number of resources available to fund expenditures in a given period of time" (Saliterer et al. 2018, p. 146).

The classic budget is usually represented as a financial plan, especially in its classic form of an annual revenue-expenditure budget. In this form it serves several main purposes:

a. Planning document—statement of expected pattern of income and anticipated expenditure. The planning process takes place before the budget is implemented.
b. After authorization, and especially in its more detailed form, the budget serves as a control device.
c. In addition to its main role, the budget also frequently performs other functions—in particular it can serve as a policy document and communication tool.

Budgets as operating financial plans need to be real and accurate, and include at least inter-year comparisons, indicators of financial performance for budgeted to actual dates, indications of performance via activity statistics (unit costs, service output measures), and projections of future operating expenses of the investment budget. In principle all spending must be within the limits provided by the budget and its sub-budgets. Any differences between actual and planned spending are known as variances, and usually represent underspending or overspending. The control process takes place while the budget is realized.

Everywhere in the world, most public-sector organizations still operate annual budgets. To ensure the timeliness of this process, they establish a regular cycle of activities, usually codified by internal norms. This budgetary cycle is repeated every year and may be steered by either a top-down or bottom-up approach, or by some mixture of the two approaches. In the top-down approach, the cycle, the main decision-making body establishes broad budget parameters, like expenditure targets, income strategies (level of used charges, fees, expected grants), use of reserves (increase or decrease of the scope of reserves), key priorities for the organization, and expected budget limits for all budget departments.

Standard budgeting is the process, or collection of processes, through which the decisions regarding the budget are made. Budgeting is in itself aimed at determining the amount of funding for programs and agencies so they can perform and fulfill those purposes. It is about negotiations and procedures preceding taking decisions about the allocation of scarce resources to those programs and agencies.

In practice, the outcomes of budgeting are on the one hand pretty predictable as the budgets in a given year are mostly a fixed mean percentage of the appropriation for agencies and programs in the previous year plus an increment or minus a decrement. The margins in the budgeting, the increments or decrements for programs and agencies, are predominantly political and much less predictable as they are determined, among other factors, by the request of the program/agency, the relationship between the agency and the funding party, the difference in the appropriations and requests in the previous year, special circumstances, and the smartness of the requesting agency in politics, gaming and influencing the funders prioritizations (Wildavsky 1964).

The classic incremental budgeting process can be characterized as shown in Fig. 1.1. It is a simple approach but does not cover the complexity of budget tasks.

Because of the limitations of incremental budgeting, governments tried to develop more sophisticated schemes, like zero-based budgeting, cash-limited budgeting, resource-restricted budgeting, contingency budgeting, planning, programming and budgeting system, and performance budgeting. The last two represent attempts to connect financial figures with performance.

Following the famous analyses of Wildavsky (1964, p. 7), for instance in his book on a comparative theory of the budgeting process, the term

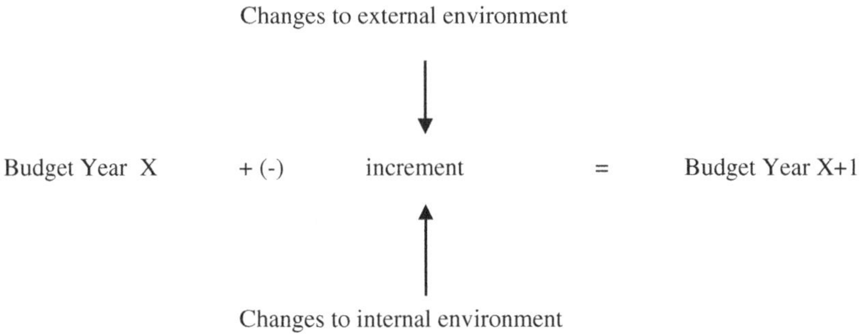

Fig. 1.1 Classic incremental budgeting

performance budgeting comes out as a pleonasm, as he defines budgeting as such as the process through which financial resources are translated into human purposes.

The willingness to connect financial allocations and performance must be always limited in its realization. This is because defining performance and measuring performance is a classic "wicked problem." Performance carries multiple and often ambiguous meanings and there are various opinions on how it should be defined. Performance measurement is the collection of deliberate activities, which includes defining a measuring object, formulating indicators, collecting data, analyzing data, and reporting (Van Dooren et al. 2010). Problems immediately arise at the first step, when measurability is usually discussed as a crucial factor in determining the quality of performance data and performance measurement. This dimension of performance research deals with questions related to the validity of the measurement of performance, such as:

1. What should be measured, and how should it be measured?
2. How should the measurement criteria be made operational?
3. Does measurement measure what it is intended to measure?

The international literature clearly shows that efficiency—performance measurement in the public sector is a complex and challenging issue, for many reasons. For example, see Andrews et al. (2006). Some of these reasons lie in the fact that in the public sector social and non-financial costs and benefits are also expected to be included in the measurement.

This makes such measurement a complex exercise, because it needs to combine objective and subjective measures, often drawn together by using data from various sources.

1.3 Alternative Ways to Link Performance to Budgeting

The discussion about budgets, budgeting and performance measurement shows that linking information about the performance of an agency or program and deciding about a budget for that agency or program is a far from obvious and simple task. This reflects the several options that have arisen in the literature for linking performance to budgeting. The different ways to incorporate performance measures in budgeting are discussed below.

The first option is to ***abandon the idea of performance-based budgeting***. There have been numerous scholars who wanted to abandon performance management and performance budgeting completely. Van Dooren and Hoffmann (2018, p. 221) conclude that because of the lasting problems "organizational structures and cultures must be revisited. Control mechanisms would need to be replaced by trust mechanisms." They arrive at this conclusion, because as they say performance measurement is a form of accountability and "the more accountability the more dysfunctional effects" (ibid., p. 220). Following Hirschman (1991), they see three such side effects of performance management: its perversity effect—e.g. manipulation of performance outputs and the gaming involved; its futility effect—e.g. the non-use of the performance information; and its jeopardy effects—e.g. the costs involved in juggling statistics that could better have been invested elsewhere (Van Dooren and Hoffmann 2018, p. 214). Van Dooren and Hoffmann (2018, p. 214) also argue that while in theory goals are assumed to be defined clearly and their achievement easily measured, this is often not possible in public governance where goals are volatile, difficult to measure, often vague as responsibilities are shared, outcomes often elusive and unpredictable, data are either unavailable or inaccurate, and the politics involved inhibits direct action when goals are not achieved. Similarly, Van Thiel and Leeuw (2002, p. 271) talked about the performance paradox, that is, the weak correlation between performance indicators and performance itself. The main point is that it is not always possible in the public sector to clearly specify intended outcomes and their relationship with outputs and activities. Putting prices on outcomes and incentivizing achievements may result in adverse behavioral distortions (Smith 1995).

The second option is to confine the link between performance and funding to a presentation of performance measures in the budget, without linking the decisions about funding to such measures. In such ***presentational performance budgeting***, the budget becomes a presentation of achievements and targets compared to the costs. The intention is to increase the transparency and accountability generated by that document. This usage has changed the definition of performance budgeting, from one where performance measures in budgeting are emphasized, to one that focuses on the reporting of performance measures in public budget documentation (Jordan and Hackbart 1999) or "a performance budget as any budget that represents information on what agencies have done or expect to do with the money provided to them" (Schick 2003, p. 201). Based on his comparative study of performance budgeting, Schick concluded that country experts usually characterize their systems as "presentational performance budgeting." Performance data are presented in the budget, but without a clear or consistent link to decision-making (Schick 2014). Most chapters in this book deal with this form of performance budgeting.

The third option is ***performance-informed budgeting***. In performance-informed budgeting there is a loose/indirect link between performance and budgeting (OECD 2007, p. 21). Performance information is to be part of the budgeting process, as it provides arguments that could be used to counter the politics usually involved in such processes. Such performance-informed budgeting is not to replace the politics involved, nor to let the technical information to be decisive, but serves other goals, namely to increase the probability that information about the efficiency and efficacy of expenditures is taken into account. This is emphasized by Donald Moynihan (2008) when he suggests that there is and should be at least a dialogue on the performances as measured, before they can be incorporated into the budgeting process. In that dialogue and in the politics involved in the budgeting, performance information can be relevant. That an agency does a good or bad job, that the money is well spent or spilled, that results are or are not visible, that goals are achieved or not, and that important outcomes are furthered by the actions of a program or agency, poses a strong, although not always decisive, argument in discussions about the new budgets for that agency or program. Again, such performance-informed budgeting does not replace the politics involved but does make it harder to have decision-making solely be based on political whims. Economic-technical rationality becomes part of the debate and this adds to the quality of the debate.

Scott (2010, p. 32) agrees with this argument when he states that "what all attempts at performance budgeting have in common is the attempt to increase the influence of policy analysis, strategic decision support, and performance information in the budget system." ...and, "It should also be remembered that while better budget systems can promote better decisions by politicians, budgeting is about politics, and a well-designed budget system may be used to make decisions that are good or bad in the views of budget officials.... Good budget systems do not lead by themselves to strong fiscal stances and optimal final outcomes. At the end of the day sound policy decisions make the difference and mastering both the technical and political side of the equation is paramount" (ibid., p. 11).

Other scholars support these views. Borst et al. (2014) pointed out that performance-informed budgeting might be the last resort for public officials. It can be seen as a countervailing power tool, for disputed public programs and their managers, especially in an adverse political context, as it provides a means to counter the whims of politicians in their decision-making, when officials` performance is looked down upon, and when bureaucrat-bashing prevails. They conclude (ibid., p. 930) that, "officials who are positive about the applicability of performance measures are found particularly in organizations that are controlled directly by politicians .... by individuals in complex managerial positions, those having positive judgments about the quality of the performance of colleagues within their organization, and those who have experience with performance management." They conclude also that "The officials see this as a desired tool to 'prove' to the hostile outside world that they work hard, effectively, and efficiently and meet their objectives" (ibid., p. 931).

In all these views performance-based budgeting is promoted as a compensation for the irrationality of political budgeting through including more technical-rational arguments. This conforms to the desire to inject more "rationality" (measurement and evaluation) into "budgeting decisions" (cf. Willoughby and Benson 2011, p. 1) and the ideas from the OECD that “Information on performance can help in managing and controlling public services, as well as in enabling parliament to check whether it is getting value for money from the executive branch of government. This information is also useful in meeting increased public pressure for accountability, as it enables the government to fulfill its duty to publicly disclose and take responsibility for its actions” (OECD 2005, p. 2).

The OECD (2008, p. 1) promotes such use, because it believes that, “performance budgeting can be combined with increased flexibility for managers in return for stronger accountability for the results, so as to enable them to decide how to best deliver public services.... it generates a sharper focus on results within the government. The process also provides more and better understanding of government goals and priorities, and how different programs contribute to them. At the same time, performance information encourages greater emphasis on planning and offers a good indication of what is working and what is not. This tool also improves transparency, by providing more and better information to legislatures and the public.”

The fourth option is what nowadays is called ***direct performance-based budgeting*** or ***performance financing***, based on awarding or sanctioning agencies according to the level of their performance through formula-based budgeting (see, for example, Robinson 2007 or OECD 2007). The reasoning is that unlike private sector enterprises, most government programs are not designed to yield a profit. Without the profit motive, it is difficult to know which programs are generating benefits and which are not. Performance measurement can help with this problem by producing quantitative evidence that shows which programs are accomplishing their purposes. Performance budgeting integrates the results of performance measurement into the budget process, ideally resulting in budget allocations that more closely reflect the relative merit of the programs (Gilmour and Lewis 2006, p. 742). It has six direct advantages:

a. Performance budgeting invites performance audit;
b. It helps to attain the objectives in a scientific manner;
c. It motivates improved performance since the input-output relationship is maintained;
d. Correct steps can easily be taken since continuous comparisons can be made between the target and the actual performance;

e. If there are insufficient funds, those available can be allocated between various activities in relation to their relative importance; and
f. All the activities can easily be analyzed and the unimportant ones eliminated.

A typical example of direct performance budgeting (performance financing) is the Dutch system of financing the judicatory. 95% of the budgets are directly related to the number of judgments in courts, distinguishing between different kinds of criminal cases. Every three years, the council for the judiciary negotiates with the ministry of justice about the financial remuneration of 10 types of criminal cases. This concerns their average costs. When these negotiations are concluded, the council distributes the agreed finances across the existing courts, distinguishing between up to 53 case categories. The finance system takes into account whether one or more judges are needed in a court case and the costs of in-service judicial training. Despite the seemingly technical nature of this type of financing, it has not removed all politics from the process of financing the judiciary, because their budget is still part of the overall budget of the Ministry of Justice, and so is dependent on the overall resources available to the minister.

Another example of direct performance budgeting is the financing of higher education, which in many countries has become output (performance)-based. An increasing part of the financing in higher education is based on the number of students enrolled in a program and the number of degrees awarded. Although this is a standard practice in many countries, it is also contentious, as it might result in grade-inflation and a lower quality of curricula as institutions try to increase the number of degrees awarded.

A third example is found in the health-care system, where funding has sometimes become directly related to performance (Eldridge and Palmer 2009). This is seen in the British National Health Service, where funding of hospitals is directly related to the activities they undertake, according to the adage "payment for results." In international aid is it visible in donor programs, where, for instance, the Global Fund to Fight AIDS, Tuberculosis and Malaria (GFATM) releases funds based on demonstrated achievements against agreed immunization targets (ibid., p. 162).

A fourth frequently discussed form of its use is found in so-called "student vouchers", with the (hardly achievable) aim to improve quality via "quasi-market" competition (Cullis and Jones 2009). The success of student vouchers is doubted by most researchers. For example, Ladd (2002) concludes that based on the available evidence from both the United States and other countries, the effects of competition on overall student achievement from a large-scale voucher program are at best likely to be small. Performance financing is also used in a limited way in providing state grants to universities (see the respective chapter) and in funding sports (for example, Pavlik and de Vries 2014) in many countries.

1.4 The Role of Performance-Based Budgeting in Post-NPM Era?

The issue in the literature has been whether performance budgeting should be seen as an alternative to the politics involved in the budgeting process, or whether it could be seen as a tool mitigating the political nature of budgeting. The latter could perhaps be accomplished by providing rational arguments in favor of or against continued, increased or decreased funding of a program or agency. The most outspoken proponents aim at using performance-based budgeting as an alternative to the politics normally involved in budgeting. In that sense such performance budgeting is related to what is called New Public Management (NPM), for both phenomena gained momentum in the 1990s.

The NPM idea was to make government competitive by injecting competition into public service delivery. In this perspective, the government should be mission-driven instead of rule-driven, and results-oriented through the use of performance measures, with an emphasis on output and controls that objectives are met. Within the public sector, politicians should let managers manage, and the government should be more market-oriented with hands-on management, copying private sector management styles and input discipline (Nemec and de Vries 2012). That performance budgeting fits in this idea was confirmed by Schick (2014) when he stated that performance budgeting is increasingly viewed as a subset of performance management rather than simply as a process for spending public money. In contrast to earlier approaches that carved out budgeting as a separate process, it is now widely understood that governments cannot budget for results unless they manage for results.

New Public Management itself was related to the ideology of neo-liberalism and the Chicago school of economics in which economic-rational people were assumed but the rationality of government actions was disputed. Within this school, Milton Friedman was a leading scholar. He was in favor of "laissez faire" government and propagated that the public sector should be as small as possible, leaving as much as possible to the free market, that taxes were to be minimized, and much of the public service delivery should be privatized or outsourced. Important for performance budgeting is his famous saying (1975) that [o]ne of the great mistakes is to judge policies and programs by their intentions rather than their results.

Partly because of its ideological base and partly for its negative side-effects, fierce discussions emerged about the pros and cons of this approach. Opponents pointed to the special character of the substance of delivering public sector services, which is not about value for money, but about value for many. These scholars refer to the "raison d'etre" of government in having to take care of people who cannot take care for themselves, irrespective whether the outcomes of a cost-benefit analysis show a positive or negative sign. They point to the multiple and often conflicting goals of public decision-making, and the delivery of collective goods as opposed to commercial, individual goods. They also pointed to the context in which the public sector has to function, as seen in its political leadership, the power-disparities involved, the complex, often multi-level networks in which it has to operate, and the need to deal with a multiplicity of conflicting interests in which stakeholders have a different amount of resources, are de jure independent, but de facto dependent on one another with regard to the outcomes of decisions. They also point to the specifics of the work of public officials, of whom a *Public Sector Motivation* is expected in which charity, care, and intrinsic work motivation are crucial. Hence, the critics argue that government is completely different from the private sector in which profitmaking, returns on investment, and cost-benefit analyses, egocentrism and external motivators dominate the decision-making.

The problems in using performance-based budgeting in the public sector mainly relate to the constant interplay between political rationality and economic-technical rationality. This brings us back to the classic writings of Wildavsky (1964) and his main point that in the margins, in determining the increments and decrements in budgets for agencies and programs, politics dominates, as most practical budgeting may take place in a twilight zone between politics and efficiency.

The chapters of this book demonstrate that also in the "governance" era, properly implemented performance-based budgeting systems have the potential to improve government performance, but also point to the fact that there exist many less successful or totally unsuccessful attempts to use this tool in practice, in countries at all levels of development.

1.5 Issues Surrounding Performance-Based Budgeting

As simple as performance-based budgeting seems to be, a historical anecdote about the Chinese K'ang-shi Emperor ruling China around 1700, is illustrative for the issues involved in this regard. This Confucian emperor ruled over a huge country and part of the job was, of course, delegated to provincial officials. Naturally, their performance had to be controlled, rewarded if the job was done well and punished if the official failed. The emperor based his judgments on what he institutionalized as the "Palace Memorial System", that is, reports produced by the officials and sent to him for evaluation. He intended to handle these reports scientifically, at least according to the dominant scientific theory of the time. As a good Confucian, he saw the weather as a heaven-sent portent and as the main criterion to judge the performance of the provincial officials (Finer 1997, p. 1138). If the weather in the province had been bad, the provincial official had to have done a bad job also, and if the weather had been favorable, it must be a sign from heaven that the official had been doing an excellent job. As the provincial officials also knew about the weather being a reflection of heaven's judgment, no report ever mentioned bad weather conditions. Indeed, during the reign of this emperor, the weather in China seems to have been the best ever.

The anecdote points to two issues surrounding performance-based budgeting: (1) performance budgeting is much older than often assumed and is not something supposedly invented by presidents or by the US Congress at the end of the 1940s (Schick 2014 or Robinson and Brumby 2005), but—as stories from holy scriptures and from other ancient empires reveal—something that has troubled leaders from the beginning of time; (2) It has always been and is still difficult to get valid and reliable information about performance relevant for the budgeting process.

1.5.1 Budgeting Has Always Partly Been Performance-Based Budgeting

As to the first point, public budgeting has always been at least partly based on performance. Departing from collective action theory (Olson 1965) that government's "raison d'etre" is to provide collective goods out of an awareness that there are collective problems, such endeavors have always needed a budget in order to accomplish and maintain those goods. In ancient times this may have been limited to securing public order and safety, the construction and maintenance of public and religious buildings, and funding the military. The idea was nonetheless unequivocal: budgets were provided in order to accomplish something, that is, to perform. The results were unambiguous. Buildings, temples, palaces—were or were not built and maintained; the people were passive and quiet, or full of unrest and oppositional; and armies lost or won wars. That was indicative of performance and resulted in keeping one's job and salary or having one's budget reduced to zero, or worse. Such performance budgeting was, for instance, also seen in the Napoleonic era, as this Emperor claimed that the burden of the costs and the spoils of wars should be on the armies themselves. If his army won a fight, the soldiers would be remunerated by the spoils of the win. If the army lost, there would be no spoils and the soldiers would not be paid. Easy performance budgeting indeed. Budgeting in general was a kind of performance-based budgeting in many empires, as the amount of money allocated to the army was contextualized. It depended primarily on whether it was peacetime or wartime and thus on the question of what kind of performance was required.

1.5.2 Issues Surrounding Performance Measurement

The existing academic and professional literature provides sets of potential benefits, but also of potential bottlenecks of performance-based budgeting. The validity and reliability of performance indicators and performance measurement itself is one core subject of this debate. The basic idea behind performance-based budgeting was to change the focus from budgets reflecting inputs—how much will be spent—to a focus on outputs and outcomes—what do we get for that money. As easy as this seems, many pitfalls, ambiguities and dilemmas are involved in determining whether or not one gets value for money in the public sector. This subsection addresses some of the issues involved.

The first issue relates to the question what people involved in the budgeting process should focus on. At an abstract level systems theory distinguishes inputs, process, outputs, outcomes, and feedback. Proponents of performance-based budgeting propose to shift the emphasis from inputs (spending revenues) and process (seeing that the way funding is spent is according to the rules) to outputs and outcomes, but what does that entail? de Kruijf and de Vries (2018) found that at least seven different meanings can be attached to outputs and outcomes. Originally, outcomes were not part of the equation. In Easton's model of the political system (1957) outcomes are defined as changes in the input to the system. A system (for instance a funding institute) receives inputs (in our case revenues and requests for funding) and converts these inputs through a (budgeting) process into binding decisions (budgets). The output results, through a feedback process, in changed demands and support (input). In this example, the budget itself is the output of the budgeting process.

Other interpretations of outputs and outcomes are (1) that outputs refer only to achieving the intended effects for which budgets were provided, while outcomes refer to all intended and unintended consequences related to such output; (2) that outputs refer to everything delivered by the system, while outcomes are context-oriented and refer to developments in the contexts of the system that add to the effects; (3) outputs as immediate effects and outcomes as effects on the intermediate or long term; (4) outputs as what is actually done and outcomes as the evaluation of what is done; (5) outputs as intentions and words, the broad decision, and outcomes as actual changes, the implementation; or (6) outputs as easily measured results and outcomes as fuzzy or hard to measure results (de Kruijf and de Vries 2018, p. 68).

Thus, a budget for the police is either seen itself as the output resulting in the outcomes of a number of policeman on the streets and a percentage of crimes solved, or the number of policemen on the streets and percentage of crimes solved is the output, with less crime and (a feeling of) safety among the residents as possible outcomes. Another interpretation is that the number of policeman on the streets, and the percentage of crimes solved, occur immediately as a direct consequence of being funded, while crime rates and (feelings of) safety occur later in time, being not only a consequence of the number of policeman on the streets and the percentage of crimes solved, but also of the valuation of that output and contextual developments.

These varying distinctions between outputs and outcomes result in the emergence to at least five dilemmas.

1. A focus on outputs is easier when it is about whether the budgets are spent as intended, then in case it is about the outcomes generated, but such a focus has the side-effect of shifting attention away from achieving the desired outcomes. This refers to what Merton (1936) called goal-displacement, or the unanticipated consequence of purposive social action. It involves the tendency that narrow and formal goals (outputs) become more important than substantive goals (outcomes) and "an instrumental value becomes a terminal value." A focus on outcomes could avoid this, but in that case the link to the budget provided becomes more ambiguous and indirect as contextual developments might also have contributed to such effects and the budget is only one among many factors that could have contributed to those outcomes.
2. It is sometimes not so easy to determine whose priorities regarding the output and outcome of a program or agency should be taken into account. Especially in the public sector many interest groups are involved in policy making, each with their own goals and proposed ways to achieve them. This might result in a fuzzy set of multiple goals for agencies and programs, making it hard to measure those goals, to establish whether each one of those goals is achieved, and to weigh off the goal-achievements against another. The emerging dilemma relates to whose desired outputs and outcomes are measured and translated in the new budget. Is the budget for the police to be based on the output and outcomes as achieved according to the police force, or is it to be based on the achievement of output and outcomes as desired by, for instance, the citizens? Denhardt and Denhardt (2007, p. 173) illustrate this issue by presenting an initiative in Iowa to involve citizens in the performance assessment of public services. It showed that these citizens were interested in outputs and outcomes, but not singularly so. Their concerns were especially about process indicators—that the city better communicates information, for instance what happens after they file a case, and about the courteousness of civil servants, e.g. being treated respectfully,

professionally and without discrimination. The dilemma is that taking measurements of all the outputs and outcomes as desired by all stakeholders into account would be equitable but could result in a costly operation with probably diffused results. Taking only the outputs and outcomes as desired by the funded agency or the funding organization into account would be less righteous, but more pragmatic.

3. Focusing on outputs as effects that have to be established before the next budgets are determined, could result in short-term policies with all the negative side effects involved. Focusing on long-term effects (outcomes) would make it problematic to incorporate those effects in yearly budgets as the discussion will arise whether or not it is too soon to make judgments about the achievements that would affect the budget.
4. The more relevant the conceptualization of outputs and outcomes, the more dimensions may be involved, and the more difficult it becomes to measure them in a valid and reliable way. In a program of Public Administration, we can measure how many students enroll, the staff–student ratio and how many students graduate within the required time, as determinants of the outputs for which the program is funded. It is, however, more complicated to judge the quality of such a program. Quality can refer to multiple aspects, such as knowledge, skills, and attitudes, and each of these three aspects has again multiple dimensions as one can ask about knowledge of and skills in applying theories on organization and management, the policy process, governance, and research methods. And again, multiple dimensions emerge when operationalizing goals on the subject-level. The dilemma relates to the negative relation between what can be easily measured and what is relevant to measure.
5. The more direct the linking of performance to budgeting, the higher the probability that reported performance will be manipulated (our chapter on universities is rather a good example of what can happen). The scores on performance measures produced by the funded agency or program might become biased in the scores on measurement scales and, or in the selection of measurement scales provided, or in changes in the actual practice. It could also be that undesirable actions will be taken to get seemingly better outcomes. Local police offices might become reluctant to

assist adjacent forces because it would result in a relatively more favorable performance of that adjacent corps and thus possibly less money for themselves. A university program funded based on output (number of graduates) might suffer from grade inflation. A hospital that is financed based on the number of consultations may increase the number of times a patient has to visit the specialist before something is actually done about the complaints. The indicators for performance linked to a budget could provide undesired incentives to maximize performance as measured by those indicators, instead of actions to contribute to performance as desired. This results in the dilemma of making budgeting performance-based resulting in less trustworthy information about actual performance and/or unintended and desirable changes in the agency's behavior to maximize on the criteria, or, having a budgeting process which is not performance based and receiving information of which one can be confident that the measures and scores are valid and reliable, and a program that aims to achieve the desired goals, but without any funding consequences because the performance will not affect the budget.

Whether these five dilemmas are real or not is disputed. Robinson and Brumby (2005) argue that the negative effects may be hypothesized in theory, but that evidence of their existence in practice is merely anecdotal. They ask where the evidence is that such effects are widespread in reality.

The World Bank emphasizes that deficiencies in performance budgeting are not due to the concept itself, but to the varying, and often bad ways in which it is introduced and managed. In a World Bank report on the topic, Schick (2008, pp. 45–46) claims that governments should err on the side of simplicity and concentrate on critical public services that are provided directly to citizens… that the reform agenda should be to remove barriers to performance…. That governments need to be selective and not blanket all of the public sector with performance budgeting. … that governments should make serious investments to strengthen internal controls…. That the capacity of government departments and agencies for self-management depends on the reliability of internal controls…. that governments should modify existing budget rules and practices… and that just adding performance budgeting to the stockpile of procedures will not work.

Nonetheless, the five dilemmas result in doubts about the applicability of performance-based budgeting in the public sector. As Serban and Burke (1998, p. 161) argue, "performance funding is easier to define than to operationalize." This is partly because "selection of performance indicators is probably the most difficult task of performance funding." So, we can laugh about the methods used by the late Chinese emperor but have to ask ourselves if we are able to do much better today.

1.6 The Structure of This Book

The exposition given above argued that very different positions can be taken with regard to performance-based budgeting. That makes one inquisitive about the experiences of countries in using performance measures in their budgeting. What happens? Do the dilemmas materialize? How do those countries handle them? And what recommendations flow from those experiences? This book contains case studies on the topics noted above from many countries in the world—including most developed countries such as the USA, Australia, and Western European countries, but with a focus on transitional, developmental conditions, where implementation failures often limit the success of realized reforms, and where the noted dilemmas might be extremely prominent. In-depth evaluation of real cases should serve as an important learning tool both for the academic and professional field. Implementation mistakes should be prevented and not repeated—the book may help in this way. It starts with two chapters about countries that are seen in the literature as front-runners in using performance-based budgeting; Australia and the Netherlands. It continues with the reluctant introduction of performance-based budgeting in Germany, Austria and Switzerland. Then we turn to transition countries, such as Russia and South Africa. All these countries have had some experience with performance-based budgeting, but although they adopted interesting approaches to the dilemmas mentioned, many gaps remain. Other countries still face major dilemmas without having found solutions to them. This is true for countries like Ukraine, Italy, Slovakia, Slovenia, the Czech Republic, and Bulgaria. The problems they face are the ones mentioned above, that is, the perversity effect; the futility effect; and the jeopardy effects. Their case studies illustrate the issues, but also point to potential solutions, and to solutions tried in different countries. In the conclusions we will return to these issues and to the question of how to fulfill the promise of Performance Budgeting.

References

Andrews, Rhys, George A. Boyne, and Richard M. Walker. 2006. Subjective and Objective Measures of Organizational Performance: An Empirical Exploration. In *Public Service Performance: Perspectives on Measurement and Management*, ed. George A. Boyne, Meier Kenneth, Laurence J. O'Toole, Jr., and Richard M. Walker, 14–34. Cambridge: Cambridge University Press. https://doi.org/10.1017/cbo9780511488511.002.

Behn, Robert D. 1994. The Wrong Way to Motivate. *Governing* 8: 70.

Borst, Rick, Christiaan Lako, and Michiel S. de Vries. 2014. Is Performance Measurement Applicable in the Public Sector? A Comparative Study of Attitudes Among Dutch Officials. *International Journal of Public Administration* 37 (13): 922–931. https://doi.org/10.1080/01900692.2014.944988.

Breul, Jonathan. 2007. GPRA—A Foundation for Performance Budgeting. *Public Performance & Management Review* 30 (3): 312–331. https://doi.org/10.2753/pmr1530-9576300301.

Brusca, Isabel, Eugenio Caperchione, Sandra Cohen, and Francesca Manes-Rossi. 2018. IPSAS, EPSAS and Other Challenges in European Public Sector Accounting and Auditing. In *The Palgrave Handbook of Public Administration and Management in Europe*, ed. Edoardo Ongaro and Sandra van Thiel, 165–185. Basingstoke: Palgrave Macmillan. https://doi.org/10.1057/978-1-137-55269-3_8.

Cullis, John, and Philip Jones. 2009. *Public Finance and Public Choice: Analytical Perspectives*, 3rd ed. Oxford: Oxford University Press.

de Kruijf, Johan A. M., and Michiel S. de Vries. 2018. Contextualizing the Trend from Output to Outcome Measurement: The Dutch Pension System. *Public Money & Management* 38 (1): 65–72. https://doi.org/10.1080/09540962.2017.1389544.

Denhardt, Janet V., and Robert B. Denhardt. 2007. *The New Public Service: Serving, Not Steering*, Expanded ed. Armonk, NY: M. E. Sharpe.

Easton, David. 1957. An Approach to the Analysis of Political Systems. *World Politics* 9 (3): 383–400. https://doi.org/10.2307/2008920.

Eldridge, Cynthia, and Natasha Palmer. 2009. Performance-Based Payment: Some Reflections on the Discourse, Evidence and Unanswered Questions. *Health Policy and Planning* 24 (3): 160–166. https://doi.org/10.1093/heapol/czp002.

Finer, Samuel E. 1997. *The History of Government*. Oxford: Oxford University Press.

Friedman, Milton. 1975. Interview with Richard Heffner on *The Open Mind* (7 December 1975).

Gilmour, John B., and David E. Lewis. 2006. Does Performance Budgeting Work? An Examination of the Office of Management and Budget's PART

Scores. *Public Administration Review* 66 (5): 742–752. https://doi.org/10.1111/j.1540-6210.2006.00639.x.

Hirschman, Albert O. 1991. *The Rhetoric of Reaction: Perversity, Futility, Jeopardy*. Cambridge, MA: Harvard University Press.

Jordan, Meagan M., and Merl M. Hackbart. 1999. Performance Budgeting and Performance Funding in the States: A States Assessment. *Public Budgeting Finance* 19 (1): 68–88. https://doi.org/10.1046/j.0275-1100.1999.01157.x.

Ladd, Helen F. 2002. School Vouchers: A Critical View. *Journal of Economic Perspectives* 16 (4): 3–24. https://doi.org/10.1257/089533002320950957.

Merton, Robert K. 1936. The Unanticipated Consequences of Purposive Social Action. *American Sociological Review* 1 (6): 894–904. http://www.jstor.org/stable/2084615.

Moynihan, Donald P. 2008. *The Dynamics of Performance Management: Constructing Information and Reform*. Washington, DC: Georgetown University Press.

Moynihan, Donald P., and Ivor Beazley. 2016. *Toward Next-Generation Performance Budgeting: Lessons from the Experiences of Seven Reforming Countries*. The World Bank. https://doi.org/10.1596/978-1-4648-0954-5.

Nemec, Juraj, and Michiel S. de Vries. 2012. *Public Sector Dynamics in Central and Eastern Europe*. Bratislava: NISPAcee.

OECD. 2005. *Modernising Government: The Way Forward*. Paris: OECD Publishing.

OECD. 2007. *Performance Budgeting in OECD Countries*. Paris: OECD Publishing.

OECD. 2008. *Performance Budgeting: A User's Guide*. Paris: OECD Publishing.

OECD. 2014. *Budgeting Practices and Procedures in OECD Countries*. Paris: OECD Publishing.

Olson, Mancur. 1965 [2009]. *The Logic of Collective Action*. Cambridge, MA: Harvard University Press.

Pavlik, Marek, and Michiel S. de Vries. 2014. The Voucher System as an Alternative for Allocating Sports Grants. *Central European Journal of Public Policy* 8 (2): 4–27.

Robinson, Marc. 2002. Financial Control in Australian Government Budgeting. *Public Budgeting & Finance* 22 (1): 80–93. https://doi.org/10.1111/1540-5850.00067.

Robinson, Marc, ed. 2007. *Performance Budgeting: Linking Funding and Results*. Basingstoke: Palgrave Macmillan. https://doi.org/10.1057/9781137001528.

Robinson, Marc, and Jim Brumby. 2005. Does Performance Budgeting Work? An Analytical Review of the Empirical Literature. IMF Working Papers 5 (210), International Monetary Fund (IMF), Washington. https://doi.org/10.5089/9781451862294.001.

Saliterer, Iris, Mariafrancesca Sicilia, and Ileana Steccolini. 2018. Public Budgets and Budgeting in Europe: State of the Art and Future Challenges. In *The Palgrave Handbook of Public Administration and Management in Europe*, ed. Ongaro Edoardo and Sandra van Thiel, 141–163. Basingstoke: Palgrave Macmillan. https://doi.org/10.1057/978-1-137-55269-3_7.

Schick, Allen. 2003. The Performing State. *OECD Journal on Budgeting* 3 (2): 71–103. https://doi.org/10.1787/budget-v3-art10-en.

Schick, Allen. 2008. *Getting Performance Budgeting to Perform*. Washington: World Bank.

Schick, Allen. 2014. The Metamorphoses of Performance Budgeting. *OECD Journal on Budgeting* 13 (2): 49–79.

Scott, Graham. 2010. Performance-Informed Budgeting: Experiences and Opportunities. In *Results, Performance Budgeting and Trust in Government*, ed. Arizti Pedro, Jim Brumby, Nick Manning, Roby Senderowitsch, and Theo Thomas, 31–40. Washington, DC: The International Bank for Reconstruction and Development/The World Bank.

Serban, Andreea M., and Joseph C. Burke. 1998. Meeting the Performance Funding Challenge: A Nine-State Comparative Analysis. *Public Productivity & Management Review* 22 (2): 157–176. https://doi.org/10.2307/3381031.

Smith, Peter. 1995. On the Unintended Consequences of Publishing Performance Data in the Public Sector. *International Journal of Public Administration* 18 (2–3): 277–310. https://doi.org/10.1080/01900699508525011.

Tarschys, Daniel. 2002. Time Horizons in Budgeting. *OECD Journal on Budgeting* 2 (2): 77–104.

Van Dooren, Wouter, and Cornelia Hoffmann. 2018. Performance Management in Europe: An Idea Whose Time Has Come and Gone. In *The Palgrave Handbook of Public Administration and Management in Europe*, ed. Edoardo Ongaro and Sandra van Thiel, 207–226. Basingstoke: Palgrave Macmillan.

Van Dooren, Wouter, Geert Bouckaert, and John Halligan. 2010. *Performance Management in the Public Sector*. Oxford: Routledge.

Van Thiel, Sandra, and Frans L. Leeuw. 2002. The Performance Paradox in the Public Sector. *Public Performance & Management Review* 25 (3): 267–281. https://doi.org/10.1080/15309576.2002.11643661.

Wildavsky, Aaron B. 1964 [2015]. *The Politics of the Budgetary Process*. Oxford: Oxford University Press.

Willoughby, Katherine, and Paul Benson. 2011. *Program Evaluation, Performance Budgeting and PART: The US Federal Government Experience*. Atlanta: Andrew Young School of Policy Studies Working Paper.

World Bank. 2010. *Results, Performance Budgeting and Trust in Government*. Washington, DC: The World Bank.

PART II

Performance-Based Budgeting in Developed World

CHAPTER 2

Budgeting in the United States: From Theory to Practice Using Higher Education

Aziza Zemrani

2.1 Introduction

The literature on budgeting and public sector productivity traces the advocacy and use of modern governmental performance measurement (PM) back to the beginning of the twentieth century.

The common unproven hope or assumption in the budgeting literature is that PBB improves program efficiency by bringing rationality into the resource decision-making process (Newman et al. 2004; Melkers and Willoughby 1998, 2001). In this chapter we look on the above issue from two points of view—by assessing historical developments of PPB in the US and by delivering own in-depth research on the impact of PPB in higher education in the US.

A. Zemrani (✉)
University of Texas Rio Grande Valley, Edinburg, TX, USA

M. S. de Vries et al. (eds.), *Performance-Based Budgeting in the Public Sector*, Governance and Public Management,
https://doi.org/10.1007/978-3-030-02077-4_2

2.2 Developments of PPB in the United States

Public budgets describe what governments do by listing how governments will spend their money (Rubin 1998). A budget links tasks to be performed with the amount of resources necessary to accomplish those tasks. Moreover, the essence or core of budgeting is that it allocates scarce resources implying choice between competing activities or alternatives. If resources were not scarce, there will be no need for budgeting (Schick 1971).

The examination of the evolutionary aspect of the budget in the United States shows that this evolution is fragmented or divided into different eras. Each era reflects the concern for the control of the role of the executive or a more aggressive role for the legislative (Lynch 1995; Lynch et al. 1996; Wildavsky 1964; Rubin 1998). However, one can argue that the search for rationality for the allocation of resources is a major factor that can count for the successive reforms, as well as in the formulation of public policy (Koven 1999; Shelley and Swanson 1998: in Koven 1999). The search for rationality through different approaches to budgeting is reflected in a series of reforms especially the performance budgeting, which is the focus of this research (Miller et al. 2001).

Budgeting reforms in the US can be classified according to some historical and political influences. Swan (1983) identified different eras to explore the historical background of budgeting and its evolutionary aspect. They reflected the struggle to develop an approach most likely to lead to a more rational allocation of resources. Swan (1983) and others (Lynch 1995; Jordan and Hackbart 2000; Wildavsky 1964) contended that one cannot overlook the historical background of budgeting. As the philosopher George Santayana suggests, "Those who do not remember the past are condemned to relive it" (Quoted in Shirer 1960: cited in Swan 1983). Such is often the case in the field of budgeting. According to Merewitz (cited in Lynch and Martin 1993) for example, ZBB was first mentioned in the literature in 1924 and was then proposed as a new approach to budgeting in the Carter Administration of the 1970s (Merewitz and Sosnick 1971).

The traditional incremental approach dominated budgetary practices in the US government until the twentieth century. Until the early part of the twentieth century, executives and legislators approved budgets using line items (Lynch 1975; Lynch and Martin 1993; Swan 1983; Wildavsky 1964, 1985). For the most part, Congress controlled the items and projects they would fund and the amount of the funding using incremental decision-making. The 1912 Commission on Economy and Efficiency played an important role in changing the system. The Commission's report argued the need for establishing an executive budget using a program orientation. The report gave as much emphasis to budget execution and management as to budget formulation. Outputs became as important as inputs. In essence, the 1912 report recommended a performance-type approach to budgeting. Nevertheless, acceptance of this rational approach was quite slow and certainly not immediate.

Significant reforms in budgeting occurred between 1910 and 1920 (Lee and Johnson 1998). These reforms mostly intended to hold the executive responsible and accountable for the budget process. Firstly, these reforms took place at the state level followed by the federal around 1921 with the Budget and Accounting Act. The Act established the new federal system. The rationale is the control of government spending. The report of the Taft Commission submitted in 1912 to the President that recommended the direction of the budget process under the control of the president (Lee and Johnson 1998).

Additionally, the 1921 Act brought two significant modifications in the budgeting field (Smith and Lynch 2004). The first is the creation by the president of a national budget and the establishment of an independent audit agency the General Accounting Office (GAO) as a congressional agency. Literature reports that this legislation strengthened the executive and created the Bureau of Budget (BOB).

By 1949 and 1955, the Hoover Commissions were still recommending the "performance budget" (Burkhead 1956; Wildavsky 1985). The time for serious rational budgeting in government started to arrive after the 1950s with the adoption of the PPBS approach for the entire federal government during the Johnson administration in the 1960s and continued with ZBB approach during the Carter administration in the 1970s.

The Johnson Administration introduced PPBS into the federal government (Lynch 1975). The strength of PPBS lies in its emphasis on policy analysis to increase effectiveness (Wildavsky 1985). This approach to budgeting embodies horizontal comprehensiveness comparing alternative expenditures in order to select the best that is likely to contribute to large programmatic objectives. However, despite its comprehensiveness and rationality, PPBS operated without any limits on spending (Wildavsky 1964).

ZBB is characterized by its vertical comprehensiveness. ZBB is an approach to public budgeting decision makers that appropriate money on a yearly basis without reference to the previous year (Smith and Lynch 2004). The primary criticism of this approach is the amount of work in terms of budget preparation. Both budgeting approaches failed despite their effort to bring rationality into the budget decision.

However, despite these differences, both approaches, PBBS and ZBB, share the characteristic of their reliance on rationality, with the former emphasis on the bigger picture and the latter on a single program. Other budget approaches followed like Management by Objectives (MBO) and Target-Based Budgeting (TBB) but did not last long (Smith and Lynch 2004).

As was previously stated, at least since the 1950s when performance budgeting reform ocame in vogue (Lee and Burns 2000), reformers have advocated the use of PM of government programs accomplishments. In the 1990s, performance budgeting and performance measurement received national attention in the context of the high visibility of budget reform. The expectation of that reform was that state governments that were already using some form of performance budgeting at the early beginning of the decade would be making greater use of PM by the end of the decade. Lee and Johnson (1998) contend that the use of PM was long advocated as a component of budget reform.

Despite the often disappointing results of performance budgeting efforts of the 1950s and the PPBS experiments of the 1960s, reformers continued to advocate the use of PM. In the 1970s, the budget reform of the moment was ZBB, which used PM as a key component of the reform. The Reagan/Bush administration of the 1980s stand out as a relatively quiet period regarding budget reform and the quiet use performance measurement (Lee and Burns 2000). The Clinton 1990s showed renewed attention to performance measurement. The reinventing government movements sought, among other things, to reorganize and often downsize government in order that it met the needs and demands of the citizenry but at relatively lower costs. In that reform movements measuring what government does or fails to do was key (Schachter 1995; Snell 1998; Lee and Burns 2000).

Performance budgeting is easier to define than to do (Carter 1994) partially because lawmakers and agencies must agree on performance measures. In a more general way, PBB is a budgeting method that links appropriations ultimately to the outcomes of the programs. Despite the difficulties, more than half the states have taken up the challenge. From 1998 to 2001, 18 legislatures adopted performance reforms that stress accountability for results through the budget (Willoughby and Melkers 2001a, b). The trend in the adoption of more accountability in budget decision is on the rise.

The proponents of the implementation of PBB claimed that governmental decisions and resource allocations would be improved (Posner 1999; Forsythe 2000). Reviewed literature and selected case studies on states' use of PBB reported that this budgeting approach had many compelling factors in its favor (Hager et al. 2001). Reformers assume that if only there were more planning and rational thinking, governmental decisions would improve. Reformers claimed that the introduction of PBB in the federal government would significantly change and improve American public administration. As noted before, this reform had a strong precedent in earlier measures. Secretary Robert McNamara's introduction of program budgeting in the Defense Department in 1961 preceded the 1965 presidential directive establishing PPB and the later 1990s legislation established the current PBB use of PM (Lynch 1975). The "all important thing in budgeting is the work or service to be accomplished and what the work or service will cost" (Schick 1971). This statement, enunciated by the Hoover Commission in 1949, set the initial tone for performance budgeting, which continued as the philosophical underpinning for its various changes or "reincarnations" through the years (Jordan and Hackbart 2000).

In contrast to incremental budgeting, performance budgeting emphasizes the systematic examination of the purpose and goals of a program and the assessment of program efficiency and effectiveness using PM. Following the Hoover Commission recommendations, performance budgeting proponents argued that the shifting of the focus from the budget process to performance would change the behavior of the budget participants and their decisions as well (Jordan and Hackbart 2000).

Hager et al. in their report (2001) stated that elements of PBB have been around for decades and almost all states use some aspects of this approach, such as developing performance measures for purposes of strategic planning and evaluation. However, the concept of PM and its operationalization pose problems to decision-makers. The major problem is that PM requires that the vague concept of program output and outcome need to be translated into indicators that make longitudinal and comparative analysis possible. The next section will address the concept of performance measurement and the issues related to this concept in terms of definition, agreement on measures.

As previously mentioned, there are several budgeting reforms that have failed throughout the history of the United States. Smith and Cheng (2006) propose that one reason reforms might fail is because of the lack of post-assessment review. They tried to establish a framework through which a reform can be viewed, to measure its efficiency and provide an effective assessment of the net benefits of the reform. The framework proposed by Smith and Cheng (2006) is contingent on two dimensions: first, type of fiscal reform (rules vs. judgment) and second, life cycle (innovators, early adopters, maturity). They conclude by making three policy suggestions (a) legislators should focus on incentives for managers to report performance measures, (b) researchers and reformers should consider how performance budgeting could be done on a comparable basis across states, and (c) influential actors such as legislators and the media should be studied in greater detail (Smith and Cheng 2006).

Another example of this is the one stated by Andrews (2004), he establishes that in order to implement successfully a reform, an organization has to have three factors, authority, ability, and acceptance. These three consistently intersect to ensure the positive implementation of a reform. In his article, Andrews mentions that three aspects of organizational ability are central to the implementation of a reform, these aspects are "performance evaluation ability, personnel ability and technical ability" (Andrews 2004). Followed by this, is the second factor, authority. He relates the implementation of a reform to a second factor, authority mechanisms in governments. And lastly, "The final factor regularly mentioned in the literature on … adoption is acceptance.

Resistance to reform on the part of public officials, department heads and employees may be the biggest obstacle to the implementation and use of performance measures" (Andrews 2004).

Another example of failed or miss-implemented reform is the one of performance budgeting (PB), as stated by Schick (2014). "PB originated as a movement to transform budgeting from means of purchasing inputs to a process that allocates money according to actual or estimated results by changing the structure and content of budget accounts" (Schick 2014). The primary aim of PB was to eradicate the line-item focus and move to a more performance oriented focus, this would include basing spending decisions on the work that was to be performed. However, this reform was promptly dismissed because some governments were just not ready for it; this was because countries and players in the budgeting area were not ready to make the change needed to implement this reform. Some of the backtracks of PB as stated by Schick (2014) are that PB reforms are a tough sell in good times, and even harder in bad times; By itself, PB cannot compensate for a shortage of fiscal space; PB cannot reverse the decline in public trust; growth would improve the market for PB-driven budget, but it cannot ignite the needed growth; valuing performance yields better results than the procedural motions of PB; and consolidating items may be a precondition for effective implementation of PB.

As already stated, the rational approach to budgeting did not go without criticism. Scholars such as Lindblom (1959) and Simon (1946) challenged the appropriateness of the rationalistic approach to budgeting. Simon introduced the idea of "bounded rationality" followed by another group of scholars contending that decision-making—more specifically budgeting—is influenced by factors other than economic, namely politics. There is a large literature that addresses the issue of the impact of politics on budgetary decisions. Lewis (1952), Mises (1944), Key (1940), and Wildavsky (1964) initiated the debate on the influence of politics on budgetary decisions.

This research argues that the main objective of the current performance budget reform is to remove the political aspect from budgeting and move the decision-making process to a more rationalistic approach. Authors such as Schick (1971) and Lewis (1952) support this rationalistic approach to budgeting. Such approaches they argue will most likely bring more objectivity into public sector budgeting and lead to an optimum use of public resources.

2.3 Performance Measurement as the Core PPB Element

The concept of PM evolved in the United States over time as public concern for increased government productivity became a major issue. The literature documents the historical background or origin of the use of PM and the various definitions associated with PM (Hatry 1999; Hatry et al. 2001; Rosen 1997; Holzer and Nagel 1984; Holzer, 1992; Epstein 1984; Gilmore et al. 1992). PM attempts to answer questions that are of great concern to taxpayers regarding the amount, quality, and effectiveness of goods and services that their taxes dollars purchase. In the private sector, if a company wishes to stay in business, it must address concerns regarding the satisfaction of its customers. For centuries, however, the government did not have the tools to address customer satisfaction concerns. For example, few government officials could tell policymakers the quantity and quality of the services they provided. Citizens and even policy analysts could not determine whether they received good value in return for the taxes paid (Blodgett and Newfarmer 1996).

In the ongoing debate on performance budgeting, the specific meaning of "performance" is normally the program's contribution to a stated objective, such as an increase in the number of graduates in educational programs. Alongside this issue of the definition of performance emerges the issue of what is to be measured. Haoran (1998) argues that there are different levels in performance to be measured. The authors make the distinction between inputs, activities, efficiency, outcome, and effectiveness. Hatry et al. (2001) defines performance as a measurement on a regular basis of the results and efficiency of services or programs. Typical types of PM are inputs, process, outputs, and outcomes. In addition, the ratio of the amount of outputs to the amount of inputs is labeled *efficiency* (in italics in the text). This topic will be elaborated later in this section.

In a general sense, GASB (2000) defines PM as the regular collection and reporting of information about the efficiency, quality, and effectiveness of government programs. Thus, reformers consider PM as an important means for improved government decision-making. As such, reformers worldwide in budgeting and public management promote PM as a key tool to improve efficiency, effectiveness, and organizational responsiveness (Schick 1990; OECD 1995: cited in Nyhan and Martin 1999).

In the public sector, reformers advocate PM as part of the effort to restore public confidence in government by increasing accountability through transparency of government operations (Halachmi 1999; Zumeta 1996, 2000, 2001; Ruppert 1997; Posner 1999; Frederickson 2001). The aforementioned statement appears to be true regardless of the level of government: federal, state, or local (GAO 1993; Willoughby and Melkers 2001a, b; Jordan and Hackbart 2000; Posner 1999).

The government enacted in 1993 the "*Government Performance and Results Act*," which laid a solid foundation for the federal government performance management. Nevertheless, the law had several weaknesses, such as insufficient outcome-oriented goals, insufficient use of performance information to make decisions that ultimately impede its progress (Shea 2008). The Government Performance and Results Act, required that federal agencies to consult with the United States congress about their mission statement, long term goals, and the strategies to reach them (Shea 2008). Further, Shea (2008) stated that the law also required agencies to draft strategic plans, and measure and produce annual performance reports.

Given that failure of implementation of the Government Performance and Results Act, the President's Management Agenda included a government-wide initiative titled "*Performance Improvement Initiative*" (PII) aimed to guarantee the best results with the federal taxpayer's money, and to overcome the implementation weaknesses of the Act. The President's Agenda designated that the federal agencies together with the Office of Management and Budget (OMB) to collaborate in identifying which programs are functioning properly, which are failing, which programs will be chosen if necessary to divert part of its funding to other programs, and draft recommendations on what has to be done to improve the performance of these programs (Shea 2008). The ultimate decisions related to budget reallocation are made by the President and the Congress, regardless the Federal agency and the OMB analysis is used to make an informed decision (Shea 2008).

The success of the PII can be measured in two ways. First, improved program performance which consists of identifying the weaknesses in program management and design of ongoing programs, to develop and implement improvement plans (in collaboration with the OMB) to get more results with the tax dollars. Second, greater investment in successful programs which consist of reallocation scarce resources to higher performing programs, also the programs that are performing poorly but that provide critical services need to improve their results. Nevertheless, Congress and the President don't take into consideration performance by itself to make decisions for funding programs, they can decide to consider performance as a critical factor and invest in programs that deliver the highest return and achieve measurable results (Shea 2008).

The United States Government (agencies and the OMB) uses the Program Assessment Rating Tool (PART) to evaluate the programs that are in place, and guarantee that they are effective and improving each year. Shea states that the PART evaluate each program's purpose, design, planning, management, results and accountability, this is achieved using the PART four-part questionnaire, each part has series of 25 questions tailored to the program category. The first part ponders about the program's design and purpose. The second set of questions inquiries about the program's strategic planning and the annual and long-term goals of the plan. The third, will be used to rate the management of an agency's program (financially, and improvements). The last segment of questions will inquire about the accuracy and consistency of the results of a program (Shea 2008).

The results of each section will be shown in a score rate from 0 to 100, programs with not acceptable performance measure or that has not collected performance data can receive a rating of "results not demonstrated" or "Ineffective," in some instances it means that further funding is needed. On the other hand, programs rated "effective" can have their funding cut for not being a priority, or for achieving their mission, or it can only mean they are functioning properly and no drastic changes are needed (Shea 2008). Further, the results of the PART evaluation will not end in an automatic decision about the program's funding; these results will be one of the many data used by the President and Congress to make decisions.

By 2007 the executive branch using the PART assessed 1004 programs (approximately 96% of the federal budget), given the results of the PART performance and transparency in programs has improved. Similarly, most programs have increased their rates to effective, moderately effective, or adequate. Shea (2008) argues that these performance and transparency improvement is the results of the consistent and clear standards of success set by the PART, and the commitment of the agency's programs to do whatever is necessary to achieve these standards. Thus, demonstrating the PI Initiative on focusing agencies on results, to produce maximum results with the federal dollars. Nevertheless, there are programs that the PART cannot asses given their limited impact or large activities, for these reason alternatives methods are being considered to determine an appropriate unit of analysis. Unfortunately, with the second PI Initiative "greater investment in successful programs" similar satisfactory results have not been achieved (Shea 2008).

The enactment of GPRA reinforced the efforts to implement PM. As previously stated, this Act encourages the use of PM by federal government agencies as well as to improve public accountability, service delivery, and congressional decision-making (Jordan and Hackbart 2000). The Act requires the specification of objectives, standards, and goals for programs (Melkers and Willoughby 1998). In addition, the Act requires the reporting of performance and that constitutes the major and critical issue for the full implementation of this legislation.

The major problem that arises with the concept of PM is the quantification of the performance measures. Some argue that the quantification of performance measures constitutes one of the main causes behind the lack of success of successive rational reforms. However, since 1993, with the enactment of the GPRA, scholars, and practitioners alike, assert that the current reform of budgeting is most likely to bring greater rationality with regard to resource allocations (Posner 1999; Lee and Burns 2000).

Furthermore, Caiden (2010) states that in Schick's works he argues that there is little justification that guarantees that accurate information in budgeting yields to a good decision-making process, given that this information can be useful for analysis purposes, but is not the best match for the "*decision rule*" practice used to allocate the budget. Schick's recommends the government to use budget performance instead as an analytical tool, and not as a decision-making one (Caiden 2010). As a result of Schick's studies on governmental budgeting, he is convinced that in the next 20 years additional fundamental changes in the budgeting process will take place, to create more effective, efficient, responsive, stable, and accountable government budgets (Caiden 2010).

2.4 Case Study: PB in Higher Education

Higher education—America's thirteenth largest industry, with total costs approaching $120 billion annually—is not exempt from reforms to increase productivity. The combined influences of competing demands, escalating costs, and greater public scrutiny resulted in a search for approaches that reinvent or reform higher education in terms of the rational model of decision-making (Penâ 2000). Policymakers, in their efforts to do more with less, foster and sometimes even mandate the use of accountability measures designed to increase efficiency and raise productivity. Performance indicators, which are a central feature of these initiatives, provide tangible evidence of results (Ruppert 1997). Bouckaert (1992) discusses productivity in the public sector from different perspectives defined in terms of disciplines. This research uses his theory where the concept of productivity that sometimes coincides with efficiency, given that this article addresses only the efficiency component of PBB leaving out the effectiveness for future research.

Despite the abovementioned trends in the use of PM, there are few studies that address PBB in higher education. Traditional line-item budgeting is still the well-established major means to budget in higher education. Borgia and Coyner (1995) surveyed chief academic officers at colleges and universities to explore the budgeting systems in higher education institutions. The survey was developed with the objectives to find budget characteristics by the approach to budgeting (traditional, PPBS, ZBB, PBB, formula approach, and cost-center approach). These characteristics range from the integration of PM in the budget, the allocation of funds and the planning, and other characteristics that concern the budget process for each approach. The findings of Borgia and Coyner confirm that the characteristics of traditional budgets, such as control of expenditure, the increase or decrease of the previous year's appropriations, and line-item control dominate higher education budgets. However, such characteristics are mostly associated with lower levels of appropriations and less sophisticated higher education institutions (Borgia and Coyner 1995). Increasingly, PBB or something very similar to it is replacing line-item budgeting in higher education (Burke 1998a, b). The current trend in higher education is that PBB or something very similar is replacing line-item budgeting in higher education (Burke 1998a, b).

When higher education institutions were under financial strain in the early 1990s due to declining enrollments, eroding purchasing power, and reductions in federal and state funding, Borgia and Coyner (1995) conducted a survey in which they explored the magnitude of the move in comprehensive colleges and universities toward more rational budgeting systems. The study showed a vast majority of the budgeting systems at institutions of higher education use budgeting strategies drawn from more than one budget approach (Boyd 2000; Hovey 2000; Zumeta 1999). The call for more rationality in the budget system continues into the twenty-first century because rational budgeting mechanisms are believed to help higher education institutions cope with the "economic realities of the times" (Borgia and Coyner 1995, p. 468). Reformers see PBB with its advantage of using the concepts of productivity as critical to improving higher education today and in the future.

Performance funding for public higher education became an issue in the first half of the 1990s. In late 1994, a survey of SHEFOs found that nine states linked some funding for public colleges and universities to their achievement of priority goals or objectives (Layzell 1998), while another 10 were considering such an approach. Two surveys in 1996 suggested a growing interest in budgeting for results. However, by 1997, the issue of performance funding for public colleges and universities became clouded in several states as they encountered practical and political problems with those reforms (Burke and Serban 1997a, b). These problems included (a) implementation difficulties, (b) campus opposition, and (c) political shifts.

The 1997 survey by Burke and Serban distinguished between performance funding and PBB. They defined performance funding as "special state funding tied directly to the achievements of public colleges and universities on specific performance indicators" (p. 1). They describe performance budgeting as "state governments considering reports of achievements on performance indicators as a factor in setting budget levels for public higher education and its institutions, without tying designated amounts directly to performance on specific indicators" (p. 1).

Burke and Serban (1997a, b) showed that 35% of states had either performance funding or performance budgeting at the time of the survey. Overall, the survey indicated that a performance component in the budgeting for public higher education was an attractive concept in a large and growing number of states, but that there were some difficulties in implementation as described above.

2.5 Data and Methodology

2.5.1 Data

This research uses data extracted from the National Center for Education Statistics (NCES), the Integrated Postsecondary Education Data System (IPEDS), the Rockefeller Institute, Washington Research Institute, and the Carnegie Classification of Higher Education. NCES carries out an annual survey of all institutions of higher education. IPEDS also conducts an annual survey on higher education institutions according to their characteristics including variables such as completion, enrollments, and financial information. The Rockefeller Institute gives information on the implementation of PBB in higher education. The Washington Research Institute provides information on the characteristics of the states. The Carnegie Classification of Higher Education identifies and classifies higher education institutions according to their mission, characteristics of the students, and faculty members.

This research uses the Carnegie Classification as it appears in its 2000 version. The 2000 Carnegie Classification includes all colleges and universities in the United States that are degree-granting and accredited by an agency recognized by the US Secretary of Education. The 2000 edition classifies institutions based on their degree-granting activities from academic years 1995–1996 through 1997–1998. However, the description of the procedures of classification is beyond the scope of this research. The classification comprises six categories with subcategories.

The unit of analysis in this research is the various institutions of higher education commonly called public universities and colleges. This research follows the McMillan and Datta (1998) and Calhoun (2003) approach that categorizes data into three major groups: (a) doctoral-Granting Universities, (b) Master's-Granting Universities, and (c) others. The variable is categorical with two classes. The logic behind this choice is that this research is exploring whether or not the use of PBB alters the efficiency of institutions of higher education, as such, the universities are the unit of analysis. The states are used in this research as a tool to explore the research question as states determine the magnitude of the implementation of PBB, as previously mentioned. The use of this approach to resource allocation is either a legislative, administrative, or a mandated requirement (Burke and Minassians 2001; Melkers and Willoughby 1998). The different state agencies, including public higher education institutions, are then required to use PBB in their budgeting approach, which was prompted by a demand for increased public accountability. The frequency table below illustrates the universities as grouped by category in the fifty states (Tables 2.1, 2.2, and 2.3).

Table 2.1 Group 1—Doctoral and research universities I and II

	Frequency	*Percent*
Otherwise	104.0	69.3
Advanced	46.0	30.7
Total	**150.0**	**100**
Otherwise	115.0	76.7
Advancing	35.0	23.3
Total	**150.0**	**100.0**
Otherwise	115.0	83.7
Backsliding	26.0	17.3
Total	**150.0**	**100.0**

Table 2.2 Group 2—Master's colleges and universities I and II

	Frequency	*Percent*
Otherwise	178.0	65.4
Advanced	94.0	34.6
Total	**272.0**	**100.0**
Otherwise	212.0	77.9
Advancing	60.0	22.1
Total	**272.0**	**100.0**
Otherwise	229.0	84.2
Backsliding	43.0	15.8
Total	**272.0**	**100.0**

Table 2.3 Group 3—Baccalaureate and other institutions

	Frequency	*Percent*
Otherwise	429.0	66.9
Advanced	212.0	33.1
Total	**641.0**	**100.0**
Otherwise	505.0	78.8
Advancing	136.0	21.2
Total	**641.0**	**100.0**
Otherwise	113.0	17.6
Backsliding	180.0	28.1
Total	**641.0**	**100.0**

2.5.1.1 Dependent and Independent Variables

The dependent variable is the efficiency score or ratio of output to input. The major explanatory or independent variable is the categorical variable measuring the magnitude of the implementation of PBB in the fifty states as computed from the Rockefeller Institute over six years (1997–2002). Based on previous studies, this research identifies some control variables (Lee and Burns 2000; Melkers and Willoughby 2001). The objective is to see whether these control variables influence the relationship between the dependent and the independent variable. The control variables are state characteristics and profile, governance, per capita income (PCI), and gross state product (GSP).

The major independent variable is the use of PBB by the institutions of higher education as reported by the Rockefeller Institute survey. Because the implementation of PBB and the use of PM vary among the states, the primary independent variable is a categorical variable reflecting the use of PBB. In other words, this research will be able to explore whether the use of PBB with its required use of PM will induce greater efficiency in public higher education institutions. The use of PBB as an independent variable is possible because of a study of Burke (1998a, b). The Rockefeller Institute conducted a series of surveys from 1998–2003 on the status of the implementation of PBB in the institutions of higher education. The series of surveys is the basis for the operationalization and computation of the explanatory variable the degree of implementation of PBB. This research uses the number of years of implementation as an indicator to measure the independent variable.

As already mentioned, the independent-variable (PBB) is an indicator variable and is constructed from the Rockefeller Institute series of surveys on higher education use of PBB by the 50 states. Given the variability of the degree of implementation of PBB as it appears in the trend displayed in these surveys, this research uses the rationale adopted by Lee and Burns (2000) to construct an index to identify three different levels ("advanced," "advancing," and "backsliding") of states reflecting their implementation and steady use of PBB, The rationale of Lee and Burns provided a better understanding and insight into the overall status of PM use in the states. First, the 50 states have been classified according to the number of years of use of PBB. Second, and based on the Rockefeller survey over the six years, the "advanced," "advancing," and "backsliding" states have been identified. The category "advanced" comprises the states that the survey reported have been using PBB for five to six years in a row without interruption. The "advancing" category comprises the states that the survey reported have been using PBB for three to four years. "Backsliding" comprises the states that the survey reported have been using PBB and stopped using this approach. The three groups identified do not include all the 50 states because 15 states reported that they are not using PBB. For the purpose of this research, this group will be included in the analysis given the inclusiveness and comprehensiveness of this research.

The remaining question regards classifying the states according to their degree of implementation: advanced, advancing, and backsliding. The classification is done based on the number of years of implementation and the assignment of the states a score or scale of one through four. The numbers do not have a ranking or order. For purposes of analysis in this paper, the data from the four tables are collapsed into a categorical variable with four levels. The factor time is the criterion that is used to collapse the states according to the number of range years.

A variable time will be integrated into the regression to examine the difference, if any, between the states.

In statistical theory, Neter et al. (1996) argue that there are many ways to quantify the identified classes of a qualitative variable. However, the rule of thumb is that an indicator variable with classes is represented by c-1 indicator variable, each taking on the values of zero and one.

The major independent variable is the degree of implementation of PBB. As previously stated, the classification of the states is done according to the number of years the state/institution has used PBB. Previously introduced as an indicator variable, the independent variable consists of three classes (X_1, X_2, and X_3) each of which takes on the value of zero and one for the purposes of analysis. This subsection classifies the universities within the groups of the states: the advanced, the advancing, the backsliding, and the states that did not adopt PBB.

The independent variable is primarily based on the surveys of SHEFOs. The high response rate of all the surveys is evidence that budgets officers have regarded the survey as important. The data is self-reported by the budgets offices and it is understood that biases may exist with such data, but these validity threats are less likely given the consistency in the responses reported from the states in the surveys from year to year.

Table 2.4 summarizes data related to the use of PBB from 1997 to 2002. The information reported in the table helps to understand and capture the trend in the use of PBB (Table 2.5).

The comparison of the level of efficiency of institutions of higher education between the states that use PBB and the ones that do not use PBB

Table 2.4 States with performance-based budgeting

Surveys	*Number (percentage)*
First 1997	16 states (32)
Second 1998	21 states (42)
Third 1999	23 states (46)
Fourth 2000	28 states (56)
Fifth 2001	27 states (54)
Sixth 2002	26 states (52)

Source Processed by the author
The Nelson A. Rockefeller Institute of Government. (2000–2003). *Annual Surveys*. Albany, NY: The Nelson A. Rockefeller Institute of Government

Table 2.5 Degree of implementation of performance-based budgeting

Number of states	*Number/years*	*Percentage*
11	6	22
3	5	6
5	4	10
9	3	18
4	2	8
4	1	8
15	None	30

is the core focus of the methodology in this research. The computation of an efficiency index for the different states remains the focus of the methodology. The main purpose is to use the index as the dependent variable showing the respective level of efficiency of the different universities. The independent variable is the use of PM in the higher educational institutions. This research examines descriptive interactions about the use of PBB in higher education to enhance the exploratory aspect of this empirical research.

The research dependent variable of this research is the efficiency score or ratio of output to input. The computation of the dependent variable efficiency is done by dividing the outputs by inputs and the score obtained is the level of efficiency. There are different approaches used for the computation of efficiency including ratio analysis, simple regression analysis, and data envelopment analysis. Ratio analysis is the ratio of inputs to outputs using the systems concept. The systems concept components include inputs, process, outputs, and outcomes. However, in the higher education sector, it is sometimes difficult to distinguish between outputs and process (McMillan and Datta 1998). For example, in some instances, the use of student enrollments is used as an output and some may argue that this is an input. To address this challenge, this research adopts the theory of McMillan and Datta, which uses students' enrollments, converted into full-time equivalent (FTE) and research expenditures as an output.

For the purpose of the analysis of the dependent variable, this research uses scores of efficiency for institutions of higher education in the three groups of states (advanced, advancing, and backsliding) in the computations. This provides a comparison of the use of PBB and PM in order to assess the impact of PBB, if any, on higher education budgeting among the states. Given the variability among the states and the different categories of institutions, this research computes average scores for the three groups of states.

The computation of the efficiency score is obtained using the traditional approach of ratio analysis as explained by Nyhan and Martin (1999), especially for comparative performance measurement. It is the ratio of outputs to inputs as displayed in Table 2.6. The input is generally dollars, though in some instances it might be measured in work hours or other resources. For this particular research, the input is total expenditure in dollars.

The table contains the components to compute efficiency. The components are inputs and outputs as they appear in the surveyed literature. As previously stated, the inputs and outputs of institutions of higher education are generally recognized but how to use these measurements is disputed (Brinckman 1990). For the purpose of this research, we assume that universities provide teaching, research, and services. To measure teaching, this research uses as proxy for outputs students' enrollments and degrees awarded adopting the approach used by McMillan and Datta (1998) and Rhodes and Southwick (1986).

This research addresses only the issue of efficiency, leaving out effectiveness which is a subject for future research. This decision is due in part to the issue of operationalization and measurement of such a construct, especially in higher education. The main objective of this research is therefore limited only to efficiency to make the research manageable for a preliminary investigation of the impact of PBB on resource allocation. Although the study of productivity in higher education encompasses

Table 2.6 Dependent variable components

Dependent variable	*Method of analysis*	*Source*	*Level of measurement*
Efficiency		Bifulco and Duncombe (2000)	Continuous (index)
1-Inputs: Expenditures (aggregated or disaggregated measure)	Ratio analysis	Hopkins (1990), McMillan and Datta (1998), and Calhoun (2003)	Continuous
2-Outputs: Student enrollment in courses degrees awarded			

the constructs efficiency and effectiveness (Gates and Stone 1997), the measurement of the latter is a huge task for organizations. Furthermore, the measurement and the analysis of effectiveness require a longitudinal study of at least ten years to be able to measure the impact of higher education on the states (Grosjean and Grosjean 2000). The authors contend that in the case of comparative performance in higher education, a longitudinal study is required which is beyond the scope of this study.

2.5.1.2 Control Variables

In analysis, control variables are used to cancel out or neutralize the effect of other factors that might otherwise explain the observed dependent phenomenon (Tuckman 1978; Bickman and Rog 1998). The control of extraneous variables means that the influence of independent variables extraneous to the purpose of the study are nullified, minimized, or isolated. Different methods are available to control for this type of variable. For example, they can be built into the design as independent variables. Once included, it makes it possible to extract from the total variance of the dependent variable, the variance due to that variable. Kerlinger (1986) argues that building these variables into the model helps to isolate the effect on the dependent variable (efficiency) as well as their possible interaction with the independent variable (PBB Implementation).

For the purpose of this study, based on the literature surveyed, the variables to be controlled for are state characteristics and governance. The National Information Center for Higher Education Policy and Analysis is the major source for variables associated with state characteristics. The center took over the work done by the Research Associates of Washington, and conducts studies on the profile of the fifty states with regard to their tax effort, tax wealth, and appropriations allocated to higher education from the collected taxes. These measures permit the exploration of the influence of state profiles on the performance of higher education institutions. In their assessment of PBB, Melkers and Willoughby (1998) and Lee and Burns (2000) use these variables to study the variability among the fifty states.

Governance

Governance is one of the variables listed in the literature to address the issue of the universities' characteristics. Governance is the variable that reflects the state university system structure. McGuiness (1999) define the state system of higher education as the system that includes the public and private postsecondary institutions within a state as well as the arrangements for regulating, coordinating, and funding them. The variable is an important factor while dealing with higher education institutions (McGuiness 1999), especially when it comes to resource allocation and budgeting. Additionally, governance has been identified as one of the influences that shape higher education performance.

McGuiness (1999) characterize state governance structures for higher education systems as segmented, unified, or federal. In most segmented systems, multiple governing boards are each responsible for one or more institutions. States determine the level of appropriations for each institution. In unified systems, a single governing board manages all degree-granting institutions and the states represent these institutions in discussions and negotiations with governments and legislators. Federal systems have a statewide board responsible for the collection, and distribution of information, and advising on the budget. McGuiness (1999) agree that governance is important and they conducted case studies on different states to explore this issue, especially on the matter of budgeting, which is the focus of this research. Controlling for this variable allows for the isolation of the effect of governance on resource allocation, or at least mitigating its influence. The governance model determines the level of control over the institutions and their ability to manage their activities freely without strong control from an outside authority.

State Characteristics

The literature reports variability among states that might be influencing factors (Willoughby and Melkers 2001a, b). Lee and Burns (2000) identified seven variables most likely to have a relationship with the use of PBB. These variables are: (1) state population, (2) percentage of population that is urban, (3) non-agricultural employment rate, (4) per capita income, (5) tax capacity, (6) tax effort, and (7) the state's unemployment rate.

Of the above, this research is using state population, tax capacity, tax effort, and population. The rationale in the use of these selected variables is derived from the specificity of higher education. State population is variable and in general, the larger the population, the greater the use of PM. Lee and Burns (2000) used this variable to assess the difference in the use of PM.

Tax capacity refers to the potential ability that each state has to raise revenues. This variable is computed by dividing state and local government relative tax capacity by the total population. This is a measure of the ability of a state to raise revenues to be allocated to higher education and other public purposes. The national average tax capacity is set at 100, and then each state's relative wealth is gauged in terms of being above or below that figure. A state that is relatively poor would have a low tax capacity score, but if that state taxed itself heavily, then the state would have a high tax effort score. According to the National Information Center for Higher Education and Policy analysis, tax capacity is a key variable in policy decisions regarding financing for higher education, especially decisions about the relative share to be borne by the students and the states.

State tax effort refers to the state and local tax revenue collected as a percentage of state and local tax potential. Tax effort is a percentage that measures how much of state and local government tax potential is actually used. The tax revenue collected for all states equals total tax capacity nationwide, so that the national effort, by definition, is 100%. This variable demonstrates how each individual state compares with the national average. This variable is computed by dividing state and local government actual tax revenues by the total tax resources.

2.6 Findings and Results

This research started by addressing the research question: Does the use of PM in PBB, as a rational approach to resource allocation, alter the efficiency of higher education institutions in the U.S? In an article published by the World Bank (2003, p. 1), the author argued: "Despite the widespread claims, the likely benefits of PBB are not always clear." PBB has long been a recommended reform both in industrialized and developing countries, yet considerable ambiguity remains on the relative impact of this resource allocation approach.

This research hypothesizes that PM as a component of PBB has a positive influence on the efficiency of higher education institutions. In addition the research hypothesizes that there is a difference in efficiency between the states that use PBB and the states that do not use PBB, with the states with PBB experiencing higher rates of efficiency. Because of the variability among the states in terms of the level of implementation of PBB the time factor becomes important in terms of its impact on the level of efficiency.

The analysis conducted in this research uncovered some interesting results. Firstly, the difference of means was used to test for the hypotheses first by year for hypotheses 1 and 2, and for hypothesis 3 by aggregating the six years for the three groups of universities. The findings were different for the two hypotheses that PBB exerted an influence on the level of efficiency of the institutions of higher education for the advanced states. Groups 1 and 2 of universities but not Group 3, showed a difference between the means of efficiency with an *F*-test equal to 5.513 (*p*-value 0.020) and 7.152 (*p*-value 0.008) for Group 1 and Group 2, respectively.

There is a statistical difference among the different levels of implementation of PBB. For Group 3, the researcher could not reject the null hypothesis of equal means (*F*-test: 0.002 with *p*-value 0.965). It is important to mention that the results were conflicting or maybe that the factor of time played a major role. The confusion remained with the advancing states in Group 2, which showed a downturn curve giving evidence that PBB exerted a negative influence. This observation may be explained, as already stated, that time played a role, or possibly maturation.

Hence, there is insufficient evidence to declare that PBB status has an impact on the level of efficiency of the institutions of higher education with respect to Group 3. In other words, the category of universities made a difference in terms of using PBB. However, the overall results confirmed hypothesis 1, that PBB exerts an influence on the level of efficiency of the institutions of higher education, positive for the advanced states, and negative for the advancing states. The analysis also revealed that this study rejected the null hypothesis that there is no difference between the states and the level of implementation of PBB. Still, the paradox concerns backsliding states whose difference may be due to chance or other confounding factors. These findings coincide with the observations of Calhoun (2003). The author, although using a different methodology, found that the difference in the level of efficiencies is a function of the category of universities. Calhoun used a nonparametric methodology (frontier analysis) to compare the level of efficiency of higher education institutions. As he found some differences, the author controlled for the style of management and drew the conclusion that management was a key variable in impacting the level of efficiency among institutions of higher education.

Being aware of the factor of time, the difference of means was conducted on the six years combined in order to evaluate the pattern for the categories of states in terms of the trend of efficiency scores. The advancing states still showed a downturn curve revealing that there is a difference between the advanced and the advancing states. These results were tested in the context of regression, controlling for the contextual variables. The findings confirmed that the state characteristics, especially tax capacity, were a key variable in showing a negative impact on the level of efficiency of the institutions of higher education. These findings substantiate the results obtained by Lee and Burns (2000) in terms of state characteristics involving the variables that might have an influence on the degree of implementation of PBB.

The findings revealed the use of PBB exerts an influence on the efficiency of higher education. However, the university category does make a difference. The results in Models 1 and 3 for Groups I and III showed that there is a statistical evidence that PBB and 0.028, respectively. The results showed at the same time that it is significant for the advancing. The exception is that this influence is negative (*p*-value 0.023) and this confirms the results of the analysis done with the difference of means. The conclusion to be made at this level is that the factor of time plays a role in the magnitude of this influence. The states should be steady in their implementation of PBB and be more consistent in terms of using the rational approach in allocating resources. This finding corroborates the issue of time lag as an important factor in public policy. The implementation of PBB requires consistent efforts and is time-consuming. Our findings show the PBB efforts are worth the reform effort.

In Group 3 of universities, the results showed that the advancing and backsliding states are significant statistically (*p*-values 0.050 and 0.019, respectively). The interpretation for this result confirms what has been stated above regarding the category of the university, which does make a difference. The level of expenditure for Group 3 is very limited and possibly this places strain on the institutions. The hypothesis could be reformulated to test the difference in the level of efficiency among the three groups of institutions along with the magnitude of PBB, and by testing for the level of expenditure.

The variable of *time* is significant for Groups 2 and 3 of universities. These results concur with the recommendations addressed by Lee and Burns (2000). The difference in the results incorporating the variable of time remained the same for the implementation of PBB. Overall, the results showed statistical evidence that PBB made a difference, but that difference is a function of the type of universities.

In summary, the control variables were found to be significant in some instances in which results or findings were different from the Lee and Burns (2000) study. Given the specificity of the higher education sector, tax effort and tax capacity were found to be significant as they had a negative impact on the level of efficiency. The variable governance (segmented and consolidated systems) was found statistically significant for Group 1 and Group 2 of universities, with a negative sign meaning that the type of governance does have an impact on the performance of a university. The federal system as a governance type makes a difference whereas both consolidated and segmented are not significant.

Wellman (2002, p. 1) emphasized the importance of the role of the governing system given the challenges facing higher education. The author contends that public colleges and universities confront "a double *whammy*: the challenge of doing more—for many more—with much less." The author stresses the importance of governance in the context of the fiscal crisis facing the states (Canto and Webb 1987). This research suggests that higher education governance is also critical for the performance of the institutions of higher education.

Overall, the findings of this study revealed that PBB exerts an impact on institutions of higher education. However, the results did raise questions about the time lag in terms of the implementation of PBB, especially for the advancing states. The variable time is crucial in the assessment of this impact. As already stated, states should be more consistent in their efforts of adopting PBB as a rational approach to resource allocation.

In conclusion, in addition to the historical evolution of budgeting in the United States, this chapter provided empirical data that can help reformers to more intelligently speculate on the question of the viability of PBB as a budget reform tool. The budget format needs consistency in the endeavor of implementation; other budget reforms have been tried and failed due to the inconsistency in the efforts. Nyhan et al. (1999) stated that such approaches failed earlier because of a lack of consistency, and called on decision-makers to stick to this approach. The bottom line is that the introduction of PBB reforms in general does positively impact productivity in higher education institutions.

With the perception primarily from conservatives that government is inefficient, ineffective, and unaccountable (Haoran 1998), the findings of this research on performance budgeting reform is crucial. This research provided empirical evidence that the adoption of such an approach can lead to greater government program efficiency and showed that such an approach is a viable tool to policy leaders seeking efficiency in government programs. The Federal Accounting Standards Advisory Board (FASAB) states in its Standards No. 4: "Measuring costs is an integral part of measuring performance" (Mercer 2002, p. 5). The findings of this research affirm that declaration.

References

Andrews, Matthew. 2004. Authority, Acceptance, Ability and Performance-based Budgeting Reforms. *International Journal of Public Sector Management* 17 (4): 332–344. https://doi.org/10.1108/09513550410539811.

Bickman, Leonard, and Debra Rog. 1998. *The Sage Handbook of Applied Social Research Methods*. Thousand Oaks, CA and London: Sage.

Bifulco, Robert, and William Duncombe. 2000. Evaluating School Performance: Are We Ready for Prime Time? In *Developments in School Finance, 1999–2000*, ed. William Fowler. Washington, DC: National Center for Education Statistics, Office of Educational Research and Improvement.

Blodgett, Terrell, and Gerald Newfarmer. 1996. Performance Measurement: (Arguably) The Hottest Topic in Government Today. *Public Management*, January, 6.

Borgia, Carl R., and Randolph S. Coyner. 1995. The Evolution and Success of Budgeting Systems at Institutions of Higher Education. *Journal of Public Budgeting, Accounting & Financial Management* 7 (4): 467–492. https://doi.org/10.1108/jpbafm-07-04-1995-b001.

Bouckaert, Geert. 1992. Public Productivity in Retrospective. In *Public Productivity Handbook*, ed. Marc Holzer. New York: Marcel Dekker Inc.

Boyd, Donald J. 2000. *State Fiscal Issues and Risks at the Start of the New Century*. Albany, NY: The Nelson A. Rockefeller Institute of Government, State University of New York.

Brinckman, Paul T. 1990. Higher Education Cost Functions. In *The Economics of American Universities*, ed. S. A. Hoenack and E. L. Collins, 107–128. Albany, NY: SUNY Press.

Burke, Joseph C. 1998a. *Campus Budgeting for Tough Times: Lessons from the First Half of the 1990s*. Albany, NY: Nelson A. Rockefeller Institute of Government, State University of New York.

Burke, Joseph C. 1998b. *Funding Public Higher Education for Results: Fad or Trend? Results from the Second Annual Survey*. Albany, NY: Nelson A. Rockefeller Institute of Government, State University of New York.

Burke, Jospeh C., and Andreaa M. Serban. 1997a. *Performance-Funding and Budgeting for Public Higher Education: Current Status and Future Prospects.* Albany, NY: Nelson A. Rockefeller Institute of Government, State University of New York.

Burke, Jospeh C., and Andreaa M. Serban. 1997b. *Performance Funding for Public Higher Education: Fad or Trend?* New Directions for Institutional Research. San Francisco: Jossey-Bass. Spring.

Burke, Joseph C., and Henrik Minassians. 2001. *Linking Resources to Campus Results: From Fad to Trend: The Fifth Annual Survey.* Albany, NY: Nelson A. Rockefeller Institute of Government, State University of New York.

Burkhead, Jesse. 1956. *Government Budgeting.* New York: Wiley.

Caiden, Naomi. 2010. Challenges Confronting Contemporary Public Budgeting: Retrospectives/Prospectives from Allen Schick. *Public Administration Review* 70 (2): 203–210. https://doi.org/10.1111/j.1540-6210.2010.02148.x.

Calhoun, Joseph. 2003. *Data Envelopment Analysis of Relative Efficiencies of Higher Education Learning.* Paper Presented at the 28th Annual Conference of the Association for the Study of Higher Education, November 12–16, Portland, Oregon.

Canto, Victor A., and Robert I. Webb. 1987. The Effect of State Fiscal Policy on State Relative Economic Performance. *Southern Economic Journal* 54 (1): 186. https://doi.org/10.2307/1058814.

Carter, Karen. 1994. *Performance Here By.* State Legislatures. December, 22–25.

Carnegie Foundation for the Advancement of Knowledge. 2000. Comparative International Review. *Education Policy Analysis Archives,* 8 (30). Retrieved from http://www.carnegiefoundation.com/.

Epstein, Paul. 1984. *Using Performance in Local Government: A Guide to Improving Decentralization, Personal, and Accountability.* 1st ed. Van Nostrand Reinhold.

Forsythe, Dall. 2000. *Performance Management Comes to Washington: A Status Report on the GPRA.* Albany, NY: Nelson A. Rockefeller Institute of Government, State University of New York.

Frederickson, G. 2001. Measuring Performance in Theory and Practice. *Public Administration Times* 23 (8).

GAO/AFMD-93-41. 1993. Performance Budgeting: State Experiences and Implications for the Federal Government. *Report to the Director of the Office of Management and Budget.* Washington, DC: U.S. General Accounting Office.

Gates, Susan, and Ann Stone. 1997. *Understanding Productivity in Higher Education.* Santa Monica, CA: Rand, Institute on Education and Training.

Gilmore, Jeffrey L., and Duc-Le To. 1992. Evaluating Academic Productivity and Quality. *New Directions for Institutional Research* 75: 35–47. https://doi.org/10.1002/ir.37019927505.

Government Accounting Standard Board (GASB). 2000. Introduction to Performance Measurement. Retrieved from www.gasb.org.

Grosjean, Atkinson J., and Garnet Grosjean. 2000. The Use of Performance Models in Higher Education: A Comparative International Review. *Education Policy Analysis Archives* 8: 30.

Hager, Greg, et al. 2001. *Performance-Based Budgeting: Concepts and Examples.* Research Report No. 302. Legislative Research Commission.

Halachmi, Arie. 1999. Mandated Performance Measurement: A Help or a Hindrance? *National Productivity Review* 18 (2): 59–67. https://doi.org/10.1002/npr.4040180211.

Haoran, Lu. 1998. Performance Budgeting Resuscitated: Why Is It Still Inviable? *Journal of Public Budgeting, Accountability, and Financial Management* 10 (2): 151–172.

Hatry, Harry P. 1999. *Performance Measurement: Getting Results.* Washington, DC: The Urban Institute Press.

Hatry, Harry P., Elaine Morley, and Scott P. Bryant. 2001. *Comparative Performance Measurement.* Washington, DC: The Urban Institute Press.

Holzer, Marc. 1992. Public Productivity Handbook. *Public Administration and Public Policy* (45) New York: Marcel Dekker.

Holzer, Marc, and Stuart Nagel. (Eds.). 1984. *Productivity and Public Policy.* Beverly Hills, CA: Sage.

Hopkins, D. (1990). The Higher Education Production Function: Theoretical Foundations and Empirical Findings. In *The Economics of American Universities*, ed. S. Hoenack and E. Collins, 11–32. Albany, NY: SUNY Press.

Hovey, Harold A. 2000. *State Spending for Higher Education in the Next Decade: The Battle to Sustain Current Support.* San Jose, CA: State Policy Research, National Center for Public Policy and Higher Education.

Jordan, Meagan M. and Merl M. Hackbart. 2000. Performance Budgeting and Performance Funding in the States: A Status Assessment. *Public Budgeting and Finance: New Brunswick* 19 (1): 68–88. Spring.

Kerlinger, Fred N. 1986. *Foundations of Behavioral Research.* 3rd ed. New York: Holt, Rinehart and Winston.

Key, Valdimer O. 1940. The Lack of a Budgetary Theory. *American Political Science Review* 34 (December): 1137, 1140.

Koven, Steven G. 1999. *Public Budgeting in the United States: The Cultural and Ideological Settings.* Washington, DC: Georgetown University Press.

Layzell, Daniel T. 1998. Linking to Funding Outcomes for Public Institutions of Higher Education: The U.S Experience. *European Journal of Education* 33 (1): 103–111.

Lee Jr., Robert D., and Robert C. Burns. 2000. Performance Measurement in State Budgeting: Advancement and Backsliding from 1990 to 1995. *Public*

Budgeting and Finance 20 (1): 38–54. https://doi.org/10.1111/0275-1100.00003.

Lee Jr., Robert D., and Ronald Johnson. 1998. *Public Budgeting Systems*, 5th ed. Gaithersburg, MD: Aspen Publishers.

Lewis, Verne B. 1952. Toward a Theory of Budgeting. *Public Administration Review* 12 (1): 42–54. https://doi.org/10.2307/972827.

Lindblom, Charles E. 1959. The Science of 'Muddling Through'. *Public Administration Review* 19 (2): 79–88. https://doi.org/10.2307/973677.

Lynch, Thomas D., Y. W. Hang, and Cynthia E. Lynch. 1996. Cycle of History and Twenty-First Century Budget Reform: Performance, Entrepreneurial, and Competitive Budgeting. Paper Presented to International Spryer Workshop on Assessing and Evaluating Public Management Reform Held at Spryer, Germany.

Lynch, Thomas D. 1975. *Policy Analysis in Public Policymaking*. Lanham, MD: Lexington Books.

Lynch, Thomas D. 1995. *Public Budgeting in America*. Englewood Cliffs, NJ: Prentice Hall.

Lynch, Thomas D., and Lawrence L. Martin (Eds.). 1993. *Handbook of Comparative Public Budgeting and Financial Management*. New York: Marcel Dekker.

McGuiness, A. C. 1999. The States and Higher Education. In *American Higher Education in the Twenty-First Century: Social, Political, and Economic Challenges*, ed. Philip G. Altbach, Robert O. Berdahl, & Patricia J. Gumport. Baltimore, MD: The Johns Hopkins University Press.

McMillan, Melville, and Debasish Datta. 1998. The Relative Efficiency of Canadian Universities: A DEA Perspective. *Canadian Public Policy* (24): 485–511.

Melkers, Julia E., and Katherine G. Willoughby. 1998. The State of the States: Performance-Based Budgeting Requirements in Forty-Seven Out of Fifty. *Public Administration Review* 58 (1): 66–73.

Melkers, Julia E., and Katherine G. Willoughby. 2001. Budgeters' Views of State Performance-Budgeting Systems: Distinctions Across Branches. *Public Administration Review* 61 (1): 54–61.

Mercer, John. 2002. *Performance Budgeting for Federal Agencies. A Framework*. International Business and Technology Consultants.

Merewitz, Leonard, and Stephen Sosnic. 1971. *The Budget's New Clothes: A Critique of Performance-Based Budgeting and Cost Benefit Analysis*. Chicago: Markham.

Miller, Gerald, William Bartley Hildreth, and Jack Rabin. 2001. *Performance-Based Budgeting. An ASPA Classic*. Boulder, CO: Westview Press.

Neter, John K., Christopher J. Nachtsheim, and William Wasserman. 1996. *Applied Linear Statistical Models*. New York: McGraw-Hill.

Newman, Frank, Lara Couturier, and Jamie Scurry. 2004. *The Future of Higher Education: Rhetoric, Reality, and the Risk of the Market.* San Francisco: Jossey-Bass.

Nyhan, Ronald C., and Lawrence L. Martin. 1999. Comparative Performance Measurements. *Public Productivity & Management Review* 22 (3): 348–364.

Penã, Deagelia M. 2000. *Higher Education Finance Variables: An Analysis.* Almanac of Higher Education. Washington, DC: National Education Association.

Posner, Paul. 1999. Performance Budgeting: A Critical Process. *Public Manager* (28) 3: 8.

Research Associates of Washington. 2000. State Profiles. Retrieved from http://www.rschassoc.com/. Information Is Then Passed on to the National Center for Higher Education Information and Policy at http://www.higheredinfo.org.

Rhodes, Edwardo L., and Lawrence Southwick. 1986. *Determinants of Efficiency in Public and Private Universities.* Columbia: Department of Economics, University of South Carolina.

Rosen, Ellen D. 1997. *Improving Public Sector Productivity: Concepts and Practices.* Newbury Park, CA: Sage.

Rubin, Irene S. 1998. *Class, Tax, and Power: Municipal Budgeting in the United States.* Chatham, NJ: Chatham House.

Ruppert, Sandra S. 1997. Roots and Realities of State-Level Performance Indicator Systems. In *Public Policy and Higher Education*, ed. Lester F. Goodchild, Cheryl D. Lovell, Edward R. Hines, and Judith I. Gill, 315–324. New York: Simon & Schuster, Custom Publishing, and Sage.

Salerno, Carlo. 2003. *On the Technical and Allocative Efficiency of Research-Intensive Higher Education Institutions.* Unpublished doctoral dissertation. The Pennsylvania State University: University Park, PA.

Schachter, Hindy Lauer. 1995. Reinventing Government or Reinventing Ourselves: Two Models for Improving Government Performance. *Public Administration Review* 55 (6): 530. https://doi.org/10.2307/3110344.

Schick, Allen. 1971. *Budget Innovation in the States.* Washington, DC: Brookings Institution.

Schick, Allen. 1990. Budgeting for Results: Recent Developments in Five Industrialized Countries. *Public Administration Review* 50 (1): 26. https://doi.org/10.2307/977291.

Schick, Allen. 2014. The Metamorphoses of Performance Budgeting. *OECD Journal on Budgeting* 13 (2): 49–79. https://doi.org/10.1787/budget-13-5jz2jw9szgs8.

Shea, Robert J. 2008. "Performance Budgeting in the United States." *OECD Journal on Budgeting* 8 (1): 2–3.

Simon, Herbert. 1946. The Proverbs of Administration. In *Classics of Public Administration*, ed. Jay M. Shafritz and Albert C. Hyde, 3rd ed. Pacific Grove, CA: Brooks/Cole Publishing Company.
Snell, Ronald K. 1998. Reinventing Government, Not Easy, but Possible. *State Legislatures* 24 (2): 34–38.
Smith, Kenneth, and Rita Cheng. 2006. Assessing Reforms of Government Accounting and Budgeting. *Public Performance & Management Review* 30 (1): 14–34. https://doi.org/10.2753/pmr1530-9576300101.
Smith, Robert, and Thomas D. Lynch. 2004. *Public Budgeting in America*. Englewood Cliffs, NJ: Prentice Hall.
Swan, Wallace K. 1983. Theoretical Debates Applicable to Budgeting. In *Handbook on Public Budgeting and Financial Management*, ed. Jack Rabin and Thomas D. Lynch. New York: Marcel Dekker.
The Nelson A. Rockefeller Institute of Government. 2000–2003. *Annual Surveys*. Albany, NY: The Nelson A. Rockefeller Institute of Government.
Tuckman, Bruce W. 1978. *Conducting Educational Research*, 2nd ed. Newbury Park, CA: Universities Bloomington. Mimeo, School of Environmental and Public Affairs, Indiana University. Unpublished doctoral dissertation, University of Pennsylvania.
Von Mises, Ludwig. 1944. *Bureaucracy*. New Haven: Yale University Press.
Wellman, Jane. 2002. *Flip Flop in Florida*. Higher Education Policy.
Wildavsky, Aaron. 1964. *The Politics of the Budgetary Process*. Boston: Little Brown.
Wildavsky, Aaron. 1985. *The New Politics of the Budgetary Process*, 2nd ed. New York: HarperCollins.
Willoughby, Katherine G., and Julia E. Melkers. 2001a. Performance Budgeting in the States. In *Quicker, Better, Cheaper? Managing Performance in American Government*, ed. Richard Nathan and Dall Forsythe. Albany: The Rockerfeller Institute.
Willoughby, Katherine G., and Julia E. Melkers. 2001b. Assessing the Impact of Performance Budgeting: A Survey of American States. *Government Finance Review* 17 (2): 25–30.
World Bank. 2003. Performance-Based Budgeting: Beyond Rhetoric. PREMnotes. Public Sector 78. Retrieved from www.worldbank.org, www.highereducation.org.
Zumeta, William. 1996. Meeting the Demand for Higher Education Without Breaking the Bank: A Framework for the Design of State and Higher Education Policies for an Era of Increasing Demand. *Journal of Higher Education* 67 (4): 367–425.
Zumeta, William. 1999. *Fiscal Prospects for Higher Education*. Almanac of Higher Education. Washington, DC: National Education Association.

Zumeta, William. 2000. *Accountability: Challenges for Higher Education*. Almanac of Higher Education. Washington, DC: National Education Association.

Zumeta, William. 2001. *Higher Education Finance in the Nineties: Lessons for the New Millennium*. Almanac of Higher Education. Washington, DC: National Education Association.

CHAPTER 3

Performance Monitoring in New South Wales Australia

Roberta Ryan and Joseph Drew

3.1 Introduction

The most difficult issue connected with performance budgeting is effective performance monitoring—with dozens of years of its use, it still tends to be unsophisticated and inconsistent in practice, both on central and local government levels. Concerning the local level, which is the focus of our chapter, across the six states and one territory that operate systems of local government in the Australian federation, most jurisdictions employ a handful of financial ratios accompanied by arbitrary benchmarks, with no attempt to adjust for environmental constraint (external need such as a high proportion of aged residents, or population density) or expenditure factors (such as high road maintenance unit costs due to unfavourable climate or substrate). This is despite the fact that

R. Ryan (✉) · J. Drew
Institute for Public Policy and Governance,
University of Technology Sydney, Sydney, NSW, Australia
e-mail: Roberta.Ryan@uts.edu.au

J. Drew
e-mail: Joseph.Drew@uts.edu.au

M. S. de Vries et al. (eds.), *Performance-Based Budgeting in the Public Sector*, Governance and Public Management,
https://doi.org/10.1007/978-3-030-02077-4_3

Australian academics have set out the empirical and theoretical considerations which must be met for a competent PM regime (see, for instance, Drew and Dollery 2014a, 2015a; Drew et al. 2017).

This case study not only provides important examples of the problems that can arise when dangers raised in the PM literature are ignored (including implications for performance budgeting), but also a glimpse into how a competent PM system might be subsequently developed in consultation with key stakeholders. PM, for accountability and transparency of New South Wales (NSW) local government has existed for decades in the form of comparative data reports compiled by the state government regulator, the Office of Local Government (formerly known as the Department of Local Government [DLG]; see, for example, DLG [2003]). However, in September 2014 the NSW state government transformed PM into a high stakes game when it announced that it would require local governments in NSW to self-assess according to just seven financial ratios and propose 'voluntary'[1] amalgamations in the event that they failed to achieve the arbitrary benchmarks set for all seven metrics (without Constitutional protection, Australian local governments are subject to legislative control of respective state jurisdictions). Moreover, the PM regime was also employed to determine whether councils would receive access to cheaper finance through the NSW Treasury and to guide performance improvement plans against which councils would be assessed in future years. The PM regime became known as Fit for the Future (FFTF).

Data for FFTF was sourced from audited financial statements in addition to the unaudited Special Schedule 7 (which is an appendix to the financial statements), and unaudited and estimated intercensal population data. It is important to note that Australia employs full accrual accounting, and this has long been known to give rise to distortion in audited financial data—particularly for depreciation accrual estimates (see, for example, Drew 2017). There was thus a rather large audit hole associated with the PM regime. There was also a good deal of synecdoche (in this case pars-pro-toto—taking a part to stand for a whole) which the literature warns may give rise to seriously misleading conclusions and increased opportunity for gaming (see, for example, Bevan and Hood 2006;

[1]Whilst nominally a 'voluntary' process, councils were directed that they must fill in an amalgamation proposal if they failed to meet all seven metrics in addition to the ill-defined 'adequate scale and capacity' criteria.

Walker et al. 2010). Combined with high stakes incentives, these problems meant that the PM regime was inherently non-robust and prone to distortion, gaming and manipulation.

The remainder of this chapter is set out as follows. Next we examine, in greater detail, the causes and scale of distortion arising from the FFTF PM regime. Thereafter we detail the development of a sector-led PM regime created in the aftermath of FFTF. We conclude with some remarks on the importance of good PM design.

3.2 Gaming Arising from Poor Performance Monitoring Design

As noted in the introduction, FFTF was characterised by an audit hole, reliance on known unreliable accruals estimates, reliance on estimated intercensal data and extreme synecdoche. Table 3.1 lists the seven metrics employed in FFTF. The audit hole occurred particularly with respect to the inputs for the Infrastructure Backlog and Asset Maintenance ratios which were derived from the unaudited appendix to the financial statement. The main use of unreliable accruals estimates related to depreciation data (from the audited financial statements) which was employed in three of the seven ratios (Operating, Building and Asset Renewals and 'Efficiency' ratio). Moreover, reliance was placed on intercensal population estimates[2] for the 'Efficiency' ratio and this was problematic because the benchmark was set at a positive linear trend line that was particularly sensitive to population size (because in most cases the actual distribution of data was parabolic and the gradient for the 'fitted' line was often very close to zero). Extreme synecdoche was evident in the fact that just seven ratios—for the most part spanning just three years of data[3]—were used to describe the performance of an entire council. The scholarly literature notes that extreme synecdoche of this sort is a poor representation of performance and is likely to give rise to both seriously misleading conclusions and high levels of gaming (Drew et al. 2017). Indeed, because the final version of the performance indicators was assessed over just three years (with the third year of data being prepared as on 30 June 2015,

[2] In intercensal periods the Australian Bureau of Statistics (ABS) merely estimates population size and these estimates have been shown to contain errors of up to 15.2% (Drew and Dollery 2014b).

[3] The exception was the 'efficiency' ratio assessed over five years.

Table 3.1 Fit for the future financial ratios for NSW councils

Criteria	*Definition*	*Benchmark*
Operating performance	(Operating revenue[a]—operating expenses)/operating revenue[a]	Greater or equal to break-even over 3 years
Own source revenue	Rates, utilities and charges/total operating revenue[b]	Greater than 60% average over 3 years
Building and asset renewal	Asset renewals/depreciation, amortisation and impairment of building and infrastructure assets	Greater than 100% averaged over 3 years
Infrastructure backlog	Estimated cost to bring assets to a satisfactory condition/total WDV of infrastructure assets	Less than 2%
Asset maintenance	Actual asset maintenance/required asset maintenance	Greater than 100% average over 3 years
Debt service	Cost of debt service (interest expense and principal repayments)/operating revenue[a]	Greater than 0% but less than or equal to 20% average over 3 years
Efficiency/ real operating expenditure	Operating expenditure/ population	A decrease in real operating expenditure over time (as measured by a linear regression over five years of data)

[a]Revenue excludes capital grants and contributions
[b]Revenue includes capital grants and contributions
WDV = written down value
Source Adapted from IPART (2015)

many months after the announcement of metrics and benchmarks in September 2014) there were ample opportunities for distortion.

In addition to these serious problems, one of the ratios—the 'Efficiency' ratio—failed to faithfully measure what it purported to assess (FFTF measured efficiency as operational expenditure per capita). Efficiency is the conversion of inputs into outputs and clearly local governments contribute more than one input (for instance staff in addition to money) and do not produce people (instead many services are delivered to properties, and others—such as roads, which are the single largest item of expenditure for most councils—are in fact negatively correlated with population; see Drew and Dollery 2015a).

Unaudited, unreliable data employed in the presence of an audit hole and extreme synecdoche made FFTF particularly *prone* to gaming (which can be defined as the distortion of PM indicators with the intention of creating a more favourable impression of performance that might be warranted). However, for gaming to actually *occur* it is necessary for there to be some conjunction between extant public sector motivations and incentives.

A good start for understanding public service motivations is Julian Le Grand's (2003) classic dichotomy of knights and knaves. Le Grand (2003) defines knights as those who altruistically pursue the public interest, and knaves as those who are motivated principally by their own self-interest. The scholarly literature assumes that gaming is entirely due to the activity of knaves (Le Grand 2010; Bevan and Hood 2006). However, we believe that some incentives might also tap into knightly motivations. To demonstrate this point we can borrow from the fraud literature[4] (see, for instance, Rezaee 2005) which lists incentives as egocentric (mainly personal prestige), economic (in the corporate world this is interpreted in terms of the need to keep investors happy, in local government keeping the state government happy) and ideological apologetics (the 'explaining away' of behaviour by reference to some perceived 'superior' moral cause). In the NSW PM regime incentives took the specific form of the need to keep one's job (amalgamation results in elected representatives and senior management losing their jobs upon the Governor's proclamation of a new boundary; egocentric incentives), the need to keep the State government regulator happy (economic incentives) and a legitimate concern for the future of the local community (this was particularly important for small rural communities where the local government can be the largest employer and the mainstay of the local economy; ideological apologetics). Clearly the first two incentives strike a chord with knaves. What is interesting about the NSW FFTF PM regime was that strong ideological apologetics were also in ample supply—people genuinely feared that amalgamation, particularly in rural areas, had the potential to destroy a local community and turn it into a 'ghost town' (as had occurred as a result of earlier reforms)—and in this particular instance it would seem that knights might also have been incentivised to manipulate and distort data. That is, a knight fearing deleterious outcomes for their local community may have been incentivised to the game in order to pursue the 'local' public interest. Indeed, research by Drew and Grant (2017) demonstrates wide-spread distortion

[4]It should be noted that we are merely borrowing from the conceptual framework of the fraud literature and in no way are trying to imply that fraud—rather than gaming—occurred.

in depreciation accrual data in response to FFTF (Quartile 1 (Q1) −6.3% relative to expected levels; median 0.2%), but even higher levels of distortion for the unaudited Special Schedule 7 data (Cost to Bring Assets to a Satisfactory Standard Q1 −48.6%, median −13.5%; Required Annual Maintenance Q1 −48.8%, median −11.4%). These sort of significant and pervasive distortions suggest that both knaves *and* knights may have been active,[5] responding to the incentives posed by the program. The extensive distortions also meant that the data had very little information value and it is therefore likely to have led to poor public policy decision-making (in relation to amalgamations, provision of debt facilities and performance improvement plans).

Thus, an important lesson arising from FFTF relates to the need to be aware of how extant motivations and introduced incentives might combine to distort practice. If high-stakes incentives can be avoided (for instance by not using data for amalgamation decisions), then gaming will likely be less pronounced. However, gaming is always a possibility and it would therefore have been prudent to introduce an audit process for the PM data. Specifically, if PM data is used for important public policymaking, to augment or even supplant financial statement data (as was the case in NSW), then it would seem important to ensure the integrity of the data through a process *at least* as rigorous as the financial statement audits. In similar vein, if high reliance is placed on PM for decision-making relating to important reforms (in this case a reform that cost up to a billion dollars and had significant implications for residents; Drew and Dollery 2015a) then it might have been prudent to ensure strong legislated penalties were in place to discourage deliberate distortion of performance data (similar to extant penalties for deliberately distorting accounting data).

As it turns out no additional audit effort was invested into FFTF and there were no specific legislated penalties for deliberate PM distortion. Moreover, there is some reason to believe that distortion continued to occur beyond this particular high stakes game and it may therefore have ongoing implications for the transparency and accountability of local government data—and hence for performance budgeting—far into the future (see, for example, Drew 2017).

[5] Although there remains the unlikely possibility that the public service in NSW is largely dominated by knaves.

It would also seem that more metrics were necessary to reduce the synecdochical gap and hence lead to a more fulsome and faithful depiction of local government performance (Drew et al. 2017). Indeed, metrics might have been included to act both as early warning devices and to dissuade individuals from attempting to distort data. For instance, a depreciation ratio (depreciation as a proportion of depreciable infrastructure, property, plant and equipment) would have served this purpose (see Drew and Dollery 2015b). Another remedy might have been to introduce a dialectic element—in the form of short comments by the local government and regulator—to provide important context for the empirical metrics and thus address synecdoche. Indeed, no effort was made to account for environmental constraint and all local governments were held to the same (and hence implausible) standard—for example, Gwydir Shire (which had a population of just 5068; a median wage of $39,186 and 1805 km of roads) was asked to achieve the same benchmarks as Mosman on Sydney's affluent North Shore (which had a population of 30,496, a median wage of $64,631 and just 86 km of roads; Office of Local Government 2015).

In view of these problems and evidence of distortion, it is not unreasonable to suggest that FFTF is a good case study in 'what not to do' when introducing a PM regime. This then begs the question regarding whether things might be done better—a question to which we now turn our attention.

3.3 A More Comprehensive Framework

One legacy of the poorly designed PM underpinning FFTF seems to have been reduced levels of trust. Many local governments feared that future performance data might be turned against them as evidence to justify forced regulatory actions; citizens read reports in prominent newspapers which ridiculed the integrity of local government performance data[6]; whilst the NSW Government seems to have been paralysed as a

[6] An example of this is the report in the *Sydney Morning Herald* that provocatively stated: 'Sydney's roads are getting better even without being fixed… according to the city's councils, which have recently wiped from their balance sheets a billion dollars of liabilities such as run-down old roads, often without spending a cent' (Robertson and Buckingham-Jones 2015).

result of losing its Minister and key senior staff in the fallout from FFTF (as well as having to back away from a number of the proposed amalgamations contested in the Courts).

Thus, the post-FFTF climate did not appear to be prima facie conducive to establishing a new performance monitoring framework. It therefore came as something of a surprise when the University of Technology's (UTS) Institute for Public Policy and Governance (IPPG) was approached in March 2016 by a large regional council to help guide the development and implementation of a local government sector-led performance monitoring program. The local government helped to recruit 17 councils to participate in the development and trial of a comprehensive set of metrics. The first meeting was attended by representatives from councils, peak bodies (one for councillors and one for senior staff) and the NSW state agency for local government where all parties explicated on their shared aspirations for a sector-led PM regime. The expertise of the authors was brought in for meetings during which empirical and theoretical solutions were presented to participating councils, peak bodies and the state regulatory agency.

As suggested, trust was a matter of great import to all concerned and it was therefore important to foster trust by ensuring that the process was perceived to be independent and free from any apprehension of bias. Having the independence of the University to facilitate the meetings and guide the development of the suite of performance indicators was therefore a critical ingredient. However, it was also important that all parties felt that their input was actively sought and carefully considered in the design of the entire PM regime. Thus, the process was characterised by genuine collaboration—all elements of PM were on the table and, along with facilitating the process, the role of the University was to provide expert advice on the advantages and disadvantages of various metrics, comparative strategies and contextual mediators. Indeed the final suite of metrics, along with the presentation of same, was quite different from anything that participants had initially conceived.

We also drew on our internationally-recognised expertise, knowledge of educational psychology and the broader scholarly literature to arrange performance indicators according to dimensions of performance.

In sum, performance was measured across 47 indicators spread over 11 independent dimensions. Each dimension was chosen to reflect important matters from the scholarly literature and contemporaneous local government sustainability debates.

Each dimension represented a distinct aspect of government performance which may have constituted the entire object of end-user inquiry—and for these cases ordering by dimension reduced information costs for end-users considerably. Moreover, organising metrics by dimensions also increased the utility of the PM suite for end-users interested in whole-of-local-government performance because it effectively ordered the cognitive load (thus enhancing comprehension). As such, the PM suite developed ensured that a balance was struck between the need to provide a comprehensive suite of performance indicators on the one hand, and accessibility and utility on the other.

Below is a brief outline of the performance dimensions used in the NSW pilot as agreed upon by the stakeholders. The descriptors below also include a thumbnail profile of one metric developed specifically for the dimension in question.

3.3.1 Performance Dimension One: Resilience

Resilience is a key concept in local government sustainability. We used this dimension to represent council ability to respond to economic shocks. Both fiscal and staff slack can play an important role where councils are required to respond to shocks. In the NSW pilot, the workplace health and safety hours lost per FTE ratio were developed as one such measure of staff slack (i.e. staff resources which could theoretically be drawn upon in times of economic shock). This metric may also point to trends which have implications for human resource practice. This dimension comprised seven metrics in total.

3.3.2 Performance Dimension Two: Liquidity

Liquidity is the ability of a council to honour its obligations when they fall due. In the NSW pilot, the *current ratio* was used as one measure of Council ability to fund short-run obligations. We note that a liquidity failure is generally an extreme event which comes after a long period of fiscal stress. We recommended that councils should remain cognisant of both predictable cash flows and the importance of trends when interpreting this ratio. Two metrics in total were developed for this dimension.

3.3.3 *Performance Dimension Three: Debt*

The use of debt is an expedient method for addressing council infrastructure backlogs. *Nett financial liabilities (as a proportion of revenue)* was agreed upon as the metric for assessing council debt capacity. With respect to this dimension, we highlighted that councils should be mindful of the potential moral hazards posed by debt, such as the erosion of intergenerational equity.

3.3.4 *Performance Dimension Four: Infrastructure Renewals*

Whilst commonly employed, there has been some criticism of the existing measurement of this performance dimension, which is supported by the empirical evidence. However, conclusions regarding this performance dimension can be made by comparing the change in relevant ratios over time. The *buildings, infrastructure and other structures renewal ratio* was the agreed-upon measure for this dimension in the NSW pilot. We advised that this data should be interpreted with reference to the current and past depreciation practices employed at council.

3.3.5 *Performance Dimension Five: Local Government Efficiency Proxies*

Technical efficiency is the conversion of a set of inputs (staff and operational expenditure) into a set of outputs (goods and services provided by the local government). In the NSW pilot, we provided a suite of proxies for local government efficiency, of which *Road operation expenditure per kilometre* was one. This metric expresses council road expenditure as a proportion of the length of council-maintained roads. It provides a basis for comparison of efficiency in road maintenance and construction. In using this metric, we recommended that councils should principally focus on comparing performance against itself over time after also taking cognisance of one-off expenditures which might skew results in any given year. This dimension comprises four metrics in total.

3.3.6 *Performance Dimension Six: Budget Accuracy*

This dimension measures council accuracy with respect to budgeting. *Deviation from budgeted revenue* was one metric which was trialled for this dimension in NSW. A positive result for this measure has a favourable impact on council overall financial position. However, we stressed that frequently under-estimating council revenue could result in undesirable outcomes such as exacerbation of infrastructure backlogs. Two metrics in total were developed for this dimension.

3.3.7 *Performance Dimension Seven: Resident and Business Satisfaction with Local Government and Delivery on Community Plans*

Resident and business satisfaction with council is an important item to measure. To facilitate meaningful analysis we advocated that local governments should conduct standardised state-wide surveys on an annual basis. This would allow council to examine trends over time with respect to changes in relevant exogenous factors. Whilst *overall resident satisfaction* and *overall business satisfaction metrics* were incorporated into the NSW pilot, the lack of existing council data prevented analysis at that time. Three metrics in total represented this dimension.

3.3.8 *Performance Dimension Eight: Governance*

Under the descriptor of 'governance' NSW stakeholders agreed upon the examination of transparency, accountability, effective political representation and disaggregated staff turnover measures in turn. In NSW, the *number of council decisions made at meetings closed to the public* was used as a metric to reflect council transparency in representative decision-making. Nine metrics in total were developed as measures for this dimension.

3.3.9 *Performance Dimension Nine: Demographic Risk*

Shifts in the demographic profile of a local government area can expose council to risk due to changing resident demand and revenue capacity. The metrics for this dimension were sourced from the ABS and council-supplied data. In the NSW pilot, three areas of demographic risk were examined, one of which was a demographic risk with respect to council-supplied business trend data. 13 ABS data items and 2 council-supplied data items represented this dimension overall.

3.3.10 Performance Dimension Ten: Consistency of Accounting Accruals Estimates

Discordant practice in calculating depreciation makes it difficult for decision-makers to understand councils' true financial position. In the absence of a suitable standard metric, it is difficult for councils to know how their practice compares to that of other councils. In the NSW pilot, we developed a depreciation rate metric to represent the rate of depreciation relative to the council depreciable asset base. Whilst it is not a perfect measure, it should alert council to whether its practice is broadly consistent with that of other local councils.

3.3.11 Performance Dimension Eleven: Equity

We have developed the metrics under this dimension to indicate the level of equity in council service provision and the taxation which is properly employed to fund public goods and services. The latter is measured by the *distribution of tax burden* metric, as trialled in NSW. This metric allows council to understand whether or not the variance evident in some council taxation structures might have evolved over time without the deliberate consideration of equity or capacity to pay. Two metrics, in total, were developed for this dimension.

Countering the various problems observed in the FFTF programme was an important focus for the sector-led PM participants. As we described in the previous section, these problems included *inter alia* extreme synecdochical gap, lack of contextual mediators, failure to adjust for environmental constraint, reliance on unreliable accruals estimates and intercensal data, misleading ratios (such as the 'efficiency' ratio) and strong incentives that appealed to extant public sector (i.e. State government) motivations.

Synecdoche was perceived as the greatest problem and the greatest challenge by the sector-led PM participants. The problem occurs, in large part, due to the trade-off between synecdoche and utility—as synecdoche is addressed by adding more metrics there is the risk that the sheer number of metrics will exceed cognitive capacity (the famous 7 ± 2

from educational psychology), and thus result in limited utility for end-users. There are at least three main solutions to this imposing problem: Reduce empirical performance metrics down to a single number for each of the distinct performance dimensions by using Factor Analysis (or variants; see Drew and Dollery 2016a), employ Cluster Analysis to 'sort' performance into performance groups (either for all performance or by distinct performance dimension), or organise performance indicators according to dimensions deemed important by stakeholders such that no dimension has more metrics than might be reasonably expected to be within the cognitive capacity of end-users. Not surprisingly the parsimonious solution (organising by dimensions deemed important to stakeholders) was chosen by participants. This reflects reticence to incur on-going costs for complex analyses, the need to be able to communicate the empirical technique to end-users and the importance of fostering trust through 'hands-on' participation in methodology.

The second problem was to provide satisfactory contextual mediators. End-users need to be able to appreciate specific challenges that may have impacted on performance over the relevant period. For instance, a flood or bush fire could be expected to increase capital expenditure and might require maintenance of infrastructure to be brought forward. The solution to this problem is very straight-forward—simply allow local governments to include a short explanation of salient events. Such use of dialectical mediators is consonant with the seminal work of De Bruijn (2007). Apart from providing important context for interpreting metrics, dialogue can also address synecdochical gap (particularly for aspects of performance that cannot be captured by empirical performance indicators) and reduce the incentives to game (because local governments can provide important information that explains unexpected changes in performance there is less incentive to game performance indicators).

A further problem faced by the sector-led PM participants was the need to address environmental constraint. The main methods for dealing with this problem are to (i) eschew benchmarks in favour of *trends* for individual local governments over time (which means that there are no comparability problems provided local conditions do not change appreciably over the short-term), (ii) conduct cluster analysis to organise councils into groups facing similar environmental constraints (see, for example, Drew and Dollery 2016b), or (iii) introduce metrics which measure and report on environmental constraint. Once again, parsimony was favoured by stakeholders (a combination of trends over time and environmental constraint indicators)—although plans were made to conduct cluster analysis for the second phase of the project.

The next problem related to unreliable data. There was no appetite or budget for additional PM audit effort so alternative strategies had to be devised. One method of at least flagging unreliable data is to include 'early warning' performance indicators. For instance, a depreciation rate indicator alerts end-users to possible distortion and may dissuade gamers from attempting to subvert PM regimes. Moreover, in the case of the sector-led PM regime, feedback from participating councils suggested that the ratio also performed an additional and critical function—to alert local government Chief Financial Officers to inconsistent depreciation practice that they had not hitherto recognised. A second strategy to deal with the problem of unreliable data was to simply replace same with more reliable estimates—for example, participants elected to replace the unreliable population input with numbers of taxable properties (not only was this input more accurate, but it was also a better proxy for actual service provision). The final strategy was to remove incentives for distortion, by ensuring that no high-stakes consequences were associated with the sector-led regime, that fair comparisons were made between the council and itself over time and that opportunities for contextual mediation were provided.

The sector-led PM participants were also keen to remove misleading metrics such as the 'efficiency' ratio which neither measured efficiency nor was reliable. The most suitable empirical methodology to precisely measure technical efficiency is data envelopment analysis (DEA) which can be applied inter-temporally (see, for example, Drew and Dollery 2015c). However, as we have already noted, sector-led PM stakeholders were keen to avoid complex empirical techniques and reliance on third parties to conduct the same. Therefore participants instead elected to replace the 'efficiency' ratio with a *series* of ratios to better reflect the costs and demands for major services—specifically ratios which measured road operational expenditure per kilometre of road; water provision operational expenditure per water connexion; sewer service operational expenditure per sewer connexion; and, residual operating expenditure (excluding the previous three items) per assessment.

In sum, forty-seven performance indicators were employed over eleven orthogonal dimensions which stood in stark contrast to the mere seven financial ratios employed in FFTF.

An important element of the sector-led PM will be the use of a peer-review process. This aspect, yet to be trialled, will involve engaging councils, developing the preferred model for performance improvement, piloting and evaluation. Councils identified this as a desirable feature of a performance improvement framework which will enable like councils to review each other's' performance by councils choosing meaningful and relevant comparators; challenging what they are doing, how and why. This focuses councils on self-reflection and learning through a 'critical friend' approach which is evidence-based and by identifying what a council is and is not good at through facilitation and dialogue. This represents a shift from a diagnostic comparison to one with a focus on council improvement through qualitative engagement, revealing findings immediately to support momentum and implementation support through follow up quarterly and annually.

3.4 Final Message

Our case study illustrates that PM done poorly—that is, PM which ignores the lessons of the scholarly literature and respectful working relationships between levels of government—is likely to give rise to gaming and other unanticipated outcomes. This suggests that PM architects must have a good knowledge of the literature as well as the time and financial resources to design a robust and reliable system, along with good working relationships with the local government sector. If any of these factors are missing then it might be better to eschew PM entirely—for our case study illustrates that the legacy of poorly designed PM may well be poor public policy decision-making, persistent distortion (with concomitant deleterious effects for performance budgeting) and reduced levels of trust and intergovernmental co-operation.

However, as the UTS IPPG project demonstrates there is an appetite from local government for PM done properly (to inform budgeting and decision-making at the local government level) and benefits will accrue from the implementation of a competent PM regime. Perhaps the most critical ingredient to a successful PM architecture is for the process to be grounded in genuine engagement with key stakeholders—a process facilitated by an independent and knowledgeable entity ensures that there is no apprehension of bias and that all reasonable solutions to PM problems are presented to decision-makers. Moreover, the input from key stakeholders ensures that a range of perspectives are taken into account in order to optimise the utility of the PM regime—that is, end-users and PM subjects are in the best position to know what data will be most valuable (for local decision-making including budgetary deliberations), and what problems must be overcome in relation to certain desired metrics.

One interesting finding from the sector-led project was the preference of stakeholders for parsimony. This should not be taken to suggest that problems cannot or should not be overcome—but rather serve as a reminder that architects of PM should keep their minds open to the possibility and desirability of simple solutions to imposing problems.

Ideally, a national approach to local government PM should be explored because the satisfactory performance of local government is critical to the prosperity of the entire nation (not least because of the fact that local government is responsible for crucial infrastructure and services such as the bulk of the nation's road network). However, lack of political goodwill, a fragmented local governance regime in Australia, lack of resourcing, turf wars between jurisdictions and inconsistent accounting practices have thus far prevented this important initiative from being progressed. Our hope is that these obstacles will be overcome in the future—if they are, then case studies of this sort, which highlight potential pitfalls and solutions, will be of paramount importance to the design of an effective PM regime.

References

Bevan, Gwyn, and Christopher Hood. 2006. What's Measured Is What Matters: Targets and Gaming in the English Public Health Care System. *Public Administration* 84 (3): 517–538. https://doi.org/10.1111/j.1467-9299.2006.00600.x.

De Bruijn, Hans. 2007. *Managing Performance in the Public Sector*. London: Routledge and Taylor & Francis.

Department of Local Government (DLG). 2003. *Comparative Information on New South Wales Local Government Councils, 2002–2003*. Sydney: Department of Local Government.

Drew, Joseph. 2017. Playing for Keeps: Local Government Distortion of Depreciation Accruals in Response to High-Stakes Public Policy-Making. *Public Money & Management* 38 (1): 57–64. https://doi.org/10.1080/09540962.2017.1389542.

Drew, Joseph, and Brian Dollery. 2014a. Estimating the Impact of the Proposed Greater Sydney Metropolitan Amalgamations on Municipal Financial Sustainability. *Public Money & Management* 34 (4): 281–288.

Drew, Joseph, and Brian Dollery. 2014b. Keeping It In-House—Households as an Alternative Proxy for Local Government Output. *Australian Journal of Public Administration* 73 (2): 235–246.

Drew, Joseph, and Brian Dollery. 2015a. Less Haste More Speed: The Fit for Future Reform Program in New South Wales Local Government. *Australian Journal of Public Administration* 75 (1): 78–88.

Drew, Joseph, and Brian Dollery. 2015b. Inconsistent Depreciation Practice and Public Policymaking: Local Government Reform in New South Wales. *Australian Accounting Review* 25 (1): 28–37.

Drew, Joseph, and Brian Dollery. 2015c. The State of Things—The Dynamic Efficiency of Australian States and Territories. *Economic Papers* 34 (3): 165–176.

Drew, Joseph, and Brian Dollery. 2016a. Summary Execution: The Impact of Alternative Summarization Strategies on Local Governments. *Public Administration Quarterly* 40 (4): 814–841.

Drew, Joseph, and Brian Dollery. 2016b. What's in a Name? Assessing the Performance of Local Government Classification Systems. *Local Government Studies* 42 (2): 248–266.

Drew, Joseph, and Bligh Grant. 2017. Means, Motive and Opportunity: Distortion of Public Policy Making Performance Management Data. *Australian Journal of Public Administration* 75 (1): 237–250.

Drew, Joseph, Janine O'Flynn, and Bligh Grant. 2017. Performing What? Exploring and Expanding the Notion of Synecdoche in Performance Management Practice. *Public Administration Quarterly* 42: 395–424.

Le Grand, Julian. 2003. *Motivation, Agency, and Public Policy: Of Knights & Knaves, Pawns & Queens*. Oxford: Oxford University Press.

Le Grand, Julian. 2010. Knights and Knaves Return: Public Service Motivation and the Delivery of Public Services. *International Public Management Journal* 13 (1): 56–71.

Office of Local Government. 2015. *Time Series Data*. Sydney: Office of Local Government.

Rezaee, Zabihollah. 2005. Causes, Consequences, and Deterence of Financial Statement Fraud. *Critical Perspectives on Accounting* 16 (3): 277–298. https://doi.org/10.1016/s1045-2354(03)00072-8.

Robertson, James, and Sam Buckingham-Jones. 2015. Sydney Councils Shift $1 Billion Repair Bill with Accounting 'Fiction' in Fit for the Future Scramble. *Sydney Morning Herald*, 22 June 2015.

Walker, Richard M., George A. Boyne, and Gene A. Brewer. 2010. *Public Management and Performance*. Cambridge: Cambridge University Press.

CHAPTER 4

Performance Budgeting in the Netherlands

Tjerk Budding, Bram Faber and Ed Vosselman

4.1 Introduction

As in many countries, in the Netherlands an important catalyst for the introduction of performance budgeting was the so-called New Public Management (NPM) movement. Compared to other countries, the Netherlands is generally regarded as a country that does not take an extreme position. On the one hand, it does not belong to the front-runners of countries that propagated NPM reforms already in

T. Budding (✉) · B. Faber
School of Business and Economics, Vrije Universiteit Amsterdam, Amsterdam, The Netherlands
e-mail: g.budding@vu.nl

B. Faber
e-mail: a.s.c.faber@vu.nl

E. Vosselman
Institute for Management Research, Radboud University, Nijmegen, The Netherlands
e-mail: e.vosselman@fm.ru.nl

M. S. de Vries et al. (eds.), *Performance-Based Budgeting in the Public Sector*, Governance and Public Management,
https://doi.org/10.1007/978-3-030-02077-4_4

an early stage (such as the USA and New Zealand), but on the other hand the reforms attracted a lot of attention (Hood 1995; Pollitt and Bouckaert 2004) and were quite influential.

One of the themes in which NPM played an important role were improvements in the planning and control structures and processes in governmental organizations. Hereby, one of the reforms aimed at connecting policy-making and the allocation of means, and, thus, a connection between political and economic considerations. Initiatives to realize this connection were already taken before the 1980s. Inspired by the US Planning Programming Budgeting System, in 1971 the Dutch central government set up a coordinating entity aimed to assess government spending by doing policy analysis, hereby using both quantitative and qualitative data. At local government level a similar initiative was initiated; the association of Dutch municipalities established a study group for policy analysis. Neither project was a success: the resulting insights were not considered useful in daily practice. At present, there are new attempts to connect political and economic dimensions that are considered more successful. An important contemporary tool for such a connection is performance budgeting: forecasting and target setting of the performance of governmental organizations and the associated funds. In this chapter we will review some of the developments in performance budgeting at two governmental levels: central government and municipalities.

As we will show, a search for the right form can be observed in the Netherlands—as in many other countries (see OECD 2014)—in how to connect policy and means. In addition to that, we also find that the Dutch public sector organizations also struggle in how to present policy objectives and results as well as financial means (to be) consumed.

4.2 Performance Budgeting in Central Government

Performance budgeting in the Dutch central government went through a range of different stages to arrive at the form we are familiar with nowadays (see Fig. 4.1).

The Compatibility Act is considered the centerpiece of the budget cycle of the Dutch central government. It establishes rules concerning the powers and procedures to be followed with regard to the budget, financial management and supervision of the minister of finance. As of 2001 the Compatibility Act also regulates the powers, duties and

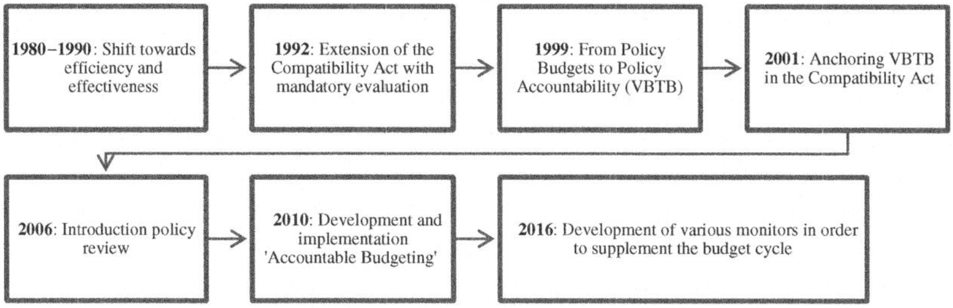

Fig. 4.1 Historical overview of the developments with regard to central government reporting since 1980

composition of the Court of Audit. The Constitution guarantees that the parliament and the senate are involved in the preparation of the budget and the annual report.

Each annual budgeting cycle takes approximately two-and-a-half years and consists of three phases: (1) budget preparation, (2) budget execution, and (3) accountability (Budding and van Schaik 2015). Budget preparation starts in year *t*–2 with state budgetary guidelines being sent by the minister of finance to ministerial colleagues. These guidelines are a further interpretation of the rules laid down in the Central Government Finance Management Act. In January of year *t*–1 budget preparation at each ministry starts. In spring, negotiations take place, both on a civil service and a political level. Over the summer months each ministry prepares its own budget and the Ministry of Finance drafts the Budget Memorandum. In mid-August the final drafts are sent to the council of ministers for a decision. The documents are presented, with great ceremony, to parliament on the third Tuesday of September, the so-called Prince's Day (*Prinsjesdag*).

Execution of the budget starts on 1 January of every year. Only after parliament has approved the budget, ministers are formally allowed to spend up to the specified ceiling. In cases where a minister wants to spend more, parliament must be asked for permission. Before doing so, the minister of finance has to be asked for his/her opinion. Furthermore, ministers are subject to rather strict budget rules, which are set at the start of each coalition period. These rules include (among others) that a minister's new policy should be covered within his/her own budget and that overruns should be compensated for within the ministry in which these take place.

At year end, each ministry prepares its own annual report and the Ministry of Finance also produces the Central Government Annual Financial Report, which combines the financial statements of all ministries. The reports of each ministry are audited by the Central Government Audit Service and are presented to parliament on the third Wednesday in May, the so-called Accountability Day (*Verantwoordingsdag*). The Central Government Annual Financial Report has to be approved by the Dutch Supreme Audit Institution. The budgetary cycle formally ends with the approval of the so-called Final Laws (*Slotwetten*) by the parliament, discharging each minister of their financial management.

Traditionally, affordability and manageability of government expenditure were found to play a key role in Dutch public spending. The 1980s and 1990s are characterized by a shift toward efficiency and effectiveness. Compliance with legislation and regulations was no longer at the core, as was traditionally the case. This happened under the influence of an emerging NPM paradigm, which manifested itself internationally as well (Groot and Budding 2008; Wiesel and Modell 2014). More and more public services were outsourced to the market. However, working in competitive relationships entailed the risk that the external party (the agent) would not take up the matters—either quantitatively or qualitatively—as intended by the government (the principal). To limit this risk, it was found to be of great importance to make clear agreements on mutual expectations by means of standards, performance indicators and contracts. It was expected that the high monitoring costs this demanded would be offset by the profit of working in a market relationship.

Accountability in just financial terms has its shortcomings. For example, costs (in more or less detail) may be indicators for resource consumption, but they do not represent the full performance of an organization or department. Costs are insufficient to fully *re*-present the performance for which an administrator or a manager is responsible. Moreover, because of a lack of concrete buyer–supplier relationships revenues can hardly be calculated. This raises the question of how the effectiveness of the programs and activities can be made visible. Many public organizations have responded to that question by complementing budgets with a system containing non-financial performance measures.

These measures further specify the desired (and realized) resource consumption and performance.

The monitoring of performance remained a red thread in Dutch government. In 1998, the report 'Evaluation research in central government' was written, because of the growing importance of non-financial policy information and the qualitative requirements that were imposed. Moreover, evaluations were often not reported to the Court of Audit, even though this was mandatory according to the revised Compatibility Act. In 1999, the government memorandum From Policy Budgets to Policy Accountability (*Van Beleidsbegroting Tot Beleidsverantwoording*, VBTB) was published, with proposals to arrive at a better understanding of the link between policy, performance and resources, as well as the link between the budget and the annual report. Through the use of systematic evaluations, performance indicators, information on goal achievement and explanatory texts, a 'body of evidence' (Van der Knaap 2006) was produced to enable the holding accountable of government.

In addition, financial information was linked to policy information and non-financial information. In 2000 the Court of Audit concluded that the evaluation function still offered room for improvement as this function was not yet clearly defined, and it was interpreted differently across the Dutch government. In order to systematize evaluation, the so-called three W-questions were formulated:

- What do we want to achieve?
- What are we going to do in order to achieve the goals?
- What will it cost?

A core priority of the VBTB reform was to increasingly make use of a list of performance indicators and policy targets in policy documents and budgets, in order to operationalize the three W-questions. This method has also been termed results-oriented budgeting (Van der Knaap 2007), and can be seen in the perspective of the shift from the (traditional) line-item budget to a program budget. The number of line-items in the budget was reduced from around 800 to 160 (De Jong et al. 2013). To highlight the programmatic aspects of policy, the 'policy section' was introduced, where policy priorities are explained by means of policy developments and their financial consequences. Accountability Day was first introduced in 2000, in order to close the circle.

The beginning of the twenty-first century announced a further extension of results-oriented budgeting, under the influence of NPM. In 2004 the VBTB method was evaluated, and it was concluded that especially *ex ante* evaluations could be further improved. The problem analysis, a baseline measurement and the expected effects of the policy, was often absent, or not elaborated thoroughly. The *ex ante* evaluations were more estimates than actual evaluation studies. Moreover, among departments there was virtually no structured and systematic consideration of policy. It was recommended that ex ante evaluations, incidentally taking place during policy preparation, should become a fixed part of the governmental policy cycle and that new policy alternatives should be identified and assessed for effects and political consequences in new or modified policies (Houppermans et al. 2015). In addition, there was little evidence that the new program classification that replaced the line-item classification led to large-scale reallocation of expenditure—while the information value of the budgets and the administrative burden for departments for a long time remained a matter of debate.

In 2006 the Policy Review was introduced: an integral *ex post* evaluation of a general policy objective. This review consists of a description of the problem analysis and the role of the central government, in addition to policy objectives and instruments used. It furthermore contains an analysis of the social effects that have occurred and a description of the resources deployed. An external expert was involved in forming the final opinion. However, it has been noted in a government-wide context that the use of external experts is often instrumental. Experts are involved in, or consulted at the end of the process. Therefore they can often only make a very limited contribution to the final product (Hoppe et al. 2016).

A need arose to reduce the number of objectives and performance indicators in budgets and annual accounts. Despite indicators and mandatory policy evaluations, insight into the effectiveness of a large proportion of government expenditure was still experienced as insufficient. Moreover, evaluations tended to stay within the fixed boundaries of policy ambitions and theories. As a result, the effectiveness and validity of existing policy programs were virtually never questioned, with the result that inefficient policy programs could continue for a long time.

In order to restore the perceived 'flaws' of VBTB, the Ministry of Finance started with the development of the new methodology of Accountable Budgeting (*Verantwoord Begroten*, VB). This form of budgeting was much more based on the powers and responsibilities of the minister. It should result in a clearer understanding of the minister's policy commitment, which in turn would ideally lead to clear policy accountability. The budget primarily became a financial document. Three new W-questions were asked, narrowing down the scope of the governmental budget:

- What does the minister want to achieve?
- What will the minister do in order to achieve the goals?
- What does the civil service apparatus resorting under the responsibility of the minister cost?

From 2013 onwards, Accountable Budgeting has been fully operative. Some of its core elements are a more detailed, centrally defined presentation of policy expenditures; separate presentation of organizational (personnel and material) and policy expenses; and stricter criteria on the use of performance targets and indicators (De Jong et al. 2013). It also links policy analyses to the annual report, in order to prevent duplication of work in this area.

The implementation of these reforms encountered some resistance. Policy directorates in particular have tried to recover their lost 'space' in budget documents by bending the new rules (De Jong et al. 2013). This is related to the idea that external pressure can make individuals and organizations decide to oppose reforms (Verhoest 2010). In practice this has led to a degree of diversity in views and mores in the governmental budget and annual report, which are partly empirically confirmed (Kraan 2010; BOR 2015; Hoppe et al. 2016; AVRo 2017) (see also Fig. 4.2).

After experiencing a lack of political interest for financial and performance information in Dutch Parliament, a member introduced a systematic approach for parliamentarians to review the country's national budget and accounts (Duisenberg, 2016). The approach draws mainly on corporate experience, and is a parliamentary version of a corporate audit committee that works with a standardized review questionnaire, looking for example at the various budgetary aspects of input, throughput, output, and (intermediate or final) outcome. Upon its first introduction in 2014, it gained some support and is presently being used by several parliamentary committees.

Fig. 4.2 Innovations in monitoring performance in Dutch Parliament

The Study Group for Budgetary Space (2016) found that in less than half of the policy reviews (to some extent) statements are made about the effectiveness of the policy pursued. For this reason, it was advised to start the operation Insight Into Quality (*Inzicht in Kwaliteit*). Among others, the project focuses on the following directions: (1) a greater role for independent parties in the evaluation system, (2) improved knowledge sharing between departments, (3) more flexibility and customization in the deployment and application of budgetary instruments, and (4) the development of new approaches within existing instruments.

In recent years, some innovations were implemented with respect to evaluation processes and foundations of public decision-making. In 2016 the Compatibility Act was supplemented with regard to non-financial information. An additional obligation came into effect that proposals, intentions and commitments should contain an explanation of the objectives, effectiveness and efficiency that are being pursued. At the moment, the Ministry of Finance is also initiating a number of changes that promote and consolidate improvements of (the use of) budget and accountability information, under the title of 'Towards a Digital Budget'. An example of this is the website rijksfinancien.nl, which experiments with respect to an informative display and visualizations of budgeted and actual data, and also tries to link this to an increasingly larger selection of outcome indicators.

A final development is the emergence of thematic approaches to performance information, rather than the perspective of the budget cycle. In 2017, a temporary parliamentary committee recommended the development of an annual Monitor Broad Welfare (*Monitor Brede Welvaart*). Its first edition was published in 2018. In this context, the Dutch Ministry of Health, Welfare and Sport developed a monitor to make the state of Dutch health care more transparent.

4.3 Performance Budgeting in Municipalities

As described in the introduction section of this chapter, Dutch municipalities began discussing performance budgeting systems already in the early 1970s (see Fig. 4.3). Inspired by the US Planning Programming Budgeting System (PPBS), Dutch municipalities looked for ways to connect policy-making, goal setting and reporting. However, a project to actually make the connection between these aspects was not considered successful.

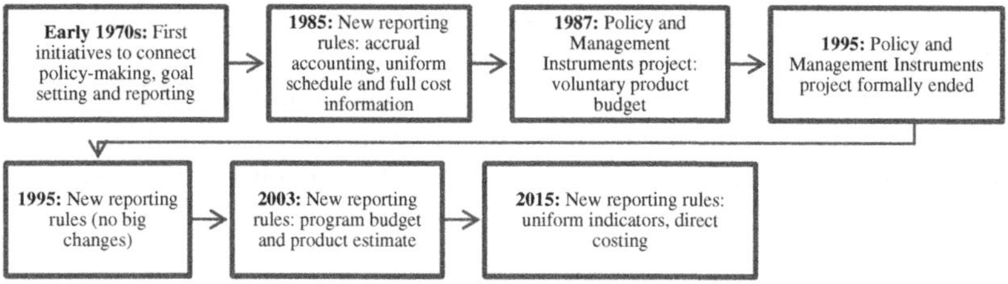

Fig. 4.3 Historical overview of the developments with regard to municipal reporting since 1980

In the 1980s two new initiatives were taken. The first is the implementation of new reporting rules in 1985. These rules prescribed that municipalities had to use accrual accounting. Moreover, as part of these new rules an accounting scheme was introduced that forced municipalities to distinguish 80 major policy areas, so-called functions, in their yearly budget and annual report (Bac et al. 1991; VB Groep 1995). This uniform scheme aimed to promote comparability between municipalities. The second initiative was the introduction of the Policy and Management Instruments (*Beleids en Beheers Intrumentarium*, BBI) project by the Ministry of the Interior and Kingdom Relations. This project provided ideas about how information could be improved to effectively support planning and control decisions in municipalities (Van Helden 1998, 2000; Houwaart et al. 1995). The BBI project was introduced in 1987 and stimulated municipalities to apply private sector tools, such as output budgeting, responsibility accounting and cost allocation (Ter Bogt 2004). Municipalities were encouraged to change the traditional budget format that was structured according to policy areas (e.g., social security, education, infrastructure) into a product-based format, facilitating the identification of specific services (e.g., primary education and maintenance of canals), their related costs and revenues and related performance indicators. The BBI project also stimulated employees of municipalities and other people involved (e.g., consultants) to share knowledge and best practices with regard to planning and control practices. Many civil servants indeed followed courses or participated in workshops, consultancy firms were frequently asked to assist, and the (professional) media paid a lot of attention to the project. In 1995, the BBI project formally ended. Several studies have been published which showed that whereas municipalities have put a lot of effort in implementing BBI measures, the actual improvements lagged behind (Van Helden 1998; Aardema 2002). After analyzing several studies on BBI, Aardema (2002) found that in many instances municipalities did not really use performance indicators to show policy results, but rather used them for illustrative purposes.

In 2002, central government enacted the new act Dual Municipal Administration (*Wet Dualisering Gemeentebestuur*). This dual system distinguished between the municipal council on the one hand—expected to focus its attention more on policy-making and evaluation of policy execution—and the board of mayor and aldermen on the other hand—expected to focus its attention more on the daily management of the municipality and its civil servants (Hendriks and Tops 2003). Although this new law mainly applied to the political system, it also brought about changes for the civil servants and the planning and control processes. As a result of these changes also the external reporting regulations had to be adapted. A new act Decision Budget and Accountability for Provinces and Municipalities (*Besluit begroting en verantwoording provincies en gemeenten*) came into effect in fiscal year 2004 and prescribed that municipalities had to publish both a program budget and a product estimate. The program budget is the municipal council's policy document that stipulates political priorities, future activities, the resources involved and the outcomes to be achieved. It is supposed to contain clear information on the municipal council's political program, enabling political decision-makers to focus on the main political issues in coherent policy programs. The board of mayor and aldermen is responsible for the execution of the program budget, and is held accountable by the municipal council. Municipalities are free to determine their own programs. However, the Ministry of the Interior and Kingdom Relations advises that three questions be answered for each program:

- What do we want to achieve?
- What are we going to do?
- How many resources are we going to use?

The first question has to be answered by defining goals and effects. When this has been done, programs and activities have to be specified that aim to realize these goals and effects (question 2). Finally, the resources that are needed for that need to be budgeted (question 3).

After the municipal council has made its final decision on the program budget, the product estimate is prepared. In this document, the program budget is translated into a specific work program for the civil servants, including information on the necessary municipal output and the associated costs. The program budget and product estimate are intended to delineate more clearly the political and managerial responsibilities of the municipal council and of the board of mayor and aldermen. Both documents enable each actor to exercise control more effectively: the municipal council uses a program budget to control policy execution while the mayor and aldermen use a product estimate to control the service and output provision of the civil servants. Although application was mandatory from 2004 onwards, the actual changes in the documents varied in practice, especially in the first years of the new regulation (Dekker and Budding 2005).

In practice, the distinction between the program budget and the product estimate turned out to be rather problematic. A formal evaluation study commissioned by the Ministry of the Interior and Kingdom Relations showed that none of the municipalities that were visited for this study used the product estimate in the way it was intended. In many instances the product estimate was not only offered to the board of mayor and aldermen, but also to the municipal council. Furthermore, the board of mayor and aldermen hardly used this document. Finally, the researchers found that in some municipalities both documents were combined (Schilder et al. 2010). In sum, the evaluation study concluded that the added value of a separate product budget could be questioned.

Another finding of the evaluation study was that the program budgets mostly contained 'story telling' information on policy issues, rather than laying a direct link between means and policy. A survey that was conducted as part of the evaluation study showed that only 28.6% of the respondents to this survey answered positively on the question 'The indicators in our program budget play an important role in the discussion about this document in the council' (Schilder et al. 2010, p. 37). One of the reasons that it seemed hard in daily practice to link policy objectives and results on the one hand and financial means on the other is that it is considered difficult to properly select and use performance indicators. In a project analyzing the catalysts and barriers for the implementation of performance measurement, Budding and Hopstaken (2010) found that the main obstacles for the implementation of performance measurement

Table 4.1 Main barriers for implementing performance measurement

Barriers	*Percentage*
1. Definition problems	55.7
2. Measurability problems	29.6
3. Inappropriate cooperation middle management	29.4
4. Limitations information system	19.8
5. Too time consuming	19.8
6. Low priority civil top management	19.7
7. Low priority politicians	16.4
8. Inappropriate training employees	5.5
9. Inappropriate means for reforms	3.2

Source Budding and Hopstaken (2010)

are problems related to properly defining and measuring performance indicators (Table 4.1).

Another issue that turned out to be problematic was the allocation of overhead costs. The accounting regulations that were in force in the period between 1985 and 2013 prescribed that municipalities had to allocate these costs to all policy areas (called 'functions') in a fair and consistent way. The expectation of the Ministry of the Interior and Kingdom relations was that in this way municipalities could get a better insight into the costs municipalities makes for their policies and services. By having this insight, it would be better able to compensate the municipalities according to their cost structure. For the municipalities themselves, full cost information was thought to be useful for a good overview of the costs of each policy and service, and making it possible to take better decisions. However, the accounting rules that came into force in fiscal year 2004 did not prescribe the allocation of overhead costs anymore. The result was that some municipalities decided to continue allocating these costs, whereas other municipalities grouped these costs into a program called 'operational management' (*bedrijfsvoering*). This development—among others—made it difficult to compare costs and performances between municipalities.

In 2015, the reporting rules were changed once again. The main reason for this was precisely the problems municipalities encountered when they wanted to compare costs and performance. The solution that was designed for these problems was twofold. First, the new rules prescribed that municipalities were not entitled anymore to allocate the overhead costs to their policy areas (i.e., programs and products) in their published budgets and annual reports. All overhead costs should be visible under the heading of the program 'operational management'. Second, the new rules prescribed that municipalities had to publish uniform indicators, more specifically five financial indicators and 39 policy indicators. The financial indicators mainly try to provide a somewhat broader and more in-depth insight into the current and future solvency of the municipality.[1] An example is the indicator 'tax capacity' that provides information about the extent to which local taxes can be increased. The policy indicators relate to many issues, ranging from information about the extent to which the municipality hires external personnel to information about the percentage of inhabitants that don't play sports.[2]

4.4 Discussion

4.4.1 What Gets Lost in Translation?

This chapter has shown that when it comes to performance measurement in the Netherlands, there exist some similarities and some differences between the municipal and the central government level. At both levels a search can be observed to connect policy and means. In terms of the OECD study that was introduced in the introduction of this book a move in the direction of direct/formula performance budgeting was aimed for, but in practice the level of presentational budgeting seems to be reached. At the level of central government, under the influence of the NPM movement the focus shifted from justification of payments toward the control of effectiveness and efficiency of activities and programs. At present, in line with this shift, budgeting has now developed into Accountable Budgeting that holds ministers accountable for a proper execution of their policies and for an effective and efficient use of the apparatuses the ministers have at their disposal. At the level of municipalities, line-item budgets were replaced by program budgets and product estimates. Program budgets stipulate political priorities, future activities, the resources involved and the outcomes to be achieved on the

[1] Staatscourant 2015, No. 20619, 17 July 2015.

[2] Staatscourant 2016, No. 16004, 1 April 2016.

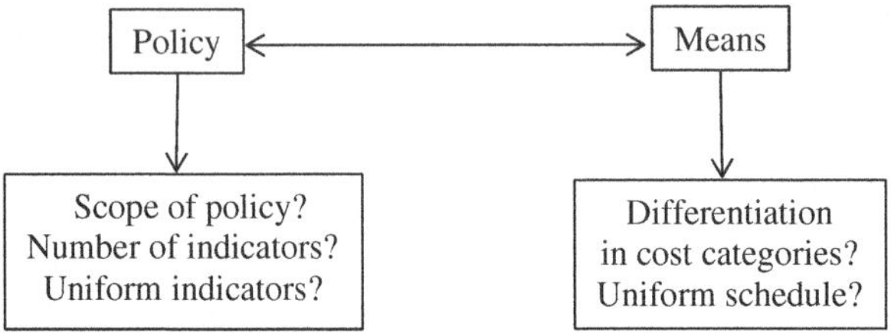

Fig. 4.4 The connection between policy and means

level of municipal programs. Product estimates do the same, but they focus on a more specific level: the product level.

This divergence in practices is illustrated in Fig. 4.4. It shows that the connection between policy and means is not the only interrelation that is at stake. Both central government and municipalities also struggle in how to define and measure the pursued and realized policy goals. We have shown in this chapter that a search can be discerned in how many and which indicators can be used for this aim. On the plane of policy, the argument of controllability is made in favor of making a more strict selection in presented information: the argument against of information overload was clearly visible (and decisive) in the central government context, and was relevant for the introduction of Accountable Budgeting. On the local level, controllability can be seen in the tendency to uniform policy areas and indicators.

With regard to the budgeted and consumed financial means we also observe that both central government and municipalities are looking for the best way in how to present these means. Hereby, the most prominent issues are related to presenting only direct or full cost information, whether or not having prescriptions in forcing organizations to report in a uniform way and the differentiation between organizational (personnel and material) and policy expenses.

4.4.2 *Performance Budgeting: Translation and Control from a Distance*

The developments in performance budgeting as described above reveal two important movements. First, rather than staying separate domains, the financial domain is connected to the domains of policy formation and execution. Such a connection takes place through a process of translating programs, their activities and resource consumption into numbers, both financial and non-financial. This translation is not a simple linear and straightforward process. It involves the work of many, among them managers, controllers and auditors. It also involves the insights and interests of many. Although the process of translation may be guided and circumvented by rules, fundamental uncertainty and complexity require situation-specific decisions based on informed judgments. The process of translation is therefore not simply technical or apolitical. In a certain sense, *politics* is *in the process of translation*.

Second, the process of translating programs, activities and resources into numbers is related to the demand for governance and control *from a distance*. The municipal council and the parliament are not directly involved in the execution of the programs, so they need *re*-presentations and *pre*-presentations of what happens, or what is expected to happen, in the municipality or country. To distant others (municipal council, parliament) the numbers (p)re-present the world of the public organization in its absence. The distant others are not only at a space-distance from what is happening, but also at a time-distance. Numbers help the distant others to overcome the time-space distance by bringing the world of the public organization to their desks. In other words, it provides them with so-called *transparency*. But the numbers do more than just creating visibility; they also enable *acting* from a distance. Numbers have the power of turning public organizations or parts thereof into calculable spaces and to turn the responsible managers and administrators on these spaces into calculable or governable persons. These calculable persons may for example become budget holders. That is, numbers have the power to both *territorialize* and *subjectivize*, to produce both spaces and subjects (see also Miller and Power 2013). By creating calculable spaces and subjects it becomes possible to compare the performances of (parts of) public organizations and the responsible subjects. Benchmarking them creates possibilities for disciplining subjects through forms of rewarding and penalizing, the latter for example in the form of 'shaming and blaming'.

Calculable spaces and subjects can be governed and controlled from a distance, and that is precisely what is needed in a democracy. Councils and parliament (or, in more general terms, distanced principals) can overcome time-space distance by *ex ante* acting on the basis of *pre*-presentations of programs and practices by numbers (both financial and non-financial). They can act by making decisions on the allocation of resources to programs and practices. *Ex post* they can act on the basis of *re*-presentations in the form of numbers by holding the calculable administrators or managers accountable for the performances of their departments. The development toward Accountable Budgeting signifies the importance of such action at a distance.

So, the development toward performance budgeting (and Accountable Budgeting) can be placed in a context of control from a distance, where control is used in a broad sense, involving both *ex ante* and *ex post* elements. Through performance budgeting, democratic institutions such as councils and parliament are enabled to influence administrators and managers so that public resources are used effectively and efficiently. In a more general sense, a 'principal' is enabled to govern his 'agents'.

As a control instrument, a budget is an important element in a planning and control-cycle. *Ex ante*, it translates a plan for the upcoming period in financial targets (cash flows, revenues and costs, changes in assets, liabilities and equity). Through a budget, a 'principal' (for example a municipality council) may allocate resources to multiple tasks or programs and may provide managers ('agents') with the authority to acquire and/or use these resources, while also holding them accountable for the resource consumption. *Ex post,* the real resource consumption is measured and an evaluation of the difference between targets and real resource consumption is performed. If deemed necessary, *ex post* interventions by the principal may take place. For example, relevant managers are invited to explain the differences, sometimes followed by certain rewards or penalties. Such evaluations may also be learning experiences with consequences for future plans.

In sum, by placing a budget in the context of control from a distance it becomes an active part of the governance of and within a public organization. It is more than just a passive reflection of the future consequences of decisions already made. On the one hand, the budget provides administrators and managers with a certain 'bounded freedom' to decide as they think best, while on the other hand making them accountable.

4.4.3 *Questioning the Representational Qualities of Numbers*

Another problem is to produce a series of performance measures that more or less completely re-present the public value that a public organization or part thereof aims to produce. It proves very difficult, if not impossible, to come up with a workable series of measures that completely (or even sufficiently) re-present the resource consumption and performance of the organization. The search for completeness has resulted in a number of measures that is hardly manageable for principal and agents alike. There is a risk, then, that performance management is reduced to a mere form of 'presentation', a form that does not serve governance and control form a distance.

At least, the lacking representational qualities of performance indicators, both financial and non-financial, do pose a serious problem to distant others. How can the 'principal' (the municipality council or the parliament) perform its democratic task if it cannot see the real performance through all the numerical (and also non-numerical) information? If the desired transparency proves to be an illusion? How can there really be a form of democratic control in society or in the municipality if, at least to a certain extent, the promise of transparency remains unfulfilled; if the calculable spaces and the calculable subjects in fact *obscure* what is really happening in society and public organizations; if administrators and managers are held accountable on the basis of a web of circulating indicators that translate the public world in a necessarily imperfect way? In short, what if control from a distance proves to be a fantasy (Roberts 2009)? Should the principal just 'trust' the administrators and the managers then?

4.4.4 *Numbers as Mediators*

We argue that lacking representational qualities of financial and non-financial indicators do not necessarily imply their abundance. The important question is: do we conceive of numbers as 'matters of fact' or as 'matters of concern' (Latour 2005)? In other words: do we see them as answers, as direct providers of transparency, or as sources for debate and discussion, as *mediators*? In the latter case they are *indirect* providers of transparency. They provide a forum through which possibilities, failures, successes and dilemmas can come to the fore, thus opening up possibilities for socializing rather than individualizing or disciplining efforts. That is, *in the quest for answers* both principal and agents, democratic institutions and managers, come to be implicated in the continuous development of policies, decisions and actions. In the process of making visible, that is in the process of translation, numbers gain significance not because they close down, but because they have the potential to open up. They have the potential to close the time-space gap between administrators and distant others (democratic institutions) not because they offer an unquestionable base for intervening, rewarding and penalizing from a distance, but because of their ability to mediate in the arena in which both principal and agents participate. Numbers mediate in the interactions, discussions and debates between principal and agents.

Rather than distrust, *trust* (be it informed trust) is the underlying condition for numbers to become mediators. That is, participants in the arena are expected to act in the public interest rather than their (possibly conflicting) own interest until the opposite is proven. This condition is difficult to reconcile with the discourse of NPM, which expresses the connection between the principal and the agent as one dominated by potential conflicts of interest and, therefore, as one in which distrust between the principal and the agent is the legitimate condition. These assumed conflicts of interests encourage the principal to use disciplining rather than cooperative or socializing devices, as rewards, penalties and exit threats. In the discourse of NPM, numbers are therefore instruments rather than mediators. In contrast, the condition of trust enables a mediating role of numbers. Although we do not advocate a certain naivety that all agents are always trustworthy, we do however argue that in the public sector trust might be the right condition to start with. As indicated by Frey et al. (2013), administrators and managers in public sector organizations may have a so-called pro-social motivation. In such situations, numbers may mediate in rich interactions between administrators and democratic institutions.

In short, we do not advocate an abundance of performance budgeting. We do challenge, however, the possibility to reach total disciplinary control from a distance on the basis of transparency. A planning and control-cycle cannot fully capture a public organization from the outside. The cycle, and in particular the numbers that are at its core, might better be used as a mediating device, thus serving the maintenance and development of a network consisting of democratic institutions and multiple administrators and managers. As such, it might open up, rather than close down, thus serving processes of continuous improvement, trust building and maintenance, learning and innovation. In short, it then becomes part of the dynamics in the public organization.

References

Aardema, Harrie. 2002. *Doorwerking van BBI, evaluatie van een veranderingsbeweging bij de Nederlandse gemeenten*. Leusden: BMC.

Advisory Committee on the Reporting System for the Central Government (Adviescommissie verslaggevingstelsel rijksoverheid, AVRo). 2017. *Baten en lasten geherwaardeerd. Voor- en nadelen van verdere toevoeging van baten-lasten informatie*. Rapportage. Ministerie van Financiën en Algemene Rekenkamer, maart.

Agency for Research and Government Expenditure (Bureau Onderzoek en Rijksuitgaven, BOR). 2015. *De macht en kracht van het budgetrecht; Het budgetrecht van de Tweede Kamer: Ontwikkelingen en verbeteringsmogelijkheden*. The Hague, 2 April, Annex to Kamerstuk II 2014/15, 33 670, nr 11.

Bac, Aad D., C.J.F. Knoop, and J.H. van Zanten. 1991. *Gemeentelijk financieel beheer; een moderne kijk op gemeentefinanciën*. Leiden: Stenfert Kroese.

Budding, Tjerk, and Jan Hopstaken. 2010. Performance Management in the Era of Public Value Management. In *Public Leadership and Citizen Value*, ed. James W. Bjørkman, Rob van Eijbergen, Goos Minderman, and Hans Bekke, 179–192. The Hague: Eleven International Publishing.

Budding, Tjerk, and Frans van Schaik. 2015. Public Sector Accounting and Auditing in the Netherlands. In *Public Sector Accounting and Auditing in Europe*, ed. Isabel Brusca, Eugenio Caperchione, Sandra Cohen, and Francesca Manes Rossi, 142–155. Basingstoke, UK: Palgrave Macmillan.

De Jong, Maarten, Iris van Beek, and Rense Posthumus. 2013. Introducing Accountable Budgeting Lessons from a Decade of Performance-Based Budgeting in the Netherlands. *OECD Journal on Budgeting* 12 (3): 71–104.

Dekker, Pieter J., and Tjerk Budding. 2005. Kostentoerekening binnen duale begroting. *Bank en Gemeente* 32 (3): 14–17.

Duisenberg, Pieter. 2016. New Development: How MPs in the Dutch Parliament Strengthened Their Budgetary and Accounting Powers. *Public Money & Management* 36 (7): 521–526. https://doi.org/10.1080/09540962.2016.1237153.

Frey, Bruno S., Fabian Homberg, and Margit Osterloh. 2013. Organizational Control Systems and Pay-for-Performance in the Public Service. *Organization Studies* 34 (7): 949–972. https://doi.org/10.1177/0170840613483655.

Groot, Tom, and Tjerk Budding. 2008. New Public Management's Current Issues and Future Prospects. *Financial Accountability & Management* 24 (1): 1–13. https://doi.org/10.1111/j.1468-0408.2008.00440.x.

Hendriks, Frank, and Pieter Tops. 2003. Local Public Management Reforms in the Netherlands: Fads, Fashions and Winds of Change. *Public Administration* 81 (2): 301–323. https://doi.org/10.1111/1467-9299.00348.

Hood, Christopher. 1995. The 'New Public Management' in the 1980s: Variations on a Theme. *Accounting, Organizations and Society* 20 (2–3): 93–109. https://doi.org/10.1016/0361-3682(93)e0001-w.

Hoppe, Robert, Jaap Woldendorp, and Nils C. Bandelow. 2016. *Sustainable Governance Indicators: 2016 Netherlands Report.* Gütersloh: Bertelsmann Stiftung.

Houppermans, Meyken, Peter van Hoesel, and Frans van Nispen. 2015. De geschiedenis van beleids onderzoek in Nederland. In *Beleidsonderzoek in Nederland. Kennis voor beleid; ontwikkeling van een professie*, ed. Peter H.M. van Hoesel et al., 1–36. Assen: Koninklijke Van Gorcum.

Houwaart, Dick, R. van der Linde, J. Post, and K. Verduijn. 1995. *Bestuurlijke vernieuwing, bedrijfsvoering en informatie; slotpublicatie Stichting BBI.* Leusden: Stichting BBI.

Kraan, Dirk-Jan. 2010. Uitgaven-heroverweging in OESO-landen. *Tijdschrift voor Openbare Financiën* 42 (2): 117–134.

Latour, Bruno. 2005. *Reassembling the Social: An Introduction to Actor-Network-Theory.* Oxford and New York: Oxford University Press.

Miller, Peter, and Michael Power. 2013. Accounting, Organizing, and Economizing: Connecting Accounting Research and Organization Theory. *The Academy of Management Annals* 7 (1): 557–605. https://doi.org/10.1080/19416520.2013.783668.

Organisation for Economic Co-operation and Development (OECD). 2014. *Budgeting Practices and Procedures in OECD Countries.* Paris: OECD Publishing.

Pollitt, Christopher, and Geert Bouckaert. 2004. *Public Management Reform; A Comparative Analysis*, 2nd ed. Oxford: Oxford University Press.

Roberts, John. 2009. No One Is Perfect: The Limits of Transparency and an Ethic for 'Intelligent' Accountability. *Accounting, Organizations and Society* 34 (8): 957–970. https://doi.org/10.1016/j.aos.2009.04.005.

Schilder, Ard, Harrie Aardema, Mark van Dam, Robert Koldenhoff, and Herrie Geuzendam. 2010. *Evaluatie financiële functie gemeenten en provincies.* Amersfoort: BMC Advies en Management.

Study Group for Budgetary Space (Studiegroep Begrotingsruimte). 2016. *Van saldosturing naar stabilisatie* (Report No. 15). The Hague, 1 July, Annex to Kamerstuk 34 300, nr. 74.

Ter Bogt, Henk J. 2004. Politicians in Search of Performance Information?—Survey Research on Dutch Aldermen's Use of Performance Information. *Financial Accountability and Management* 20 (3): 221–252. https://doi.org/10.1111/j.0267-4424.2004.00387.x.

Van der Knaap, Peter. 2006. Responsive Evaluation and Performance Management. *Evaluation* 12 (3): 278–293. https://doi.org/10.1177/1356389006069135.

Van der Knaap, Peter. 2007. Results-Oriented Budgeting and Policy Evaluation: Accountable for Learning. In *Making Accountability Work*, ed. Marie-Louise Bemelmans-Videc, Jeremy Lonsdale, and Burt Perrin, 163–180. New Brunswick and London: Transaction Publishers.

Van Helden, G. Jan. 1998. *BBI in de praktijk - Een vergelijkend onderzoek naar de planning en control bij acht middelgrote gemeenten*. Maastricht: Shaker Publishing.

Van Helden, G. Jan. 2000. A Strategy for Implementing Cost Allocation in a Dutch Municipality. In *Comparative Issues in Local Government Accounting*, ed. Eugenio Caperchione and Ricardo Mussari, 125–141. Boston: Kluwer Academic Publishers.

VB Groep. 1995. *Waardering en inzicht; de CV 1995 in breder perspectief*. Voorburg: VB-Groep.

Verhoest, Koen. 2010. The Relevance of Culture for NPM. In *The Ashgate Research Companion to New Public Management*, ed. Tom Christensen and Per Lægreid, 47–63. London and New York: Routledge.

Wiesel, Fredrika, and Sven Modell. 2014. From New Public Management to New Public Governance? Hybridization and Implications for Public Sector Consumerism. *Financial Accountability & Management* 30 (2): 175–205. https://doi.org/10.1111/faam.12033.

CHAPTER 5

Performance Budgeting in Germany, Austria and Switzerland

Christoph Reichard and Nicole Küchler-Stahn

5.1 Introduction

In the following chapter the patterns and trajectories of performance budgeting in Germany, Austria and Switzerland will be outlined. The three German-speaking countries are presented together in one chapter, as these countries are looking back on long-standing common administrative traditions and also were similarly exposed to recent managerial

The authors are grateful to Gerhard Hammerschmid, Renate Meyer, Thomas Prorok, Iris Saliterer, Kuno Schedler and Johann Seiwald for providing important information about specifics of the performance budgets in Austria and Switzerland.

C. Reichard (✉)
Department of Public and Nonprofit Management,
University of Potsdam, Potsdam, Germany
e-mail: reichard@uni-potsdam.de

N. Küchler-Stahn
Faculty of Business and Law, Frankfurt University of Applied Sciences,
Frankfurt, Germany
e-mail: kuechlerstahn@fb3.fra-uas.de

M. S. de Vries et al. (eds.), *Performance-Based Budgeting in the Public Sector*, Governance and Public Management,
https://doi.org/10.1007/978-3-030-02077-4_5

reforms like New Public Management (NPM). Performance budgets emerged in each of the three countries in the last 10–15 years at various government levels. Their concepts, implementation strategies and also their practical use are, as will be shown below, quite diverse.

5.2 Performance Budgeting in Germany

5.2.1 General Situation of Public Financial Management

Germany is a federal state with 16 states (*Länder*) and about 12,000 municipalities. The German public financial management is based on a strong legalistic *Rechtsstaat*-tradition and very long-standing legacies of cameralistic accounting. The federal states are to a large extent independent in their financial management practices; a fact that is widely recognized as one of the pitfalls of the reform of the Germany budgeting, accounting and reporting system (Mühlenkamp and Glöckner 2009). Since centuries and partly until now, German government practices a very traditional concept of financial management which is characterized by a cash-based cameralist bookkeeping system and a highly itemized annual input budget (Müller-Marqués Berger and Heiling 2015). It is only about 20 years that the worldwide reform movement of NPM arrived in Germany and started—under the label "New Steering Model" (NSM)—primarily at the local level. NPM-reforms at *Länder* and particular at federal level were only partial and selective. Reforms of the accounting and budgeting system were an explicit part of the NSM (Reichard 2003). The change of accounting and budgeting in Germany is still work in progress: while most of German municipalities have largely accomplished the move to accruals and also implemented a PB, this is only very partially the case at the *Länder* level and absolutely absent in federal government. Together with Ireland, the Netherlands and Cyprus, Germany is one of the last EU-member states with a cash-based reporting and budgeting system at central level.

5.2.2 Performance Budgeting at Federal Level

The German federal budget with a financial volume of 337 bn Euros (2018) is balanced since 2014 without incurring new debts. The total budget is split into 23 departmental budgets, e.g. assigned to a ministry (Müller-Marqués Berger and Heiling 2015). Each budget contains estimates of the revenues, expenditures, commitment authorizations and established posts. Each departmental budget is structured into chapters (task areas) and further down into titles (e.g. personnel expenditures).

The German federal budget is a one-year, highly detailed and cash-based budget which primarily informs about financials. Additionally, the MoF prepares a non-binding mid-term financial plan. In order to focus at least to some extent on (expected) results, the federal MoF introduced more recently some changes and additional tools (BMF 2017):

- top-down instead of bottom-up budget composition process (federal government decides at first on key budget figures for policy fields)
- introduction of a results-oriented component in text form and realignment of the structure of the federal budget. Goals and priorities have to be outlined in detail in the prefaces of each departmental budget (Einzelplan) and in the preliminary remarks of the respective chapters. Moreover, the first nine chapters of each section are to be summarized under a task-oriented heading.
- introduction of additional spending reviews as recommended by OECD (2014): Joint assessment of selected policy fields in terms of appropriateness, effectiveness and efficiency.

Although these adjustments may result in a modest extension of the results focus, they do not provide a sufficiently detailed picture of intended outputs and outcomes and can thus not considered being an alternative to a full-fledged PB.

Apart from these adjustments, the federal budget remains in its traditional shape. A change toward accrual accounting never was an issue of German federal government. About 10 years ago, the MoF started reforms toward an extended cameralist accounting concept with disclosure of assets and liabilities in a simplified variant of a balance sheet, with some performance information (PI) in the budget and with additional information on resource consumption. But this proposal was blocked by the budget committee of federal parliament and thus never implemented (Portal et al. 2012). With the ongoing debate on common European Public Sector Accounting Standards (EPSAS) the issue of a comprehensive reform of accounting and budgeting again came on the agenda of the German federal government. But the German MoF and various other public authorities fundamentally opposed against a possible change to accruals in general and to EPSAS based on IPSAS in particular (European Commission 2012). Thus, the opportunities of a comprehensive accounting and budgeting change at the German federal level are quite uncertain.

5.2.3 Performance Budgeting at State Level

Of the 16 federal states, only three have made the switch to resource-based accrual accounting (Hessen and the city states of Bremen and Hamburg) and have undergone some changes toward PB. North Rhine-Westphalia is on a similar track toward PB but still on the move. The majority of the *Länder* continues with cameralist accounting and traditional input budgeting, only occasionally performance indicators and/or (strategic) objectives can be detected in these budgets (e.g. Baden-Württemberg, Saarland, Sachsen-Anhalt, Schleswig-Holstein).

Hessen started its accounting reform into accruals already in 2000 and published its first financial report and a PB in 2010 (Lüder 2013). The new budget is quite conventionally structured into departments and chapters. For each chapter, a generic planning document (*Wirtschaftsplan*) is issued which includes a cash-based finance plan, an accrual-based results plan and a performance plan (*Leistungsplan*) informing about the products of the respective chapter and additionally about targets and indicators. In a separate document, the MoF issues a reconciliation budget (*Überleitungsrechnung*) which includes in a condensed mode the total cash appropriations of the respective department. The whole budget of Hessen follows therefore a dual approach (cash and accrual preview of financials) and also includes some PI. Parliament decides upon the whole budget, i.e. *Wirtschaftsplan* and reconciliation budget. In practice, however, the use of PI for decision-making is quite limited and the traditional cash-focus is still dominant (Lüder 2013).

The budget of Bremen is purely cash-based and structured into departments and chapters. For each department, an overview of product groups and products together with performance targets and indicators is offered. PI focuses on outputs, outcomes and quality. In contrast to budgeting, Bremen has changed its financial reporting to accruals.

The budget reform in Hamburg dates back to the mid-1990s, but it was not until 2003 that the city assembly decided to switch to accrual accounting and initiated a project drawing up a financial statement for the core government as of December 1, 2006. This first financial statement of a German *Land* was supplemented by a consolidated balance sheet covering all legal entities of Hamburg as of December 31, 2007 (Raupach and Hilgers 2012). The first PB (*Produkthaushalt*) was presented for 2015–2016 (bi-annual budget). It consists of 24 sections which are split-up into so-called task areas (*Aufgabenbereiche*). For the whole government but also for each task area, a cash-based finance plan and an accrual-based results plan is presented (Wagner et al. 2017). While the result plan shows aggregated expenses and revenues, the financial plan contains cash inflows and outflows. In addition to the current two budget years, the expected financials for the next two years are shown. In addition, for each product group targets, performance indicators and related figures for measuring the achievement of goals are provided. Performance data are presented as actuals as well as expected values for the four following years.

Compared to the initial reform concepts, the outcome-orientation of the budget has been reduced (Wagner et al. 2017). Today, indicators include predominantly input and output figures as well as isolated quality figures. Activity-oriented indicators are increasingly used. The amount of goals and indicators in the various product groups differs remarkably and also the quality of such data varies. According to a recent qualitative evaluation of the use and acceptance of the financials and PI, administrative as well as political decision-makers are modestly satisfied with the information provided: 70% state that the information is "important" or even "very important" for their work. In analogy to the statements made above, the respondents complain about the quality of the provided PI and demand a selection of indicators relevant for decision-making and thus the reduction of the total number of these figures. Furthermore, the interviewees ask for a more transparent link between formulated objectives and expenses for achieving them (Wagner et al. 2017).

5.2.4 *Performance Budgeting at Local Level*

Compared to the rather modest and hesitant reform developments at federal and *Länder* level, the German municipalities have been pioneers in changing their accounting and budgeting system (Müller-Marqués Berger and Heiling 2015; Burth and Hilgers 2014). After a test phase, the committee of the *Länder* ministries of interior (responsible for municipal financial management) decided in 2003 on a reform concept which encouraged all German *Länder* governments to change the municipal accounting and budgeting toward accruals and to a PB. This concept only marked the essentials of the reform and gave the *Länder* quite some discretion in standard setting and in formulating the various *Länder*-specific budgeting and reporting acts. Thus, major differences exist across German municipalities with regard to e.g. valuation of assets and liabilities or to the composition of the budget and the balance sheet.

10 of the 13 territorial states of Germany (the other three *Länder* are city states where state and local level are integrated) request their municipalities to move to accruals and to PB. The residual territorial states offered an option to move toward accruals or to maintain the cameralist concept, which resulted in a very low willingness to change.

Despite the variation of conceptual details of the municipal reforms, there are some common features of the budgeting concept of German municipalities (Hilgers and Burth 2015; Reichard 2012):

- The municipal budget is structured along the product approach in various product areas, subdivided into product groups and products. Product areas usually correspond with organizational units like departments.
- The budget follows a dual focus: It is split up into a cash-based finance plan and an accrual-based results plan. These two variants are broken down to lower layers of the municipality.
- The budget has a mid-term perspective; apart from the budget year it also informs about the expected developments in the next 3–4 years.
- The budget is a lump sum budget, i.e. the total amount of the budget for a product group is the spending ceiling and gives the respective manager discretion of shifting certain appropriations and also of carrying-over.
- The budget informs about municipal performance: it includes performance information—e.g. objectives and indicators concerning the previous and the budgeted periods at the level of product groups

The introduction of accrual reporting and of the PB was a very strenuous and time-consuming process in German municipalities which still is going on. One of the most laborious stages was the recording and valuation of all the various municipal assets and the set-up of the opening balance sheet. Further, extensive training of municipal staff took a lot of time. Hence, incorporation of the performance side of the budget often was perceived as an inferior task and consequently, many municipalities started quite late and hesitantly with identifying performance data for budget composition (Küchler-Stahn 2010). Thus, evidence from the ongoing reform process toward the municipal PB is so far quite limited (Kroll and Proeller 2012; Hilgers and Burth 2015; Reichard 2014): Municipalities tend to use input and output indicators while outcome and quality indicators still are quite rare. Less than 20% of respondents in German municipalities state to connect indicators with strategic goals (Kroll and Proeller 2012), although a few attempts of linking objectives with strategies can be found (Kientz 2013). The willingness of actors to use performance data for budgeting decisions is—although slowly rising—still modest (Hilgers and Burth 2015). Politicians are particularly hesitant in using PI for budgeting (Grossi et al. 2016). After all, there are indications that with growing PB-experience the usefulness of the PB for municipal steering is more positively assessed by politicians involved in budgeting (Hilgers and Burth 2015).

Such modest results of a widespread and profound reform are not surprising at all. Not all actors were convinced of the advantages of the reform and most of them had to manage all those change processes aside from their daily duties (Küchler-Stahn and Gelep 2015). Reformers also experienced that the superior government institutions of the *Länder* and the federation still continued the traditional cameralist mode of financial management. Even at local level, the reform movement is highly fragmented, e.g. with regard to variation of accounting and budgeting standards but also with regard to the timing of reforms. At large, the complex change process of accounting and budgeting is still in progress and various steps (like consolidated reporting) have to be done.

5.2.5 General Assessment

German experiences with PB concentrate largely on the local level, with some additional evidence at *Länder* level. The absence of PB at federal level is a serious limitation of the further expansion of PB in Germany. The majority of *Länder* governments is in waiting position, looking for first steps of the federal government. By and large, the municipal PB has informational character, its performance data is not linked with appropriations. Its structural features are more or less in line with the usual PB-standards. A big challenge is the inconsistency of the various PB-concepts. Municipal PBs from different *Länder* are not really comparable with each other. This applies more or less also to the so far three PBs at *Länder* level. The incorporation of PB into the practice of budget planning and control is a long-lasting process, but more recent experiences are moderately positive.

5.3 Performance Budgeting in Austria

5.3.1 General Situation of Public Financial Management

Austria is a federal state with 9 states and about 2100 municipalities. Similar as Germany, the Austrian public financial management is historically rooted in a strong legalistic *Rechtsstaat*-tradition and in far back reaching cameralist accounting and budgeting legacies (Rauskala and Saliterer 2015; Schauer 2016). The federal states are generally independent in their financial management practices, although some common standards have to be respected, e.g. an act for standardized budgeting and reporting principles (*Voranschlags- und Rechnungsabschlussverordnung; VRV*). The state governments regulate the financial management concepts of their municipalities. Thus, there is quite some variance in financial management among subnational and local governments in the country.

Since long time, most government entities in Austria have used a cash-based accounting and budgeting system, although since the 1980s the federal level and to a minor extent some state governments have moved to a hybrid accounting version with a mix of cash and accrual elements (*Mehrphasenbuchführung*). Since about 15 years, the financial management systems of Austria are fundamentally changing. The federal government started an extensive reform in 2004, taking full effect in 2013 (more details below). The federal reforms initiated comprehensive reform debates also on the other government layers. The federal government therefore issued an amended version of the VRV-act in 2015 which obligates the state and local governments to change their budgeting and accounting systems to a harmonized concept which is quite similar to the—already introduced—federal system. From 2020 all government entities have to apply a full-fledged accrual budgeting and reporting concept.

However, the introduction of a performance budget, i.e. the disclosure of PI in the budget, is not compulsory. In this respect, state and local governments are autonomous to design their budgeting concept. At present, there is no clear and definite picture, how many state and local governments will opt for a performance budget; most of them are still quite reluctant.

5.3.2 *Performance Budgeting at Federal Level*

Until 2008, the federal budget was a quite itemized input-oriented budget, based on a cash-focused accounting system. Since the late 1990s, some first adjustments of the budgeting concept emerged. Federal government introduced a top-down oriented budget planning process and expanded the planning focus to two years. Additionally, the Austrian Ministry of Finance (MoF) promoted pilot experiments with budget flexibilization in a number of federal agencies, granting these agencies more autonomy in their budget execution (e.g. with regard to carrying over and shifting) in return to a strengthened output-focus and an increased self-responsibility for managing their financial resources (Seiwald et al. 2013, pp. 101–108).

Encouraged by the positive results of these first reform steps, the Austrian federal government started in 2004 an extensive reform of its budgeting and accounting system. The essentials of the new concept are an accrual-based financial reporting system following IPSAS and a multi-year performance budget (Blöndal and Bergvall 2007; Steger 2010). The MoF was the central reform promotor which developed the comprehensive and ambitious project in two steps: At first, until 2009 a number of legal changes in the Austrian constitution and other important law amendments have been issued which were considered as being irrevocable or at least difficult to change. The more detailed and technical decisions were made in the second stage which resulted in 2013 in the final implementation of the whole reform package. The successful implementation of this project was the result of a subtle and well-planned change strategy which took the important stakeholders on board (Steger 2010; van Helden and Reichard 2018).

The major elements of the new Austrian federal budget concept are as follows (Rauskala and Saliterer 2015, pp. 15–20):

- a quite globalized budget composition with limited number of line items (lump sum budget)
- a four years mid-term expenditure focus of the budget with binding spending ceilings (budget year plus next three years)
- opportunities to shift and carry-over for budget executing authorities
- performance information available at the various budget layers
- budget and budgetary reporting following accrual accounting standards

The logic of the new federal budget follows a pyramid structure: At the most aggregate level, the budget consists of five headings or rubrics (e.g. employment, social services and health; education, research and culture; economic affairs, infrastructure and environment). The headings are subject of mid-term fiscal planning, thus they are part of a comprehensive budget strategy report of the MoF covering the next four years. At the next layer, 32 budget chapters are grouped, each covering a policy field and classified into several global budgets (altogether around 70 global budgets). These global budgets are again split into a few detailed budgets which are mostly conform to certain administrative units and connected with the existing cost accounting system. Only the first three layers are subject of parliamentary decision-making; the detail budgets are only binding within the intra-administrative context. Thus, the legislation only discusses and decides upon a rather condensed spectrum of 70 global budgets.

The financial part of the budget informs at first in its accrual variant (operating budget) about the expected revenues and expenses in the respective budget-element. Secondly, it also offers a cash-based version covering receipts and expenditures (cash-flow budget). Additionally to the monetary appropriations, the MoF provides a selection of PI related to the budgets at the various budget layers.

The performance budget is part of a comprehensive performance management system (PMS) of the government (Steger 2010). For each budget chapter, a mission statement and up to 5 outcome objectives are to be formulated. Additionally, several output targets and related statements should be determined for each global budget. At each layer, at least one of the targets should deal with gender equality issues. For every performance objective information should be provided about the actual performance target and the achieved actual performance results of the last budget year. Performance is measured with the help of meaningful performance indicators. The line ministries are responsible for their part of performance management, they each have a "performance mandate" which does not only cover the budget execution but also related performance issues, e.g. in the field of operational management and human resource management. The whole performance measurement process is managed and coordinated by the Federal Performance Management Office. In the Austrian parliament, a Parliamentary Budget Office (PBO) facilitates the budget debates and provides analyses and evaluations to the legislation. The PB is linked with several other performance-focused reform activities of federal government, e.g. with the results-oriented impact assessment (primarily for new legal acts), with the annual impact controlling and with the multi-annual strategy report.

To avoid an overflow of PI in the budgeting process, the number of outcome/output targets and related indicators (target and actuals level) is limited to a maximum of five targets per budget chapter and per global budget. The budget of 2013 for instance includes in total 660 performance indicators (Berger 2015). Here is an example of the budget chapter "Education and Women' Affairs" (Geppl and Kranabetter 2014):

> Outcome objective 1: Improving the education levels of pupils; Indicator 1.1: Percentage of 18–20 years old pupils having finished upper secondary education; target value (2013/2014): 88.9%; latest actual value (2009/2010): 88.5% (two more indicators available).

According to a recent IMF-review, Austria is one of the most advanced countries in practicing *Gender Budgeting* in its budgeting context (IMF 2017). As mentioned before, gender-related outcome objectives have to be disclosed in each budget chapter. These objectives should be deduced from gender analyses in the various policy fields. At the end of the budget year the Performance Management Office prepares a general impact controlling report and a gender performance report for the parliament, based on the annual evaluations by the various ministries.

As the new PB-concept is only a few years in operation, practical experiences are still quite scarce. Not surprisingly, the use of PB-practices in Austrian government has strongly increased within the last years. According to a recent OECD survey, Austria is now among the top users among the OECD countries (OECD 2017, p. 127). These are some of the experiences made so far in legislation and government (Berger 2015; Korac 2017; Steger 2016):

- performance issues are now more intensively debated in the Parliament, particularly in the budget committee (often in a policy debate and not necessarily in a budgeting context)
- members of the opposition use PI more intensively as other members of parliament (in the budget committee)
- the limitation of objectives per budget chapters and global budgets has proved itself in practice, although some objectives were perceived as too vague or simply repetition of previous targets
- ambition and consistency of PI still need improvement
- links between PI and appropriations are sometimes perceived as rather loose
- coordination of PI across ministries and agencies is underdeveloped
- unmet performance targets don't result in budgetary consequences (see also OECD 2017, p. 127).

Although comprehensive evaluations of the Austrian budget reform are still to be made, the general experiences with the new concept seem to be quite encouraging. The PB-concept has been accepted to some extent by the major actors and a kind of "performance culture" is slowly emerging at federal government level. Taking the long-lasting cameralist traditions in Austria in account, this is not a too bad intermediary result.

5.3.3 PB at State and Local Level

So far, there is high diversity in public sector accounting and budgeting both at state and at local level, but the cash-mode is dominant. Budgetary and financial reporting are usually closely connected (Rauskala and Saliterer 2015, p. 15). As already indicated, this will change in the next few years, as according to the new VRV-act of 2015 all state and local governments will move toward accruals. State governments can then choose between more compact or more detailed budgets. Currently, a few state governments and additionally several (mostly larger) municipalities have already started with financial management reforms. While the state of Vorarlberg and its municipalities have more than 60 years of experience with variants of modified accrual accounting, other states only recently started their reforms (e.g. Steiermark, Burgenland, Kärnten, and Salzburg).

The state of Styria (*Steiermark*) for instance follows largely the PB-concept of the federal government. Its budget is structured into 11 chapters, each consisting of several global budgets. A limited number of performance targets and indicators is provided for each of these budget units, including also gender equality targets (Land Steiermark 2018). Subsequent to the annual budget, the Styrian government prepares a detailed annual impact assessment report (*Wirkungsbericht*) where realized goal achievements, deviations and resulting problems are presented and discussed. At this stage, the PB-concept of Styria seems to be the most advanced at Austrian state level.

The willingness to move toward a PB seems to be so far only modestly developed: While the states of Steiermark, Kärnten, Salzburg and Oberösterreich either have already a performance focus in their budget or are intending to change in that direction, other state governments are rather reluctant in this respect. This also applies for most of the Austrian municipalities. It can be assumed that the respective authorities are hesitant to invest a lot of time, money and human resources into the development of PBs, as long as the "hard core" technical issues of the accounting change with all the valuation efforts have not been mastered. One minimum requirement is, however, mandatory: according to the constitution, the gender equality must be displayed in all budgets. The Austrian center for public administration research (KDZ) recommends that municipalities should introduce a lean version of PB with a limited number of performance targets and indicators at a quite aggregated level, following the PB-concept of Swiss cantons and municipalities (Prorok et al. 2015).

5.3.4 General Assessment

The Austrian PFM-system is in a comprehensive change process toward accruals and to new budgeting concepts. While the federal level has implemented the new system, this still has to be done in the coming years at lower government layers. With regard to implementation, the Austrian federal government is among those countries in Europe which have fundamentally reformed their financial management system (Brusca et al. 2015). According to some statements about first experiences with the new PFM-system (e.g. Berger 2015; Rauskala and Saliterer 2015; Schauer 2016; Steger 2016), the shift from an input-oriented traditional system to a complex PMS with the PB as a central part is still not finished. It would be very unlikely to assume that the underlying cultural change in the federal bureaucracy has already taken place (Seiwald and Geppl 2012). So far, there is not much evidence about effects of the federal reforms, e.g. if the limitation of performance indicators and the permission of carrying-over unspent appropriations has shown positive results. Based on a provision in the federal budget law, an external evaluation of the budget reform is currently taking place.

5.4 Performance Budgeting in Switzerland

5.4.1 General Situation of Public Financial Management

As the other two countries under review, Switzerland is a federal state. It consists of 26 regional states (cantons) and about 2350 municipalities. The Swiss public sector is characterized by a high autonomy of the cantons and municipalities, by a historically deeply rooted system of direct democracy and by strong consensus orientation in the society (Kraan and Ruffner 2005). Compared to the other two German-speaking countries, the Swiss public sector follows a more pragmatic administrative culture, driven by an economic and managerial spirit also in parts of the civil service.

Switzerland started reforming its public financial management system already quite early (Schedler 2002): Until 1978 governmental accounting and budgeting at all layers was cash-based and the budget highly itemized. Then the cantons decided conjointly to move toward accruals; the local level followed soon. In contrast, the federal government continued to report and to budget in cash-mode, it only introduced an accrual consolidated account. In the early 1990s, the NPM movement emerged in Switzerland and became a quite influential reform doctrine, particularly in the German-speaking part of the country. Performance measurement and management became a particularly strong module of the Swiss NPM-concept: outcome-oriented public management (WOV: *Wirkungsorientierte Verwaltungsführung*) was the widely used label of managerial reforms (Schedler and Proeller 2010). The focus at performance was pointing the way also in the case of accounting and budgeting reforms. Accordingly, performance budgets (PBs) have been designed and implemented at all government layers already in the 1990s.

5.4.2 Performance Budgeting at Federal Level

The federal government was more hesitant to move toward accruals, as proponents of the cash-mode were quite influential (Schedler 2002). Not least because regional and local governments already had some 20 years of experience with accruals but also as a consequence of the evolving NPM, federal government changed its reporting system in the late 1990s (Schedler 2000). At first it established an experimental clause in its administrative law to stimulate performance management activities of federal authorities by introducing performance contracts and lump sum budgets (FLAG: *Führung mit Leistungsauftrag und Globalbudget*). Later, the Swiss Federal Finance Department (EFD) developed a new accounting and budgeting concept with a dual focus at both cash and accrual figures (EFD 2008). Both the budget (*Voranschlag*) and the annual reporting (Bundesrechnung) consist of an income statement, a financing and cash flow statement and an investment statement; the reporting additionally includes a balance sheet. The new concept which came into practice in 2007, follows very closely the IPSAS. To a large extent it is consistent with the accounting and budgeting concepts at cantonal level.

The federal budget is largely a transfer budget, i.e. two third of the totals are destined for transfer payments to subnational layers and other public entities (Kraan and Ruffner 2005). Since 2003, the budget follows a strict national debt brake. Since the budget year 2017, the federal budget has been transformed into a PB: Additionally to the appropriations in financial terms, it also provides information about important products, strategic priorities, targets and indicators by following the concept of the Integrated Task and Finance Plan (IAFP) which was earlier developed at cantonal level (see below). The federal PB is composed for four years in advance and is carried forward from year to year; it also includes explanatory information about expected developments in the various departments and with regard to altogether 120 product groups of federal government (EFD 2016). The appropriations for each of the various entities and product groups can be shifted and carried over; the PB is thus a lump sum budget with regard to each product group. The new PB-version is part of a comprehensive management concept of federal government (NFB) and is connected with performance contracts between ministries and subordinated entities. Parliament approves annually all planned expenditures and expenses and takes notice of expected revenues. Additionally, at the beginning of each legislative period of four years, the Parliament approves a mid-term budget for the whole period (*Legislaturplanung*).

As the introduction of the performance component into the federal budget has been done only recently, there are so far no empirical findings about its practice and eventual changes in budgetary decision-making.

5.4.3 PB at Cantonal Level

All cantons in Switzerland practice a harmonized concept of budgeting and accounting which follows since 40 years the accrual mode. Parallel to the change of the federal accounting model, all cantons reformed their systems along a new accounting concept, based on recommendations of the association of cantonal finance directors. The concept follows the IPSAS to a large extent and also structurally conforms to the federal system (HRM2; see Bergmann 2012). 15 cantons introduced a performance budget and most of the other cantons also provide some PI in their budgets (Fuchs et al. 2015).

The IAFP is the central budgeting instrument of most cantonal governments and more recently also of federal government. It is connected with and based on the Legislative Plan (*Legislaturplan*) which serves as the political and programmatic policy concept of legislative and executive government for the whole legislative period and informs about priorities and challenges of the government. Usually, it is a rolling concept with a four years' perspective and a specific focus at the next year as budget year (in some cantons the IAFP and the annual budget are separated). The IAFP is composed along a limited number of product groups which correspond in many cases with organizational units. For each product group, the IAFP informs about strategic priorities, performance goals, expectations about future task development, planned quantities and qualities of the products, milestones of scheduled activities—and of course about the expected expenses and revenues. All these features are supported with indicators (Schedler and Summermatter 2009). The IAFP is drafted by government and approved by the cantonal parliament. It is a lump sum budget: to each product group or department a fixed amount of appropriations is allocated as a ceiling and allows for flexible spending. At the end of the budget year, an annual budget report with intensive performance data is prepared and submitted to government and parliament.

5.4.4 *PB at Local Level*

Municipalities are usually following the cantonal reforms. Most of them have moved or are currently moving toward the new accounting standards of HRM2. PBs, however, are only an issue for larger municipalities. As only about 4% of all Swiss municipalities have more than 10,000 inh., the experiences with PBs are rather limited at this level (Fuchs et al. 2015).

5.4.5 *General Assessment*

Switzerland is an early mover in public financial management reforms. Supported by a more pragmatic and managerial culture, both federal and subnational governments introduced accrual accounting already some decades ago, and the cantons and municipalities started with PB-experiments almost 20 years ago. By now, the IAFP is a well-established variant of PB which has also been accepted by elected politicians. The latter is also a result of the design of PB and of the overall PMS which pays sufficient attention to the specifics of politicians' rationalities and tries to avoid sophisticated and technocratic budgeting procedures (Schedler 2000, 2003).

Some empirical evidence about PB-practices is available for the cantonal and local level, but so far not for the only very recently reformed federal level. Some studies show that the composition of performance indicators in municipal PBs is inappropriate (Sager et al. 2010; Ritz 2007): There is a tendency to prefer indicators focusing at inputs or activities while output- and outcome-related indicators are quite rare. Furthermore, quite some indicators don't conform to the targets to which they are assigned (for similar evidence from other countries see Bleyen et al. 2017). In contrast to research findings from other countries about the (modest) willingness of elected politicians to use PI for budgeting decisions (see e.g. Askim 2007; Grossi et al. 2016), evidence from Swiss cantons is more positive about the attitudes of this actor group (Summermatter and Demaj 2012): After IAFP-introduction politicians are showing more interest in political priority setting and in identifying future challenges. However, their attitude to make short-sighted decisions primarily based on expenditures is still observable (see also Demaj 2017). Another study sheds light on the impact of certain contextual factors (e.g. type of task and interactions of politicians) on how public managers perceive the effectiveness of PB (Helmuth 2010, 2011). And yet another research examined the role change of direct democracy in Switzerland after introduction of PB, particularly in municipalities with an annual referendum on the budget by the electorate (Ritz and Sager 2010): Although the studied cases don't provide evidence so far, such effects cannot be excluded, e.g. when municipal managers are more autonomous in their spending in case of lump sum budgets.

Altogether, the PB seems to have a quite uncontested position in the Swiss financial management context. After intensive coordinated reforms driven by a relatively strong NPM-doctrine, the PB as a concept now seems to be quite settled at all government layers.

5.5 Comparative Analysis

Although coming from similar administrative traditions (legalistic *Rechtsstaat*, cameralist accounting), the three countries under review show different trajectories of changing their budgeting concepts into the direction of PB. While the Swiss governments have moved to accruals and PI at all layers, Austria has done this so far only at central level and Germany only at local and partly the regional level (Table 5.1).

The implemented PBs in the countries under review have some common features: Compared to traditional line-item budgets, the amount of budget items has been strongly reduced: The new Austrian federal budget for instance only consists of 70 global budgets which are subject of legislative decision, the respective budget in Switzerland is split up into 120 product groups. This also holds true for the local level in Germany.

Table 5.1 Status of implementation of accrual accounting and of performance budgeting

	Austria	*Germany*	*Switzerland*
Central government	Accruals and PB	–	Accruals and PB
Subnational government (*Länder*)	In future accruals in all states and in some states also PB	Accruals and PB in three of 16 states	Accruals in all cantons, PB in 15 of 26 cantons
Local government	In future accruals	Accruals and PB in most municipalities	Accruals in most municipalities, PB so far only in larger ones

For example, the model chart of products of the State of North Rhine-Westphalia—one of the frontrunners of the reforms on local level—includes 292 product groups (which is by coincident the same amount as in the budget of Hamburg; Wagner et al. 2017). Furthermore, all budgets have a mid-term perspective: They do not only focus at the next year but they also anticipate expected developments in the following three years. The dominant budgetary focus is on policy areas or product groups. And finally, all these new budget concepts follow the idea of a lump sum budget (spending flexibility within the margin of the budget sum). With regard to the kind of financial appropriations, all budgets apply a dual focus: in the accrual-based results plan they inform about the expected resource consumption and in the cash-based financial plan they provide information about expected expenditures and revenues.

In each of the three country cases, the PB is part of a comprehensive PMS incorporated in the respective government. The linkage of the PB with an overarching PMS is particularly visible in the Swiss case where the PB is on the one side linked with strategic planning and on the other side associated with performance contracting but also with performance reporting and evaluation. Similarly (although so far less systematic), the Austrian federal budget is incorporated into a broader PMS which also provides regular strategy reports and results of an annual performance monitoring. Such systematic links of the budget with strategies and with a broader PMS as in the case of the Swiss IAFP revealing the strategy for the next few years do not exist on local or state level in Germany.

Apart from a few case studies and some not very actual surveys, there is not much evidence about the practice of PB and particularly about the use of PI for budgeting decisions and budget control in the three countries. The acceptance of the PB by politicians and public managers seems to be quite high in Switzerland and less strong at the Austrian federal level and the German local level. Nevertheless the case of Germany leaves room for hope as there are indications of significant differences in the level of acceptance of PI between early and late adopters of the reform. There is also anecdotic evidence that performance data is perceived as being less relevant compared to financial data. Furthermore, empirical findings show that provided indicators are not always in line with the targets to which they are attached and that the coupling of performance data with financial appropriations in PBs is only indirect and loose. Generally, it can be assumed that observations of the OECD from their PB-surveys will be also true for the three German-speaking countries

(OECD 2016): PI is only occasionally used for budget negotiations in governments and governments only modestly draw consequences, if ministries or agencies do not meet the performance targets promised in their budgets.

What lessons can be learned from the experiences in the German-speaking countries (but also for them from international evidence; see e.g. Moynihan and Beazley 2016; Schick 2013; Sterck and Scheers 2006)? Firstly, governments need sufficient capacities and also time to initiate the performance measurement component of a PB, not least to identify meaningful and reliable targets and indicators. Cooperation of line departments and agencies is unavoidable. Secondly, a PB should be incorporated into a more comprehensive PMS, where strategic planning, contracting, reporting, spending reviews and auditing are closely connected. To keep such a system running, a vital performance culture is important. Thirdly, the collection of PI should not be overloaded, indicators should mirror their targets which themselves should concentrate on outputs and outcomes, and applied performance information should be regularly revised and updated. Fourthly, the data in the PB should be frequently used, not only for budget negotiations, but also for short-term adjustments and budget control; a mechanical exercise of the PB as a pure matter of duty should be avoided. And finally, the performance focus of the PB should not be over-emphasized as the PB is just one part of a comprehensive PMS.

References

Askim, Jostein. 2007. How Do Politicians Use Performance Information? An Analysis of the Norwegian Local Government Experience. *International Review of Administrative Sciences* 73 (3): 453–472. https://doi.org/10.1177/0020852307081152.

Berger, Helmut. 2015. *Introducing Performance Budgeting in Austria—Experiences and Lessons*. Vienna: Parliamentary Budget Office.

Bergmann, Andreas. 2012. The Influence of the Nature of Government Accounting and Reporting in Decision-Making: Evidence from Switzerland. *Public Money & Management* 32 (1): 15–20. https://doi.org/10.1080/09540962.2012.643050.

Bleyen, Pieter, Daniel Klimovský, Geert Bouckaert, and Christoph Reichard. 2017. Linking Budgeting to Results? Evidence About Performance Budgets in European Municipalities Based on a Comparative Analytical Model. *Public*

Management Review 19 (7): 932–953. https://doi.org/10.1080/14719037.2016.1243837.

Blöndal, Jon R., and Daniel Bergvall. 2007. Budgeting in Austria. *OECD Journal on Budgeting* 7 (3): 39–76.

Brusca, Isabel, et al. 2015. Comparing Accounting Systems in Europe. In *Public Sector Accounting and Auditing in Europe; The Challenge of Harmonization*, ed. Isabel Brusca, Eugenio Caperchione, Sandra Cohen, Francesca Manes Rosi, 235–251. Basingstoke: Palgrave Macmillan.

Bundesministerium der Finanzen (BMF). 2017. *Wirkungsorientierung im Bundeshaushalt – mehr als Spending Reviews*. In Monatsbericht des BMF—September 2017. Retrieved from http://www.bundesfinanzministerium.de/Monatsberichte/2017/09/Inhalte/Kapitel-3-Analysen/3-5-Wirkungsorientierung-im-Bundeshaushalt-mehr-als-Spending-Reviews.html.

Burth, Andreas, and Dennis Hilgers. 2014. Cui Bono? Depicting the Benefits of the New Municipal Budgeting and Accounting Regime in Germany. *Journal of Business Economics* 84 (4): 531–570. https://doi.org/10.1007/s11573-013-0698-9.

Demaj, Labinot. 2017. What Can Performance Information Do to Legislators? A Budget-Decision Experiment with Legislators. *Public Administration Review* 77 (3): 366–379. https://doi.org/10.1111/puar.12713.

EFD. 2008. *The New Accounting Model of the Swiss Confederation*. Bern: EFD.

EFD. 2016. *Grundlagen der Haushaltführung des Bundes*. Bern: EFD.

European Commission. 2012. *Public Consultation—Assessment of the Suitability of the International Public Sector Accounting Standards for the Member States*. Summary of Responses. Brussels: European Commission.

Fuchs, Sandro, Andreas Bergmann, Iris Rauskala, and Anna Schmitt. 2015. Public Sector Accounting and Auditing in Switzerland. In *Public Sector Accounting and Auditing in Europe; The Challenge of Harmonization*, ed. Isabel Brusca, Eugenio Caperchione, Sandra Cohen, Francesca Manes Rosi, 204–218. Basingstoke: Palgrave Macmillan. https://doi.org/10.1057/9781137461346_14.

Geppl, Monika, and Stefan Kranabetter. 2014. *Performance Budgeting in Austria. Example: Secondary Education*. Vienna: Chancellery.

Grossi, Giuseppe, Christoph Reichard, and Pasquale Ruggiero. 2016. Appropriateness and Use of Performance Information in the Budgeting Process: Some Experiences from German and Italian Municipalities. *Public Performance & Management Review* 39 (3): 581–606. https://doi.org/10.1080/15309576.2015.1137770.

Helmuth, Utz. 2010. Better Performance with Performance Budgeting? Analyzing Cases of Success and Failure in Public Administrations. *International Public Management Journal* 13 (4): 408–428. https://doi.org/10.1080/10967494.2010.524833.

Helmuth, Utz. 2011. *The Impact of Performance Budgeting on Public Management.* Dissertation, University of St. Gallen.

Hilgers, Dennis, and Andreas Burth. 2015. Nutzen-Determinanten der kommunalen Doppik aus Sicht der Haushaltspolitiker. *Der Moderne Staat* 8 (1): 173–200. https://doi.org/10.3224/dms.v8i1.19116.

IMF. 2017. *Gender Budgeting in G7 Countries.* Policy Paper. Washington: IMF.

Kientz, Jürgen. 2013. *Integration der strategischen Planung in die Haushaltsplanung einer Kommune- dargestellt am Beispiel des Landkreises Lörrach.* Dissertation, University of Kassel.

Korac, Sanja, et al. 2017. *Between Overload and Keen Eye for Detail—Performance Information Use by Politicians in the Budgetary Process.* Paper for EGPA-Conference 2017.

Kraan, Dirk-Jan, Michael Ruffner. 2005. Budgeting in Switzerland. *OECD Journal on Budgeting* 5 (1): 37–78.

Kroll, Alexander, and Isabella Proeller. 2012. *Steuerung mit Kennzahlen in den kreisfreien Städten – Ergebnisse einer empirischen Studie.* Gütersloh: Bertelsmann-Stiftung.

Küchler-Stahn, Nicole. 2010. *Leistungs- und wirkungsorientierte Budgetierung: internationale Praxis und Gestaltungsoptionen für deutsche Kommunalverwaltungen.* Berlin: BWV-Verlag.

Küchler-Stahn, Nicole, and Adrian Gelep. 2015. Die elektronische Rechnungsverarbeitung in der öffentlichen Verwaltung. *Verwaltung und Management 21* (2): 96–102.

Land Steiermark. 2018. *Landesbudget Steiermark 2018.* Retrieved from http://www.verwaltung.steiermark.at/cms/ziel/142120398/DE/.

Lüder, Klaus. 2013. Die Neue Verwaltungssteuerung des Landes Hessen - Interpretative Chronik einer Reform. In *Moderne Finanzkontrolle und öffentliche Rechnungslegung. Denkschrift Manfred Eibelshäuser*, ed. Walter Wallmannn et al., 237–299. Köln: Carl Link Verlag.

Moynihan, Donald, and Ivor Beazley. 2016. *Toward Next-Generation Performance Budgeting. Lessons from the Experiences of Seven Reforming Countries.* Washington: World Bank.

Mühlenkamp, Holger, and Andreas Glöckner. 2009. *Rechtsvergleich kommunale Doppik – Eine Synopse und Analyse ausgewählter Themenfelder des neuen doppischen kommunalen Haushaltsrechts der Bundesländer.* Speyerer Forschungsberichte 260. Speyer: DHV.

Müller-Marqués Berger, Thomas, and Jens Heiling. 2015. Public Sector Accounting and Auditing in Germany. In *Public Sector Accounting and Auditing in Europe; The Challenge of Harmonization*, ed. Isabel Brusca, Eugenio Caperchione, Sandra Cohen, Francesca Manes Rosi, 93–107. Basingstoke: Palgrave Macmillan.

OECD. 2014. *Budget Review: Germany.* Paris: OECD.

OECD. 2016. *OECD Performance Budgeting Survey Highlights*. Paris: OECD.

OECD. 2017. *Government at a Glance*. Paris: OECD.

Portal, Marine, Evelyne Lande, Rowan Jones, and Klaus Lüder. 2012. French Revolution and German Circumspection: Reforming Budgeting and Accounting in National Governments. *Public Money & Management* 32 (5): 357–361. https://doi.org/10.1080/09540962.2012.703421.

Prorok, Thomas, Peter Biwald, and Alexander Maimer. 2015. Kommunale Wirkungsorientierung - Die Position des KDZ konkret zusammengefasst. *Forum Public Management* 1: 10–13.

Raupach, Björn, and Dennis Hilgers. 2012. Quo Vadis? Die Reform des Hamburger Haushalts- und Rechnungswesens. *Verwaltung und Management* 18 (6): 283–291. http://www.jstor.org/stable/24236579.

Rauskala, Iris, and Iris Saliterer. 2015. Public Sector Accounting and Auditing in Austria. In *Public Sector Accounting and Auditing in Europe; The Challenge of Harmonization*, ed. Isabel Brusca, Eugenio Caperchione, Sandra Cohen, Francesca Manes Rosi, 235–251. Basingstoke: Palgrave Macmillan.

Reichard, Christoph. 2003. Local Public Management Reforms in Germany. *Public Administration* 81 (2): 345–363. https://doi.org/10.1111/1467-9299.00350.

Reichard, Christoph. 2012. Umsetzung und Praxis des neuen kommunalen Haushalts- und Rechnungswesens – eine Auswertung vorliegender Empirie. *Verwaltung und Management* 18 (3): 118–121.

Reichard, Christoph. 2014. Leistungsinformationen im neuen Kommunalhaushalt – welche Rolle spielen diese Daten in der Praxis? *Verwaltung und Management* 20 (3): 125–129.

Ritz, Adrian. 2007. Performance Management and Output-Based Budgeting in Switzerland. Output and Outcome Data—An End in Itself or Relevant for Steering? In *Modernizing Government in Europe*, ed. Hermann Hill, 149–172. Baden-Baden: Nomos.

Ritz, Adrian, and Fritz Sager. 2010. Outcome-Based Public Management and the Balance of Powers in the Context of Direct Democracy. *Public Administration* 88 (1): 120–135. https://doi.org/10.1111/j.1467-9299.2009.01786.x.

Sager, Fritz, Adrian Ritz, and Kristina Bussmann. 2010. Utilization-Focused Performance Reporting. *Public Money & Management* 30 (1): 55–62. https://doi.org/10.1080/09540960903492398.

Schauer, Reinbert. 2016. *Rechnungswesen in öffentlichen Verwaltungen. Von der Kameralistik zur Doppik - Einführung und Standortbestimmung*, 3rd ed. Linz: Linde.

Schedler, Kuno. 2000. Performance Measurement Challenges in Switzerland: Lessons from Implementation. *International Public Management Review* 1 (1): 84–104.

Schedler, Kuno. 2002. Government Budgeting and Accounting Reform in Switzerland. In Models of Public Budgeting and Accounting Reform, *OECD Journal on Budgeting*, 2, Supplement 1: 243–263.

Schedler, Kuno. 2003. '… and Politics?' *Public Management Review* 5 (4): 533–550. https://doi.org/10.1080/1471903032000178572.

Schedler, Kuno, and Isabella Proeller. 2010. *Outcome-Oriented Public Management. A Responsibility-Based Approach to the New Public Management.* Charlotte, NC: IAP.

Schedler, Kuno, and Lukas Summermatter. 2009. Der Integrierte Aufgaben- und Finanzplan als Instrument der mittelfristigen Steuerung in der Schweiz. *Der moderne Staat* 1 (2): 391–410.

Schick, Allen. 2013. The Metamorphoses of Performance Budgeting. *OECD Journal on Budgeting* 10 (2): 1–31.

Seiwald, Johann, et al. 2013. *Neue Wege des Haushaltsmanagements.* Berlin: Ed. Sigma.

Seiwald, Johann, and Monika Geppl. 2012. Wirkungsorientierte Steuerung: Chancen und Spannungsfelder. *Österreichisches Haushaltswesen* 53 (1–3): 38–52.

Steger, Gerhard. 2010. Austria's Budget Reform: How to Create Consensus for a Decisive Change of Fiscal Rules. *OECD Journal on Budgeting* 7 (1): 7–20.

Steger, Gerhard. 2016. *Austrian Budget Reform—Experiences Beyond Traditional Budgeting.* Charts retrieved from https://www.vkontrole.lt/bp/failai/files/03_Gerhard%20Steger.pdf.

Sterck, Miekatrien, and Bram Scheers. 2006. Trends in Performance Budgeting in Seven OECD Countries. *Public Performance & Management Review* 30 (1): 47–72. https://doi.org/10.2753/pmr1530-9576300103.

Summermatter, Lukas, and Labinot Demaj. 2012. Die Nutzung integrierter Aufgaben-und Finanzpläne (IAFP). *Verwaltung und Management* 18 (4): 171–179.

van Helden, Jan, and Christoph Reichard. 2018. Cash or Accruals for Budgeting? Why Some Governments in Europe Changed Their Budgeting Mode and Others Not. *OECD-Journal on Budgeting* 15 (1): 89–113. https://doi.org/10.1787/budget-18-5j8l804pq0g8.

Wagner, Kristin, Helge C. Brixner, Dennis Hilgers, and Jan Quast. 2017. Das parlamentarische Berichtswesen im doppischen Produkthaushalt. *Verwaltung und Management* 23 (3): 145–153.

CHAPTER 6

Public Sector Performance-Based Budgeting in Italy

Sara Giovanna Mauro

6.1 Introduction

The public sector reforms introduced in recent decades in Italy have involved all three levels of public administration—national, regional, and local—although the national level[1] has been subject to increasing attention in a climate of economic, financial, and social crisis. Since the late 1980s, the government of Italy has been swayed by fiscal and budgetary pressures, political scandals and a consequent lack of trust by citizens in their government, and increasing levels of perceived inefficiency and ineffectiveness. As a result, the Italian central government embarked on

[1] The national government in Italy is composed of the Prime Minister, line ministers, who are responsible for the actions of their ministries—complex organisations in charge of elaborating policies and delivering services to achieve the ministries' goals—and the Council of Ministers, which consists of the Prime Minister and the line ministers.

S. G. Mauro (✉)
Institute of Management, Scuola Superiore Sant'Anna, Pisa, Italy

M. S. de Vries et al. (eds.), *Performance-Based Budgeting in the Public Sector*, Governance and Public Management,
https://doi.org/10.1007/978-3-030-02077-4_6

a path towards significant reforms (Cepiku et al. 2017). The scope of these reforms has been wide, ranging from restructuring and institutional changes in the central government and moves to improve the relationship between citizens and the public administration to performance, transparency, and e-government initiatives. Specific interventions have aimed to confront growing economic and fiscal pressures (di Mascio and Natalini 2015), while performance-oriented tools have been introduced to strengthen the efficiency and effectiveness of public administration.

In this latter regard, in the spirit of the New Public Management (NPM) (Hood 1995), the buzzword 'performance' has increasingly influenced the agenda of many public sector organisations. The NPM approach involves the introduction of business principles and tools and systems modelled on the private sector into the public sector, with the goal of improving efficiency, effectiveness, and the overall performance of public administration. While reforms in English-speaking countries have been largely studied and have become a reference model, continental Europe has often been considered a 'latecomer' in terms of NPM (Kuhlmann 2010); Italy, specifically, has generally lagged behind in adopting and implementing NPM reforms (Meneguzzo and Mele 2008; Ongaro 2011). Nevertheless, over the last several decades, increasing efforts have been made to introduce managerial reforms in Italy following the international trend towards NPM. Despite the international character of these reforms, they have assumed different features in each country under the influence of contextual factors. It has been widely recognised (Pollitt and Bouckaert 2011) that the institutional context where a reform is adopted influences the reform's design, its expected goals, and its results. In the Italian context, managerial reforms have been introduced by legislation consistent with the well-known bureaucratic and legislative tradition of the Italian public sector (Anessi-Pessina and Steccolini 2005); this legislation has therefore, paradoxically, reinforced the existing administrative and prescriptive traditions (Panozzo 2000). Accordingly, the legalistic and bureaucratic model that has prevailed in the public sector over time has influenced the adoption, implementation, and current extent of use of NPM-inspired changes, including performance-based budgeting.

Within the broader wave of public sector reforms, the budgeting system represents a specific area of intervention. In the 1990s, budget reforms sought to control the growth of public expenditures and to improve public sector performance; in the 2000s, these practices developed further, in conjunction with the reinforcement of performance systems. This was the origin of performance-based budgeting.

This chapter will provide insights into performance-based budgeting in Italy in central government institutions (ministries) and, in particular, explain how the reforms have been interpreted and implemented over the last several years. The chapter relies on document analysis, examining official regulations and guidelines, budget and performance documents adopted by the central administration, official reports developed by national authorities on best practices, and secondary evidence stemming from previous studies on the topic. To contextualise the development of performance-based budgeting, the next sub-sections discuss performance and financial management within the national government in Italy. The chapter then proceeds to discuss the reforms of public budget processes that led to performance-based budgeting. Finally, it discusses the features, the state-of-the-art, and key challenges for these reforms in the Italian context and draws some conclusions.

6.2 Performance Management in Italy: The Introduction of a 'Performance Cycle'

Managerial discourse has been transmitted across the central public organisations of Italy through a series of legislative reforms. Particularly, performance management systems were the subject of reform in 2009, when law no. 15/2009 and legislative decree no. 150/2009 were adopted to mandate the introduction of a formal performance management system within the central government. Italian ministries were expected to measure and manage their performance at both individual and organisational levels and to use performance measures and metrics to enhance public services and the overall performance of public administration. This reform required central organisations to adopt an integrated and comprehensive performance system to control performance, and to use the system in order to improve overall performance (Cepiku et al. 2017). Specifically, the legislation explicitly defined the actions to be carried out in each step of a proper 'performance cycle', as briefly described below:

1. define and assign objectives, and set targets and indicators for each objective;
2. link objectives to resource allocation;

3. monitor the execution of the objectives during the year to adopt any necessary corrective actions;
4. measure and assess individual and organisational performance;
5. use awards to valorise merit;
6. report results to all internal and external stakeholders.

The legislation appears to be based on a textbook model, theoretically sound but challenging in practice. In fact, this approach relies on the ability of public organisations to identify meaningful and measurable objectives, supported by sound indicators and targets. The performance cycle must be developed in accordance with the budgetary planning cycle, with objectives linked to the allocation of resources following the enactment of budget legislation. It implies that the system must be built on directive links from political decisions, programs, and priorities, to the objectives set by the central administrative bodies. The interconnection between budgeting and strategic planning is further embodied into a broader performance management cycle (Bianchi and Xavier 2017). The initial implementation of this cycle soon revealed various challenges in translating its theoretical and normative expectations into practice, as shown for instance by the problematic time alignment across the various cycles and the difficulties in developing the complex technical and conceptual infrastructure needed for implementation.

Managerial and organisational changes were introduced to carry out these activities. Two key documents were mandated by the new legislation: the 'performance plan' and the 'performance report'. The performance plan is a three-year planning document developed and published by each ministry at the beginning of each year to identify the performance indicators and targets for each objective, set according to the policies defined by the minister. The plan is adopted based on the policy directions for each ministry and accordingly it defines strategic and operational objectives. The performance report is an annual document developed at the end of the year and published by June of the year following the reference year. It closes the performance cycle as a reporting document whereby each ministry accounts for the results it achieved, compared to those initially established in the performance plan. It mainly aims at verifying compliance with objectives and contributing to the transparency and accountability of the organisation. Various organisational changes have been introduced to support and monitor the completion of the performance cycle. First, the form of the previous internal control units has been standardised as an independent performance unit called the OIV (*Organismo Indipendente di Valutazione*), designed to monitor and control the ministry's performance. Each ministry has its own OIV in charge of supporting performance cycle completion, controlling adherence to guidelines, adoption of documents in a timely fashion and maintaining accuracy in their development, and checking and validating the final report. A national authority called the CIVIT (*Commissione Indipendente per la Valutazione, la Trasparenza e l'Integrità*) was established as an independent body in charge of monitoring, coordinating, and supporting the implementation of performance measurement and management systems in the central state organisations. CIVIT developed several guidelines and memoranda to provide more specific indications of the form and content of performance plans and reports, monitored the implementation of reforms, and created official reports to assess the extent to which the performance cycle was being implemented across the central public administration. According to the analysis offered in these reports, especially the 2014 annual report, several years after the introduction of the reform there was still a general tendency for the adoption of required documents to be delayed, and compliance with the requirements of the reform was limited. This scenario was explained in terms of the limited attention paid to performance issues by actors at the top level of complex ministries and in terms of the difficulties smaller organisations faced in implementing the reforms. The new requirements needed to be simplified and their application differentiated according to the functions and scale of the organisation in question (ANAC 2014; Ter Bogt et al. 2015).

CIVIT was then subjected to further reforms. It was renamed the ANAC (*Autorità Nazionale Anti-Corruzione*), and its functions and responsibilities in terms of performance were moved to the Department of Public Function in 2014 (Law 114/2014). In fact, the performance evaluation function was apparently deprived of its independence, being subsumed within a department within the Council of Ministries. This department is expected to support the process of innovation in public administration and is assisted in its functions by a technical commission for performance that was established in 2016 and develops technical and methodological guidelines.

6.3 Performance and Financial Management in Italy: Integrating Performance and Budgeting Cycles

With the advent of the NPM, Italy tried to fill the perceived gap between its national policies and European best practices by introducing several modifications to its budget process, although the comprehensive and complex changes attempted require a longer period of experimentation for full implementation to be achieved (Ranalli and Giosi 2011). In addition, public sector financial management in Italy has been influenced by the initiatives towards spending reviews and, more recently, towards the integration of a spending review into the budget process. Nevertheless, additional changes continue to be made to the budget process to address important weaknesses as they are identified, such as the initial lack of formal deadlines during the formulation stage and the complexity of the required procedures (Blondal et al. 2016).

Traditionally, central government budgeting, accounting, and reporting systems in Italy have been cash and commitment-based to guarantee budgetary compliance and expenditure control (Liguori et al. 2016). These systems have been subject to a long experimentation and reform process, shown in the introduction of long-term planning, the simplification of the budget structure, and the introduction of accrual accounting and cost accounting tools. Since the 1990s, line ministries have been required to focus on performance, identifying target objectives, resource requirements, and indicators through the development of 'Preliminary Notes'. The logic behind these notes was to produce more detailed performance data, including financial and non-financial information. However, the budget structure was still highly complex, with numerous expenditure items; its long-term orientation was weak and undermined by a persistent incremental logic, by the limited consideration of non-financial information, and by the emphasis on controls against outcome measures (Liguori et al. 2016). Consequently, the structure of the budget was changed to improve the connection between resource allocation and performance information. It was first modified by reducing the number of line items on which the Parliament has to vote. Then, during the 2000s, the structure of the budget was subject to a reform introduced by the Ministry of Economy and Finance (MEF) through its circulars and formalised in the law on accounting and finance no. 196/2009. The budget was structured into missions and programs: a mission indicates the final purpose for which resources are being spent and can be achieved jointly by several line ministries or by a single ministry. Each mission includes several programs, which are homogenous groups of activities by which a mission can be achieved. Unlike a mission, each program should be under the responsibility of a single administrative unit. The new classification of the budget into missions and programs is designed to improve both allocative and operative efficiency, as well as to increase the awareness of the goals of public spending and improving transparency and accountability (Servizio del Bilancio del Senato 2007).

The budget office for the central government in Italy is the Ragioneria Generale dello Stato, situated within the MEF but with a unit in each line ministry. Among their other functions, these units are responsible for communicating the line ministry's budget requests to the MEF, but they are not responsible for managing the negotiations. Consequently, one weakness of the Italian budget process is the widespread budgeting capacity limitation in each line ministry (Blondal et al. 2016). In this context, a leading role is assigned to the MEF as a coordinator of the budgeting process. This process can be divided into three main phases: budget formulation, approval, and execution. Formulation of the budget starts with the definition of the Economic and Financial Document (DEF), a high-level policy document that sets out the macroeconomic projections for the subsequent three years in an aggregate form. Then, the line ministries update their baseline while advancing their requests to the MEF. Through several meetings between the MEF and the line ministries, the submitted requests are discussed in detail; both formal and informal meetings take place to share information. The MEF then meets with the President of the Council of Ministers and they also discuss specific political priorities. The resulting decisions are formalised, and the MEF communicates those decisions to the minister concerned. Subsequently, the budget that results from the negotiations between the line ministries and the MEF and between the MEF and the President of the Council of Ministers is presented to the Parliament, which has to approve the budget. The allocation phase of the budget process is thus expressed in the budget and in the Integrative Notes to the budget, which derive from further development of the previous Preliminary Notes. The Integrative Notes are prepared by each ministry and are attached to the national budget estimates. For each program, the Notes should indicate the objectives to reach, the indicators and targets to be used to monitor their enactment, the resources allocated, and the budgeted costs, thus making evident the connection between resources and objectives. The performance information reported in the Notes should be coherent with that reported in the performance plans. A selection of indicators and targets included in the performance plans are to be included in the Notes. At the end of the year, in the Integrative Notes to the final statement, respective results are reported in terms of results achieved, resources used, and costs incurred. The cycle is thus closed coherently at the end of each reference period through performance reports.

Thus, performance-based budgeting appears to result from the coordination of two cycles, the budgeting process and the performance cycle. The effort at integrating these different cycles is one of the attempts to transform the legal framework using an organisational and managerial approach (Bianchi and Xavier 2017). Figure 6.1 provides a graphical representation of these key steps.

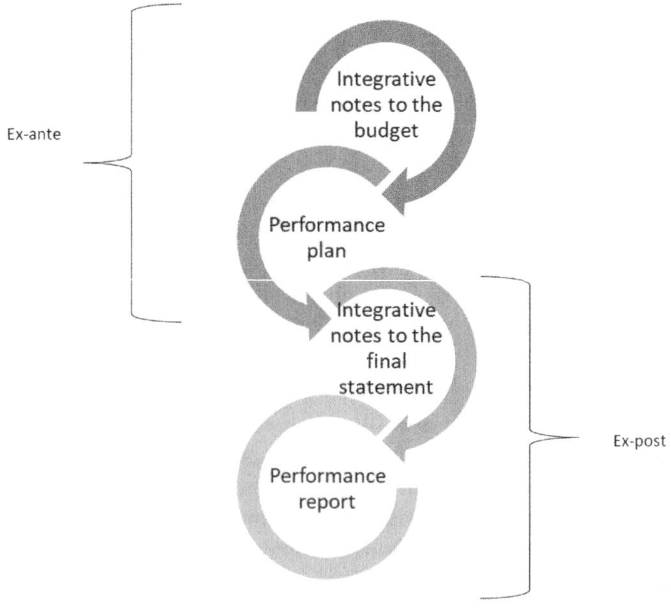

Fig. 6.1 Coordination of the two cycles: key documents

6.4 Performance-Based Budgeting Within the Central Government: Process and Challenges

The adoption of performance-based budgeting, intended as the decision to take a model into use (Johnsen and Vakkuri 2006), can be understood as a result of the pressures on the central public administration to improve its performance through improved budgeting and performance systems. The analysis of an official report published in 2009 by the MEF entitled 'Performance-budgeting, public spending and institutional context: the Italian experience' shows that a strong emphasis has been put on the need to revise the process and mechanisms of public spending in Italy and to reinforce performance measurement practices in light of international experiences.

Consequently, fragmented actions have been carried out to introduce various reforms through legislation. Specifically, the implementation of reform, as aimed at the conceptualisation, design, and development of performance-based budgeting (Johnsen and Vakkuri 2006), appears to have been segmented into the legislative reforms discussed in the previous sections. These particular changes have cumulatively tried to modify the budget process and structure, while strengthening the performance systems.

Therefore, performance-based budgeting in Italy should result from the coordination of different systems, as shown by attempts to integrate the financial, strategic, and operating planning systems (Ranalli and Giosi 2011). In the MEF official report (2009), performance-based budgeting was defined as a budgeting procedure whereby the allocation of public resources is conditioned by the results achieved towards policy goals in relation to the resources used. Hence, performance indicators are expected to influence allocation decisions. Performance-based budgeting is therefore theoretically understood as results-oriented budgeting, although the link between results and resources appears to be vague and ambiguous. On the one hand, this linkage is expressed in the coordination between the performance cycle and the budgeting cycle, which is expected to be completed through the coordination of documents and actors. However, this coordination has been challenged in practice by difficulties in aligning the timelines for the elaboration of these documents, as well as budget constraints and measurement difficulties, and has resulted in a duplication of information in multiple documents.

Several specific factors challenge the use of performance-based budgeting by the Italian central government. This reform has been comprehensive in scope, introducing wide and homogeneous requirements for all the central organisations (ministries) of the Italian state. The first consequence of this approach was evident in the challenge of creating a flexible system suitable for addressing the specific needs of each ministry. The legislation assigned each organisation the possibility of adopting a system for measuring and managing performance whereby managers could specify phases, execution times, actors, and responsibilities of the system within the broader legal framework. However, in practice, the systems established were highly similar despite their different organisational contexts. Furthermore, the reforms have been managed in a centralised fashion, requiring the national authority (ANAC) to develop guidelines for all departments of the central government. This meant that the indicators they developed could not take into consideration the specific needs of each ministry to any significant extent. In this regard, new guidelines released in 2017 for the elaboration of the performance plans by the Department of Public Function and its technical commission partially replaced the previous ANAC guidelines, attempting to address the main problems emerging from previous experimentation through an interactive approach involving active collaboration with each ministry. The first significant point concerned improving the temporal alignment between the performance cycle and the budget cycle, anticipating the elaboration of the performance plan, and attempting to make the process more informative by guaranteeing reporting of information about the past, which previous plans had often lacked.

The analysis of the documents published by the ministries shows the abundance of performance information that is now produced. However, the document analysis also shows that, in the definition of performance plans and Integrative Notes to the budget, performance information is mostly oriented towards the future, while references to information about the past remain limited. Thus, the use of information about results to influence decisions for the future appears partial and weak. Also, an analysis of the performance plans adopted by the ministries in recent years shows that in most cases the plans identify activities to perform rather than results to achieve in terms of outputs and outcomes. Examining the indicators in detail, most of them have an inherently bureaucratic nature; these targets are almost always completely achieved, which calls attention to the harmful possibility that only less challenging tasks have been incorporated into these indicators. Further, both the ANAC and the Court of Auditors recognised the duplication of documents and responsibilities, pointing out the risk that the intended managerial reform could be transformed into an additional bureaucratic burden. According to the last ANAC report about the implementation of reforms at the central government level (2014), coordination between the performance cycle and the budgeting cycle remained weak and incomplete: while 75% of strategic objectives were connected to the allocation of resources, only 16.7% of operational objectives were connected to financial resources. Further, the amount of financial resources linked to strategic objectives in performance plans and reports often differed from the amount of financial resources reported in the Integrative Notes, where resources were linked to strategic or structural objectives. In addition, it has been demonstrated that only 40% of the total spending authorised by the state budget was associated with performance indicators (Rebora et al. 2017).

The stressful financial conditions and continuous political changes the government has faced (Rebora et al. 2017) have challenged the development of coherent and consistent policies. This unstable environment does not allow comparisons to be made between the results achieved over time and accentuates the negative implications of the short-term perspectives of politicians. The strategy developed by elected officials results in a broad document that includes generalities and overall policy priorities, paving the way for ambiguity and vagueness in the definition of more precise performance indicators and targets.

These challenges reflect the limited ability of public organisations to measure and manage their performance and connect this system to the public budget. The challenges faced by the central public administration in using performance-based budgeting can be classified according to the framework developed by Andrews (2004), who grouped the key factors influencing the practice of performance-based budgeting into three macro-classes: ability, authority, and acceptance. The coexistence and interaction of these three factors contribute to the creation of a 'reform space' where performance-based budgeting can be used. In addition to challenges related to ability discussed above, the Italian experience provides insights into the other two dimensions: authority and acceptance. First, legal and organisational authority is crucial, especially in the field of public budgeting. Previous studies have claimed that the existence of legislation concerning performance-based budgeting can support the achievement of this reform (Lu et al. 2009); however, the empirical case of Italy shows that despite the existence of laws supporting the linkage between performance management and budgeting process, performance-based budgeting has not been fully implemented, as seen in other contexts (Hijal-Moghrabi 2017). The textbook, comprehensive approach has not facilitated the implementation and use of the reform. Furthermore, the legislation has created the perception of additional bureaucratic obligations, demotivating the staff of central organisations rather than diffusing a performance culture. Moreover, in the context of public budgeting, the autonomy and flexibility of the staff of each ministry are constrained, reinforcing the perception of centralised decision making with limited space for autonomy. In turn, this scenario has resulted in a lack of widespread acceptance for performance-based budgeting across ministries and organisational levels.

6.5 Conclusions

According to analyses of the use of performance-based budgeting in several OECD countries (OECD 2013), Italy has consistently scored below the OECD average. Despite the abundant production of performance information, the greatest challenges concern how performance information is used and its impact on the budgeting process. The Italian experience shows that the central administration has made several steps towards recognising the relevance of performance measurement and management systems and understanding the role of budgeting as an instrument of planning and control. However, the public budget appears to still be influenced by a traditional, input-oriented approach, enriched with performance information; the performance measures and indicators are reported in several documents but serve only with difficulty as the basis for budget decisions.

The extent to which performance information is used during the budgeting process is hence limited. Financial and non-financial information are linked in a preliminary way, where information about the future prevails over information about the past during the budgeting process. In such a situation, the path towards performance-based budgeting for results (Bleyen et al. 2017) is a long one.

Reforms to introduce performance-based budgeting have not found a supportive context in Italy because of its long tradition of prescriptive, bureaucratic, and top-down procedures, which have often resulted in an implementation and usage gap (Ongaro 2009; Ongaro and Valotti 2008;

Ter Bogt and van Helden 2000). Public management reforms have not replaced the traditional juridical paradigm but have been adapted and incorporated within the legalistic managerial culture (Kickert 2005; Panozzo 2000). Therefore, although the reform appears focused, as demonstrated by the ambitious and complex legislative framework, the introduction of coordinating bodies and the strong investments made to support the changes inspired by a performance-oriented reform movement, its results are still not satisfying (Mauro et al. 2018). The economic and financial crisis, the rigidity of expenditures, the limited diffusion of performance culture, technical difficulties in measuring performance and linking it to the budgeting process, and ambiguity in the integration between performance and budgeting cycles are all factors that contribute to the slow implementation and use of performance-based budgeting among central government organisations in Italy (Bianchi and Xavier 2017; Rebora et al. 2017), as has also been noted at the local level (Grossi et al. 2016; Mussari et al. 2016).

The ongoing changes can stimulate improvements in the implementation and use of performance-based budgeting; however, better results can be expected as political and administrative leaders collaborate to develop suitable practices in light of the needs and features of each ministry (Cepiku et al. 2017). Technical and cultural barriers can be eroded through reforms that incrementally, in a flexible way and with the involvement of the organisations, focus on simplifying procedures (e.g., eliminating the duplication of information), and on introducing feasible practices (e.g., replacing technocratic and rationalising tools with experimentation with different approaches). The reform of performance-based budgeting should overcome the duality of its design, addressing the challenges linked to both performance management and budgeting procedures. Hence, it becomes of utmost importance to empower learning processes, allow adaptive reforms, and aim for a deeper understanding of the meanings of performance and budget cycles.

References

ANAC Autorità Nazionale AntiCorruzione. 2014. *Relazione sulla performance delle Amministrazioni Centrali.*

Andrews, Matthew. 2004. Authority, Acceptance, Ability and Performance-Based Budgeting Reforms. *International Journal of Public Sector Management* 17 (4): 332–344.

Anessi-Pessina, Eugenio, and Ileana Steccolini. 2005. Evolutions and Limits of New Public Management—Inspired Budgeting Practices in Italian Local Governments. *Public Budgeting & Finance* 25 (2): 1–14.

Bianchi, Carmine, and John Antony Xavier. 2017. The Design and Execution of Performance Management Systems at State Level: A Comparative Analysis of Italy and Malaysia. *International Journal of Public Administration* 40 (9): 744–755.

Bleyen, Pieter, et al. 2017. Linking Budgeting to Results? Evidence About Performance Budgets in European Municipalities Based on a Comparative Analytical Model. *Public Management Review* 19 (7): 932–953.

Blöndal, Jón R., Lisa von Trapp, and Erik Hammer. 2016. Budgeting in Italy. *OECD Journal on Budgeting* 15 (3): 1–29.

Cepiku, Denita, et al. 2017. Performance Information Use in Public Administration: An Exploratory Study of Determinants and Effects. *Journal of Management & Governance* 21 (4): 963–991.

Di Mascio, Fabrizio, and Alessandro Natalini. 2015. Fiscal Retrenchment in Southern Europe: Changing Patterns of Public Management in Greece, Italy, Portugal and Spain. *Public Management Review* 17 (1): 129–148.

Grossi, Giuseppe, Christoph Reichard, and Pasquale Ruggiero. 2016. Appropriateness and Use of Performance Information in the Budgeting Process: Some Experiences from German and Italian Municipalities. *Public Performance & Management Review* 39 (3): 581–606.

Hijal-Moghrabi, Imane. 2017. The Current Practice of Performance-Based Budgeting in the Largest US Cities: An Innovation Theory Perspective. *Public Performance & Management Review* 40 (4): 652–675.

Hood, Christopher. 1995. The "New Public Management" in the 1980s: Variations on a Theme. *Accounting, Organisations and Society* 20 (2–3): 93–109.

Johnsen, Åge, and Jarmo Vakkuri. 2006. Is There a Nordic Perspective on Public Sector Performance Measurement? *Financial Accountability & Management* 22 (3): 291–308.

Kickert, Walter J.M. 2005. Distinctiveness in the Study of Public Management in Europe: A Historical-Institutional Analysis of France, Germany and Italy. *Public Management Review* 7 (4): 537–563.

Kuhlmann, Sabine. 2010. New Public Management for the 'Classical Continental European Administration': Modernization at the Local Level in Germany, France and Italy. *Public Administration* 88 (4): 1116–1130.

Liguori, Mariannunziata, Ileana Steccolini, and Silvia Rota. 2016. Studying Administrative Reforms Through Textual Analysis: The Case of Italian Central Government Accounting. *International Review of Administrative Sciences*. https://doi.org/10.1177/0020852315619023.

Lu, Yi, Katherine Willoughby, and Sarah Arnett. 2009. Legislating Results: Examining the Legal Foundations of PBB Systems in the States. *Public Performance and Management Review* 33 (2): 266–287.

Mauro, Sara Giovanna, Lino Cinquini, and Giuseppe Grossi. 2018. External Pressures and Internal Dynamics in the Institutionalization of Performance-Based Budgeting: An Endless Process? *Public Performance and Management Review* 41 (2): 224–252.

MEF. 2009. *Performance Budgeting, spesa pubblica e contesto istituzionale: L'esperienza italiana*. Retrieved from www.rgs.mef.gov.it.

Meneguzzo, Marco, and Valentina Mele. 2008. Designing and Implementing Innovation Policy in the Public Sector: The Italian Experience. In *Innovations in Public Management and Governance in Italy*, ed. Denitam Cepiku, Marco Meneguzzo, and Mariastefania Senese, 15–38. Rome: ARACNE Editrice.

Mussari, Riccardo, et al. 2016. Design, Trajectories of Reform, and Implementation of Performance Budgeting in Local Governments: A Comparative Study of Germany, Italy, Lithuania, and Norway. In *Local Public Sector Reforms in Times of Crisis*, ed. Sabine Sabine Kuhlmann and Geert Bouckaert, 101–119. Basingstoke: Palgrave Macmillan.

OECD. 2013. *Government at a Glance*. Paris: OECD.

Ongaro, Edoardo. 2009. *Public Management Reform and Modernization: Trajectories of Administrative Change in Italy, France, Greece, Portugal and Spain*. Cheltenham: Edward Elgar Publishing.

Ongaro, Edoardo. 2011. The Role of Politics and Institutions in the Italian Administrative Reform Trajectory. *Public Administration* 89 (3): 738–755.

Ongaro, Edorardo, and Giovanni Valotti. 2008. Public Management Reform in Italy: Explaining the Implementation Gap. *International Journal of Public Sector Management* 21 (2): 174–204.

Panozzo, Fabrizio. 2000. Management by Decrees. Paradoxes in the Reform of the Italian Public Sector. *Scandinavian Journal of Management* 16 (4): 357–373.

Pollitt, Christopher, and Geert Bouckaert. 2011. *Public Management Reform: A Comparative Analysis-New Public Management, Governance, and the Neo-Weberian State*. Oxford: Oxford University Press.

Ranalli, Francesco, and Alessandro Giosi. 2011. New Perspectives on Budgeting Procedures in Italy. *International Journal of Public Administration* 34 (1–2): 32–42.

Rebora, Gianfranco, Renato Ruffini, and Matteo Turri. 2017. A Serious Game: Performance Management in Italian Ministries. *International Journal of Public Administration* 40 (9): 770–779.

Servizio del Bilancio del Senato. 2007. *La classificazione del bilancio per programmi e missioni. Elementi di documentazione* (No. 11). XV Legislatura.

Ter Bogt, Henk J., and G. Jan Van Helden. 2000. Accounting Change in Dutch Government: Exploring the Gap Between Expectations and Realizations. *Management Accounting Research* 11 (2): 263–279.

Ter Bogt, Henk J., G. Jan van Helden, and Berend Kolk. 2015. Challenging the NPM Ideas About Performance Management: Selectivity and Differentiation in Outcome—Oriented Performance Budgeting. *Financial Accountability & Management* 31 (3): 287–315.

PART III

Performance-Based Budgeting in Transitional Countries

CHAPTER 7

Performance Budgeting in Local Government: A Case Study of eThekwini Municipality in South Africa

Nirmala Govender and Purshottama S. Reddy

7.1 Introduction

Performance Budgeting has been part of the wave of global budgetary reforms, which have been implemented by countries internationally in order to address the challenges of managing public finance (Cangiano et al. 2013). Kelly and Rivenbark (2011) point out that the roots of a performance based approach to allocation decisions can be tracked to the start of the New Public Management Movement in the 1990s. Performance information, is not new, as OECD countries have recently

N. Govender (✉) · P. S. Reddy
School of Management, IT and Governance,
University of Kwazulu Natal, Durban, South Africa
e-mail: nirmala.govender@durban.gov.za

P. S. Reddy
e-mail: Reddyp1@ukzn.ac.za

M. S. de Vries et al. (eds.), *Performance-Based Budgeting in the Public Sector*, Governance and Public Management,
https://doi.org/10.1007/978-3-030-02077-4_7

been incorporating it in the budgetary process with a view to enhancing decision-making, which is move away from just the amount being reflected to what can be actually achieved with the budget (OECD 2008). This practice supports the notion of Performance Budgeting, which assists in its conceptualisation and further development.

The International Monetary Fund Working Paper by Robinson and Brumby (2005, p. 5), states that "performance budgeting refers to procedures or mechanisms intended to strengthen links between the funds provided to public sector entities and outcomes and/or outputs". Furthermore, this is done with the assistance of information on performance thereby facilitating decision-making on resources allocation. Performance budgeting develops a linkage between the funds allocated to results that can be measured (OECD 2008).

The objective of performance budgeting initiatives according to Sterk and Bouckaert (2006) is to strengthen allocative efficiency and to improve operational efficiency. According to the OECD (2008) countries not only want to monitor what is invested in a project, but to determine how much can be achieved with the budget allocated. Consequently, the focus then shifts to activities that seek to enhance the control of expenditure, efficiency of the public sector and ultimately performance.

The OECD (2008) has determined that diverse methods of performance budgeting have been adopted which are relevant in terms of responding to the development needs of the country. South African history has put considerable pressure on cities nationally. The needs of the people are massive and quite divergent and cities are at the coal-face in responding to these needs, particularly in relation to service delivery.

According to Kumar (2017) the process of performance budgeting entails budgetary allocation to projects and programs, which have been evaluated in terms of targets and priority and these are then monitored on an ongoing basis. Siswana (2007) indicates that public sector managers must be accountable, and transparent and legally flexible so that budgets can be effectively managed.

The research study undertaken by the Collaborative African Budget Reform Initiative (CABRI) (2013) revealed that several African countries are now implementing a budgetary process where performance is a key consideration. CABRI (2013) also revealed that Performance and Program based budgeting reforms are being applied, as it improves expenditure contribution towards social sectors that are directed at poverty reduction.

The aim of this chapter therefore is to review the effectiveness of the performance budgeting system used by eThekwini Municipality, located in Durban, South Africa. As the South African environment is highly challenged, it is important to place the case study within the national government setting. The legislative context is also provided as a backdrop to the chapter.

7.2 The South African Framework

There is no specific terminology of "Performance Budgeting" within South African legislation. However, the principles and legislation implemented nationally by government departments follow the basics of the definition of Performance Budgeting as identified by the International Monetary Fund paper by Robinson and Brumby (2005), which measures the outputs and outcomes in relation to the budget allocated, through performance monitoring.

The monitoring of performance indicators and budgets was identified as critical on all levels post-1994. The legislation which gives impetus to the monitoring of performance and the budget is the Constitution of the Republic of South Africa (1996). Section 195 of the Constitution (Republic of South Africa 1996) has stipulated that public funds should be used efficiently, effectively and economically and furthermore that public services should be discharged fairly, impartially, equitably and without bias. Section 216 of the Constitution (Republic of South Africa 1996) goes on further to point out that national legislation introduces measures which ensures transparency, as well as the control of expenditure in all governmental spheres, by introducing "generally recognised accounting practice, uniform expenditure classifications, recognised accounting practice and uniform treasury norms and standards".

From a budgeting perspective, the Department of Finance (Republic of South Africa 1998) rolled out the Medium Term Expenditure Framework for a three-year budget program, as a broad budget reform process for all three spheres of government. "This three-year rolling budget framework means that departments can plan and reprioritise with greater certainty about future resource allocations than in the past" (Republic of South Africa 1998). According to the Department of

Finance (Republic of South Africa 1998), the budgetary reform process sought to deal with in a practical way, the financial challenges experienced nationally by making choices so that resources are fully utilised for the reconstruction and development priorities of Government and "to meet basic needs to the people as well as to ensure greater effectiveness in the management of public resources to deliver services more efficiently and fairly".

The National Treasury (Republic of South Africa 2001) states that the Medium Term Expenditure Framework (MTEF) provides for 3-year continuing revenue and expenditure plans for national and provincial departments. Furthermore, the MTEF also provides for transfers to local government. Utilising the Medium Term Expenditure Framework to budget revolves on certain basic principles which focuses on fiscal policy and the framework for the budget, public expenditure and policy priorities, service delivery budgeting and political oversight of the budgetary process politically (Republic of South Africa 2001).

In the year 1999, the South African National Treasury introduced the Public Finance Management Act (PFMA) (Republic of South Africa 1999), the objective of which was to "secure transparency, accountability, and sound management of the revenue, expenditure, assets and liabilities of the institutions to which this Act applies" (Republic of South Africa 1999, p. 12). The PFMA provides governance over financial management at Provincial and National Government level and was a precurser to the Municipal Finance Management Act (MFMA) (Republic of South Africa 2003), which applied to local government.

The next reform was the Framework for Managing Program Performance Information (Republic of South Africa 2007). This was followed by the publication of Quarterly Performance Information in the *Performance Information Handbook* (Republic of South Africa 2011).

The latest budget reform introduced by the South African National Treasury (Republic of South Africa 2014) is the Municipal Standard Chart of Accounts (MSCOA) which provides for a multi-dimensional classification framework, which provides local government "the method and format for recording and classifying financial transaction information in the general ledger, forming part of the books of account containing a standard list of all available accounts". These regulations are aligned with the notion of performance budgeting as the municipal information provided is uniformly recorded and classified at the transaction level in alignment with the National and Provincial government spheres. It will also facilitate national policy co-ordination/reporting, performance measurement and benchmarking at the local level.

Other legislation critical for performance budgeting is the Framework for Managing Program Performance Information (FMPPI) (Republic of South Africa 2007) and the Framework for Strategic Plans and Annual Performance Plans (FSPAPS) (Republic of South Africa 2010).

The Framework for Managing Program Performance Information (Republic of South Africa 2007) provides an indication of whether the aims and objectives are being met, and which policies and processes are working. Furthermore, for service delivery to be efficient and economical, all levels of government must formulate strategic plans, ensure effective resource allocation for plans to be implemented and which need to be monitored and reported on.

There is a positive linkage between the inputs of resources to the activities, outputs, outcomes and impacts that are likely to be accomplished. One of the critical inputs is the budget, without which no activity or output can be achieved. Therefore, in line with the definition of Performance Budgeting, outcomes and outputs are dependent on the resources. In the FMPPI (Republic of South Africa 2007) it is illustrated that what is used to do the work, ultimately determines what is aimed to change. Measurement of indicators occurs at each step of the way. The FMPPI (Republic of South Africa 2007) constitutes the basis for the performance system introduced in South Africa and includes the core explanations. According to it, the term input refers to "what we use to do the work", namely personnel, finances, equipment and buildings which are the total resources contributing to the creation and generation of outputs. Actions are then set in motion to convert the inputs into requisite outputs and ultimately outcomes thereby defining "what we do". The third component is final products in the form of outputs that is goods/services produced for delivery. Outputs are demarcated as "what we produce or deliver". The fourth component is outcomes which are medium-term results which are the resultant effect of defined outputs. "What we wish to achieve" are outcomes and the final component are the impacts, the results of attaining specific outcomes, more specifically creating jobs and reducing poverty. The FMPPI (Republic of South Africa 2007) also indicates that in securing results, budgets are created relative to inputs, activities and outputs, whilst the key objective is managing towards ensuring that the desired impacts and outcomes are achieved.

The Framework for Strategic and Annual Performance Plans (FSPAPS) (Republic of South Africa 2010) by National Treasury highlights the framework for Key Performance Indicator Concepts, which was adapted from the FMPPI (Republic of South Africa 2007) and which reflects an outcomes based approach, linking the cost initiatives to results in order to ensure value for money. In managing and budgeting for performance, budgets are drawn up taking into consideration the inputs, activities and outputs, with the intention of achieving outcomes and impacts.

7.3 Performance Budgeting at Local Government Level in South Africa

The Local Government: Municipal Systems Act (MSA) (Republic of South Africa 2000), (Section 38) enabled municipalities to measure performance so that they could administer services economically, effectively, efficiently and in an accountable manner.

In 2003, with the introduction of the Municipal Finance Management Act (MFMA) (Republic of South Africa 2003), government's reform process then moved into the performance area which was a response to the concept of performance budgeting at Local Government level. So although, the term Performance Budgeting was not used in the South African legislation, the concept of Performance Budgeting is encapsulated in the legislated requirements for local government performance and budgeting processes.

Previously municipalities placed much emphasis on the financial position, however in line with international best practices, more emphasis is now being placed on performance delivery. Siswana (2007) points out that there have been fundamental changes in the South Africa public financial management system post-1994 and the system is still evolving. More recently, the National Treasury of South Africa have identified the need for municipalities to measure performance outputs and the related budget spend and have just introduced the Municipal Standard Chart of Accounts, which is the next step in the Performance and Budgeting reform process. Siswana (2007) also highlighted the significance of performance budgeting in the Public Service, which prioritises an approach which is results-oriented and promotes management of government resources which is accountable and flexible within the stipulated legal framework.

Section 68 of the Municipal Finance Management Act (Republic of South Africa 2003), provided the framework for performance monitoring and budgeting at the local level. The Municipal Finance Management Act (Republic of South Africa 2003) Section 69, stipulated that a Budget linked to a Service Delivery Budget Implementation Plan (SDBIP) and additionally Annual Performance Agreements for the Municipal Manager and all managers, at the senior and executive level had to be developed/implemented and monitored. Section 72 of the MFMA (Republic of South Africa 2003) further required a budget and performance assessment for the Municipalities. National Treasury's Circular 13 then provided the details of how the SDBIP must be rolled out in municipalities.

The MFMA (Republic of South Africa 2003) highlights the fact that the SDBIP provides for the monitoring of budget execution and performance of senior management by the Municipal Manager, the monitoring of the Municipal Manager by the Mayor, and the monitoring by the local communities of the attainment of the strategic objectives of the Municipality. The SDBIP reflects the service delivery targets and budgets allocated and actual performance on both delivery targets and budgets which provides credible information for management decision-making, which will also determine the performance of senior managers and ultimately the municipal manager.

The National Treasury (Republic of South Africa 2005) circular on the Service Delivery Budget Implementation Plan (SDBIP) provides guidance for performance budgeting implementation at Local Government Level in South Africa. According to Circular 13 (Republic of South Africa 2005) "The budget gives effect to the strategic priorities of the municipality" whilst the SDBIP measures the objectives of implementation as detailed in the Integrated Development Plan and which has been budgeted for. Budget reforms have been occurring quite steadily since 1994, and one of the most recent reforms at local government level is the Municipal Chart of Accounts Reform. National Treasury (Republic of South Africa 2014) recognises that uniform expenditure classifications in the finance and budget process have already been implemented at Provincial and National Government level, however, this has not yet occurred at local government level. Furthermore, each municipality reports according to its own chart of accounts, which prevents National Treasury from consolidating local government information into national accounts, which in turn impedes transparency, reliability and accuracy in the planning and report processes at national government level. According to research conducted by the National Treasury (Republic of South Africa 2015), MSCOA is a "proudly South African" project focusing on practices of municipalities' policy implementation/review and reporting outcomes.

Performance information provides the oversight bodies and public a view of whether municipalities are ensuring value for money, by critically examining the performance of service delivery against budgets and to determine where corrective action is necessary. The implementation of the MFMA (Republic of South Africa 2003) has improved control over public expenditure in order to ensure that municipal management uses resources more efficiently.

7.4 Performance Budgeting at eThekwini Municipality

eThekwini City Council in Kwa-Zulu Natal, South Africa is a metropolitan Municipality and is approximately 2297 km^2, with a population of 3.5 million residents (Statistics South Africa 2016). It is the largest municipality in the Province of Kwazulu and the third largest nationally (eThekwini Municipality 2016, Para. 3).

The City vision is that "By 2030, eThekwini will be Africa's most caring and liveable city" (eThekwini Municipality 2016). The Medium-term Revenue and Expenditure Framework from 2017/2018 to 2019/2020 (eThekwini Municipality 2017) reflects that the total budget for 2017/2018 for the Municipality is R44,5 billion, equivalent to 2.98 billion euros. Furthermore, this budget was developed within an overall Planning Framework which identifies programs and projects to achieve the Municipality's Strategic Objectives. The Municipality was also impacted by the severe economic downturn over the last few years and despite the economic challenges, aims to continue with the Service Delivery agenda as detailed in the Integrated Development Plan (eThekwini Municipality 2017).

7.4.1 Performance Budgeting: Principles

The National Treasury and the Co-operative Governance Department have over the last few years introduced performance monitoring as well as budget monitoring for local government. In as much as there is regulation in performance and finance areas within government, there are still many more reforms which are being introduced.

As indicated above, the tool for performance budgeting was legislated by National Treasury and is the SDBIP (Republic of South Africa 2003). It should be noted that only projects and programs budgeted for should be included in the SDBIP. All legislations and regulations in rolling out the performance budgeting process for local government were legislated in the Municipal Finance Management Act (Republic of South Africa 2003).

In the following part of the text, the level of compliance of the current performance budgeting practice in eThekwini Municipality with the core suggestions, as provided by the academic literature is evaluated.

A: Kelly and Rivenbark (2011) comment that research has revealed that successful performance budgeting systems start with setting clear strategic goals and measurable objectives, to then measuring and evaluating progress towards meeting the goals and objectives, and to then reporting on performance outcomes. So performance budgeting has to follow strategic planning and performance measurement. According to Schick (2003, p. 79) "Performance also has both managerial and political dimensions. Without political encouragement, managers may have difficulty focusing on what their work is supposed to accomplish; without committed managers, politicians cannot make progress in implementing their vision. Because politicians and managers often speak different languages and have various interests, it is hard to get the interface between them right. When breakdowns in performance occur, it is often a question of confusion or misunderstanding over the respective roles and responsibilities of elected leaders and senior managers. Getting the relationship right is a necessary condition for the performing state."

From this point of view, eThekwini Municipality is fortunate in that the political commitment for performance and performance budgeting is a priority. The Council of the Municipality, led by the Mayor, has an Executive Committee, a Municipal Public Accounts Committee, as well as several sub-committees dealing with each aspect of the Municipality. The Mayor and all members of the Executive Committee, who are also chairpersons of the various sub-committees of Council play an active role in monitoring and providing oversight over performance budget information. The MFMA (Republic of South Africa 2003), requires the SDBIP to be submitted on a quarterly basis to Council in order for councillors to interrogate and call to account the relevant line management. All items which are budgeted for are therefore scrutinised by not only the ruling party, but also all other Political Parties who make up the Council.

This oversight ensures that Management who are accountable for the delivery of services, within the allocated budget, have to answer for non-delivery issues, over spending of allocated budgetary resources as well as all other challenges faced in the public realm in the delivery of basic services.

B: Kelly and Rivenbark (2011) also reflect that research indicates that by incorporating performance measures into financial processes, there is an increased likelihood that management will use this for informed decision-making, especially if effectiveness and efficiency indicators are included instead of just output measures.

At the eThekwini Municipality, the original roll out of performance budgeting was merely reporting on outputs on programs and projects and the budget alignment was merely the total budget allocated per focus area. There was no allocation of budget to each project and program. In order to start aligning to the principles of performance budgeting, the capital projects were then allocated the budget per project. This was more meaningful, as the budget could be tracked against the outputs. At this point in time, however effectiveness and efficiency of budget spend on outputs were not yet being measured.

Some of the other impediments to Performance Monitoring and Budgeting which has been identified over the years at eThekwini Municipality are improperly defined projects and programs resulting in poorly defined project plans and matching budgets; non-reliable data and evidence to support the projects status; lack of integration of performance to budget information; budgets cannot be allocated to operational projects and difficulty in monitoring actual spend with actual delivery of programs and projects.

National Treasury has introduced the concept of the Municipal Chart of Accounts, which was brought directly in line with the national and provincial chart of accounts to address some of these challenges. This recent introduction of the Municipal Standard Chart of Accounts (MSCOA), ensures that every item budgeted for is aligned to the Strategy of the Organisation, and is monitored in terms of not only delivery but also actual expenditure. This then assists management to ensure effectiveness and economy of projects.

C: Another performance area introduced to ensure accountability and achievement of objectives is the alignment of outputs to individual performance. Robinson and Brumby (2005, p. 46) point out that management in the public sector has over a period of time been influenced considerably by the thinking that human organisational behaviour is largely self-centred and this is a phenomenon in both the private and public sectors.

This has been the crux of the eThekwini Performance System, where organisational performance indicators are directly linked to the performance of its senior management team.

Therefore, there is accountability for budget spend on targets for service delivery and ensuring effectiveness and efficiency in the achievement of objectives which is the motivation for performance budgeting. There has to be strong alignment to individual performance, via the measurement of the organisation's performance.

D: Kelly and Rivenbark (2011) astutely point out the Performance Measurement systems may threaten Managers who now have to account for outcomes they cannot control. This could be for several reasons.

A typical example in eThekwini Municipality during 2016 was when a Business Forum called Delangekabona threatened and stopped municipal staff from undertaking critical service delivery responsibilities in certain areas, as the Forum wanted to be allocated tenders themselves. Performance measures which were impacted on were the delivery and maintenance of roads infrastructure, electricity and water supply to residents amongst other issues.

Heads of units with Key Performance Indicators were then impacted by non-performance at year end for not delivering on targets which were set at the beginning of the financial year.

These external factors are not budgeted for and are not factored into the SDBIP which is Performance Budgeting at eThekwini Municipality.

These types of incidents and political interventions, therefore influence management not to include certain indicators for measurement purposes into the Balanced Scorecard, or the SDBIP.

eThekwini Municipality, through the Performance Monitoring and Evaluation Unit, has implemented an electronic system in order to monitor the programs and the projects of the Municipality, which has a budget allocated to it. The tool used to monitor the SDBIP is called the 'Enterprise-wide Performance Monitoring Application (EPMA), which allows the direct capture, consolidation and reporting on all programs and projects of the Municipality into a single document, which details the program, the accountable manager, related projects within the program, the accountable project managers, annual and quarterly targets which are normally set before the commencement of the financial year. The EPMA also allows for evidence to support Key Performance Indicators to be uploaded for verification and audit purposes. The SDBIP is then reported to Council for monitoring on a quarterly basis, where units and accountable management are required to account for areas of performance and spend on the budget. A typical area highlighted for oversight would be where there is non-performance in relation to the pre-set targets, but overspend of the budget.

7.4.2 Performance Budgeting: Practice (on the Example of Water Management Area)

One of the priorities of the eThekwini Municipality is the provision of water to the residents of the Municipality. This is classified as basic service provision. The foundation of this process is included in the development, implementation and approval of the Integrated Development Plan (IDP). The IDP projects for the Water Department and the Water Department's previous year's actual performance against set targets, are reviewed annually, taking into consideration the input from Ward Committee meetings, Public meetings and the public sector through the Integrated Development Plan Forum.

Examples of water projects include the provision of water services to new human settlements; the provision of water to all residents, including indigent households; the building and maintenance of water infrastructure projects.

The Water projects are then captured on the Planning Module of the electronic system and the eThekwini Municipality's Water Department then provides input regarding the consolidated list. Projects are prioritised within the department, based on the Master Plans; Spatial Development Framework; Housing Implementation Plan; Asset Replacement Policy; Statutory requirements; Infrastructure plans identified in prior years; Duration of the project; Cost effectiveness of the project; if the project is a new/renewal asset; and inputs received during the IDP process.

The next step is the identification of funding sources for prioritised projects and allocating the segments of MSCOA to all prioritised projects. The Municipal Water tariffs and future implications are then calculated.

The list of Water prioritised projects is submitted to the Strategy Office, who ensure alignment to the strategy and these projects, with all other projects, are then submitted to the executive committee of the Municipal Council for ratification. The final list of projects is then included in the draft revised IDP; and the Draft Budget and the SDBIP is prepared. All projects are linked to Key Performance Indicators (KPIs) which monitor achievement of the intended outputs and outcomes. These KPIs are included in the SDBIP.

All KPIs must be accompanied by a Technical Indicator Definition document, which defines what is being measured, how and why it is being measured; and provides an indication of the data elements and evidence that will be available to show that targets are achieved, amongst other details. Without the submission of this document, the KPI and the linked project is not accepted to be included in the SDBIP.

The Project plan for the Project must also be submitted at the time the project is submitted for inclusion in the IDP. The project plan details the deliverables for the project and also provides the weighting for each deliverable of the project for each quarter of the financial year. If the project plan is not submitted at the time that the project is submitted for inclusion in the IDP, the project is not accepted.

The draft IDP, draft budget and draft SDBIP is noted by council, undergoes a public participation process and the final document is submitted to council for approval. Once approved the SDBIP is implemented.

The SDBIP delivery and budget spend is monitored on a quarterly basis and a report on the progress made towards meeting the targets set are submitted to Council within 30 days after the end of each quarter. The Council of the Municipality thereafter refers the SDBIP to each of the council's multi-party sub-committees, where areas of low performance are interrogated with the relevant heads of units. Heads of units are then requested to present the reasons why the projects targets are not being achieved and what measures have been put into place to address the low performance, in order that the project target is achieved by year end (Table 7.1).

Table 7.1 Service delivery Budget Implementation Plan: Water Connections

Sector	*Water*	
National Key Performance (National Government)	Basic Service Delivery	
Strategic Focus Area (IDP)	Quality Living Environment	
Outcome	Improved Access to Water	
Outcome Indicator	Percentage of households with access to basic water supply	
Key Performance Indicator (Output)	Number of new water connections meeting minimum standards	
Indicator Owner	Deputy City Manager for Infrastructure	
Programme	Address Infrastructure Backlogs	
Programme Owner	Head of Water Unit	
Project	The number of consumer units provided with access to AT LEAST a FREE basic level of potable WATER either by means of an individual h.h. yard supply (ground tank or metered flow limiter connected to a yard tap) or, for informal settlements, by a standpipe	
Project Owner	Deputy Head of the Water Unit	
Baseline (previous financial year)	6000	
Annual Target	7000	
	Target	Actual
Quarter 1: Target/Actual	2000	2200
Quarter 2: Target/Actual	1000	1500
Quarter 3: Target/Actual	1500	1000
Quarter 4: Target/Actual	2500	4000
Quarter 1: Budget Allocation/Spend	R75,000	R75,000
Quarter 2: Budget Allocation/Spend	R36,000	R40,000
Quarter 3: Budget Allocation/Spend	R54,000	R45,000
Quarter 4: Budget Allocation/Spend	R85,000	R90,000
Total Budget for Financial year	R250 million	

Source Authors' own

7.5 Conclusion

Schick (2003) believes that given the fact that budgeting is quantitative, makes it a perfect instrument for developing a linkage with the results generated. However, on average, very few governments have developed a real link between public funds and results in this manner, thereby contributing to the limited success of performance budgeting.

This chapter highlighted the South African framework and in its core part, it used the example of eThekwini Municipality to document the situation at local level. eThekwini Municipality, unlike many municipalities within South Africa, had a history of full political commitment and participation in the performance and budgetary processes. This has played a defining role in allowing the Municipality to be regarded as one of the top municipalities nationally in relation to financial management.

Despite many positive achievements identified there are several challenges in eThekwini Municipality—for example the absence of monitoring of the effectiveness and efficiency of budget spend against projects; projects and programs are not properly defined resulting in poor project plans and inaccurate budgets; unreliable data and evidence to support the project status; lack of integration of performance to budget information and budgets not effectively allocated to operational projects. Moreover, budgetary performance data are not sufficiently communicated to the general public.

Many of these challenges identified within the eThekwini context, are illustrative of the challenges faced by most municipalities within South Africa. eThekwini Municipality however, is a metropolitan municipality, with a much larger rate base, and therefore much larger budget. The local and district municipalities within the country experience not only the same challenges as eThekwini Municipality, but also are challenged by the lack of funding and resources to implement adequate processes and controls to implement effective performance budgeting systems.

There is still much to reform in the performance budgeting area in eThekwini Municipality, as well as most municipalities within South Africa; however, the broad budget reform process being applied at a national level will eventually lead to a stabilised performance and budgeting system. The Chief Directorate at National Treasury has indicated in recent national meetings that for any budget and performance reform process in government to be successful the following must be applied "gentle pressure, relentlessly applied, within a coherent framework".

Many of the performance and budgetary reforms being required by National Treasury within South Africa, follow the recommendations of the OECD (2008). Recently the National Treasury of South Africa in line with the OECD (2008) recommendations also introduced the following to local government: the application of a single performance budgeting model in the form of Municipal Standard Chart of Accounts; the participation of local government in appraisal sessions regarding performance and budgeting reforms and alignment, which the eThekwini Municipality has been active in; and the government-wide planning and performance framework for reporting.

It is quite clear that the process of performance budgeting is still evolving in particular in developing countries and it will be some time before the system in completely entrenched in the local government financial system.

References

Cangiano, Marco, Teresa Curristine, and Michel Lazare (eds.). 2013. *Public Financial Management and Its Architecture*. Washington, DC: IMF.

Collaborative African Budget Reform Initiative (CABRI). 2013. *Performance and Program—Based Budgeting in Africa*. Cape Town: CABRI.

eThekwini Municipality. 2016. *About eThekwini Municipality*. Durban: eThekwini Municipality. Accessed 3 September 2016. http://www.durban.gov.za/Discover_Durban/Pages/AboutEM.aspx.

eThekwini Municipality. 2017. *Medium Term Revenue and Expenditure Framework 2017/18 to 2019/2020*. Durban: eThekwini Municipality.

Kelly, Janet M., and William C. Rivenbark. 2011. *Performance Budgeting for State and Local Government*, 2nd ed. New York: M.E. Sharpe.

Kumar, Pranav. 2017. *Performance Budgeting (PB): Meaning, Purpose and Other Details*. Yourarticlelive. Accessed 6 July 2017. http://www.yourarticlelibrary.com/accounting/performance-budgeting/performance-budgeting-pb-meaning-purpose-and-other-details/62110/.

Organisation for Economic Co-operation and Development (OECD). 2008. *Policy Brief on Performance Budgeting: A Users' Guide*. Paris: OECD.

Republic of South Africa. 1996. *Constitution of the Republic of South Africa Act 108 of 1996*. Pretoria: Government Printers.

Republic of South Africa. 1998. *Medium Term Budget Policy Statement 1998*. Pretoria: Department of Finance.

Republic of South Africa. 1999. *Public Finance Management Act, No. 1 of 1999*. Pretoria: Government Printers.

Republic of South Africa. 2000. *The Local Government: Municipal Systems Act (MSA) No. 32 of 2000*. Cape Town: Republic of South Africa.

Republic of South Africa. 2001. *Medium Term Expenditure Framework Treasury Guidelines: Preparing Budget Submissions*. Pretoria: National Treasury.

Republic of South Africa. 2003. *Local Government: Municipal Finance Management Act 56 of 2003*. Pretoria: Government Printers.

Republic of South Africa. 2005. *Municipal Finance Management Act (MFMA) Circular 13: Service Delivery Budget Implementation Plan*. Pretoria: National Treasury.

Republic of South Africa. 2007. *Framework for Managing Program Performance Information (FMPPI)*. Pretoria: National Treasury.

Republic of South Africa. 2010. *Framework for Strategic Plans and Annual Performance Plans (FSPAPS)*. Pretoria: National Treasury.

Republic of South Africa. 2011. *Performance Information Handbook*. Pretoria: National Treasury.

Republic of South Africa. 2014. *Local Government: Municipal Finance Management Act 56 of 2003: Municipal Regulations on Standard Chart of Accounts*. Pretoria: Government Printers.

Republic of South Africa. 2015. *Municipal Standard Chart of Accounts (MSCOA) Circular No 1: Implementation*. Pretoria: National Treasury.

Robinson, Marc, and Jim Brumby. 2005. *Does Performance Budgeting Work?—An Analytical Review of the Empirical Literature*. Working Paper WP/05/210. Washington, DC: IMF.

Schick, Allen. 2003. The Performing State. *OECD Journal on Budgeting 3* (2): 71–103.

Siswana, Batandwa. 2007. *Leadership and Governance in the South African Public Service: An Overview of the Public Finance Management System*. Doctoral thesis (Public Affairs). Pretoria: University of Pretoria.

Statistics South Africa. 2016. *eThekwini, Stats SA*. South Africa. Accessed 16 November 2016. http://www.statssa.gov.za/?page_id=1021&id=ethekwini-municipality.

Sterk, Miekatrien, and Geert Bouckaert. 2006. *The Impact of Performance Budgeting on the Role of Parliament—A Four Country Study*. Belgium: Public Management Institute. Accessed 30 July 2017. http://steunpuntbov.be/rapport/s0406011_2TAD.pdf.

CHAPTER 8

Performance-Based Budgeting in Russia

Andrey Klimenko

8.1 Introduction

Russia may well rank highly in a relevant international rating of the formal attributes of performance-based budgeting (PBB). The Russian government has created the necessary preconditions for PBB—introducing a multi-year budget and accumulating data on performance indicators that are considered in the budget planning process. The new budget code draft currently under discussion proposes strengthening the link between the budget and programs. However, the use of PBB tools is not a guarantee of success. The experience of many countries has demonstrated that the use of performance indicators in budget discussions, spending reviews, etc. is an essential but insufficient condition for an effective budget system. This fully applies to the Russian budgeting practices. On the one hand, Russia has introduced many PBB tools, ranging from presentational budgeting to direct budgeting. On the other hand, the effectiveness of the budget spending leaves much to be desired.

A. Klimenko (✉)
Faculty of Social Sciences, National Research University Higher School of Economics, Moscow, Russia
e-mail: aklimenko@hse.ru

M. S. de Vries et al. (eds.), *Performance-Based Budgeting in the Public Sector*, Governance and Public Management,
https://doi.org/10.1007/978-3-030-02077-4_8

To characterise the development of PBB in Russia, there are known budgeting models, such as presentational, performance-informed, and direct budgeting (Performance Budgeting in OECD Countries 2007, pp. 21–22), or results-linked, performance-driven, and results-driven budgeting (Schick 2014). Program budgeting could also be singled out as a model in which information about the costs and benefits of program implementation is used to define the amount of budget expenditures (Robinson 2007).

Each of these types of models has an equivalent in Russian budgeting practice. *Key Areas of Government Activities* (KAGA) and *Reports on the Results and Main Activities of Ministries and Agencies* (RRMAs), applied in 2008–2012, can be considered as examples of presentational budgeting.

Until recently, PBB was largely a tribute to budgeting trends and an object of piloting and testing. In recent years, the implementation of PBB has become particularly relevant for Russia in light of the economic stagnation and shrinking of budget revenue in the wake of unstable energy prices and international sanctions.

8.2 Creating Preconditions for PBB in Russia

As in many other countries, the practice of budget planning and management in Russia is evolving in conjunction with the performance management system as a whole. The first systematic efforts to form legislative and organisational preconditions for performance-based management and budgeting were undertaken in the Russian Federation in the early 2000s.

In 2001, a government directive enacted the first socio-economic development program of the Russian Federation for 2002–2004, which was extended in 2006 to 2006–2008. During that period, the idea of a 'functional budget' was discussed in the context of the PBB concept, i.e. a budget aimed at government functions being performed and government services being provided on the basis of activity-based costs and activity-based management principles. In the early 2000s, discussions also centred on issues related to the development of program budgeting, using performance indicators, formula funding, and incentives. At the 2006 G8 summit, presided over by the Russian Federation, the Russian Ministry of Finance came forward with an initiative concerning good governance of public finance, which included a proposal to introduce results-oriented budgeting (Ministry of Finance of the Russian Federation).

The 2004 Russian government's resolution on *Measures to Improve the Effectiveness of Budget Spending* was directly concerned with PBB implementation. It included the *Concept of Budgetary Reform 2004–2006 in the Russian Federation* along with provisions on the *Reports on the Results and Main Activities of Ministries and Agencies* (RRMAs), which became one of the first PM tools used in the budgeting process.

RRMAs contained descriptions of targets, tasks, and performance indicators for ministries and agencies (budgetary planning entities) along with their spending obligations and revenue generation plans. Budget allocations were distributed across targets, tasks, and programs, and their performance indicators were established. The aggregate of RRMAs had to paint a comprehensive picture of how strategic goals for the country's development would be achieved.

In practice, RRMAs failed to provide adequate links between planned performance results and budgetary allocations. This was largely due to the effect of 'soft budget constraints' (Kornai et al. 2003; Desai and Olofsgård 2006), the optional nature of RRMAs as a special kind of public contract, and the lack of appropriate accountability and incentives. This partly devalued the original idea and reduced the significance of RRMAs in the budgeting process. Soft budget constraints are essentially an obstacle for PBB implementation in the public sector, not just in post-socialist economies, because the lack of effectiveness in this sector can always be justified by the existence of more important objectives that cannot be quantified.

RRMAs could have functioned as public declarations and agency mission statements, i.e. they could have become a full-fledged tool of presentational budgeting. However, they failed to perform this role fully due to their excessively complicated and bureaucratic format, understandable only to a narrow sector of public officials and experts. Other than the actual authors of these documents, it is likely that few people read them with the attention they merited. Moreover, no procedure was in place for a public discussion in which the comments of other agencies and civil society representatives could be considered.

Still, the accumulation of the experience with preparing such reports, creating a database of outputs and outcome indicators, and testing the methods for substantiating the amounts of subsidies needed to achieve the desired target and results played a positive role. The development of RRMAs helped shape the culture of evidence-based and performance-based management and budgeting and awareness of the consequences of budgeting decisions.

The 2004 concept called for the transition predominantly to program budgeting as a subset of performance-informed budgeting aimed at effectively achieving national program targets and priorities. This signified a departure from the traditional line-item budgeting.

The concept also called for the expansion of the budgeting horizon to three years, which created preconditions for implementing a performance management and program approach to budgeting. The first three-year budget was adopted in Russia for the 2008–2010 period.

The concept also stated that the budget had to be formed taking into account the objectives of public policy, while budget allocations had to be clearly linked to performance. It stipulated that national programs had to be developed with a primary focus on the substantiation of the outputs and their interconnection with the amount of budget allocations and the effectiveness of their spending.

The concept also incorporated a number of other fairly essential ideas. One idea involved a competitive allocation of funds among national programs. It proposed an experiment involving the annual competitive allocation of a portion of budget subsidies among federal ministries and agencies taking into account the anticipated results and bearing in mind the priority of the programs they were implementing and the quality of the RRMAs they submitted.

The next stage of the evolution of the target-setting system as a precondition for the application of PBB is associated with the development of the 2008 document titled *Key Areas of Government Activities* (KAGA) *up to 2012* (Rasporyazhenie Pravitel'stva RF). KAGA outlined the medium-term priorities along with 60 nationwide projects with indicators of anticipated results. The projects were subdivided into five target sectors. The first sector, called 'a new quality of life', substantiated the objectives and activities of public policy in the fields of healthcare, improvement of the demographic and environmental situation, and development of the system of education. The second sector, called 'a dynamic innovative economy', involved ensuring macroeconomic stability, creating a favourable business environment and a national system of innovations, making the industries more competitive, and creating the infrastructure for an information society. The third sector, called 'national security', was concerned with the tasks of revamping the defence industry, enhancing the country's anti-terrorist protection, ensuring greater economic security, and protecting information. The fourth sector, called 'balanced regional development', focused on aligning the federal policy with regional policies and creating new socio-economic development centres in the regions. The fifth sector was called 'an effective government' and involved administrative and budget reform and the institution of e-government.

The description of each KAGA project included objectives, indicators, and activities aimed at achieving them. Every project had its executive ministries and agencies, 'project roadmaps' designed to show the changes to occur in the economy and society as a result of project implementation and the resources required to achieve them, the volume of budget spending required to achieve the objectives, and how target indicators will change following changes in the volume of funding, and so forth.

Work on KAGA project roadmaps in 2008–2010 relegated RRMAs to the background but did not override them altogether. KAGA parameters were considered when it came to forming the budget. Notably, just like with RRMAs, PBB was implemented initially in the form of presentational budgeting rather than as performance-informed budgeting.

On the subject of presentation budgeting tools, it is worth mentioning the 'budget for citizens' system operating at the federal level under the Open Government (*Otkrytoe pravitelstvo*) since 2012. Similar systems exist in a number of regions. Taking into account specific public interests, the website answers such questions as: Which spending is prioritised now and why? Who determines the amount of subsidies for priority spending items and how? What is the share of social spending in the budget? How much do citizens pay in taxes? What is being done to make the budget less dependent on oil and gas revenue? and so forth. In addition to general information about key budget parameters, some of these portals support public opinion polls and offer citizens an opportunity to join the discussion of budget-related issues.

8.3 On the Path to Performance-Informed and Program Budgeting

An important attempt at linking programs and budgets was made in 2010. The idea was to make the federal budget entirely program-based, i.e. allocate almost the entire volume of federal budget spending among federal programs and link the amounts of budget subsidies to the performance indicators of these programs.

A total of 41 national programs were approved in late 2010. In the draft budget for 2012–2014, the expenditures of federal executive authorities were allocated among these programs (except for a small 'off-program' portion). A similar approach was also applied to budgets at the regional government level of the Russian Federation.

In the Russian president's address on the budget policy for 2014–2016, national programs are mentioned as the primary tool linking strategic and budget planning. A requirement was introduced whereby new regulatory acts (including federal laws) have to be justified bearing in mind the objectives of national programs.

There are presently 44 national programs at the federal level. Most of them were launched in 2013 for a six-year period. They cover 70% of federal budget spending and incorporate some 2000 performance indicators, some of which are target indicators of outcomes, while others are target indicators of outputs.

National programs are adopted by a directive of the prime minister. The current federal programs cover a period up to 2020. Each one of these programs includes a substantiation of public policy priorities in a specific area as well as indicators of outcomes and outputs, subsidy amounts, and implementation timeframes for the primary activities. One ministry is put in charge of the implementation of each program at the federal level. A ministry can oversee implementation of several programs. Programs are subdivided into subprograms with their own responsible ministry or agency, targets, indicators, and budgets. Information about most national programs is in the public domain and can be found on the portal of national programs of the Russian Federation (Portal Gosprogramm RF).

Federal-level national programs are subdivided into five thematic sectors: a new quality of life, innovative development and modernisation of the economy, effective government, balanced regional growth, and national security.

The planned program targets and subsidies are updated annually for the remaining period of their implementation, which is more often associated with changes in budget revenue and less with any failure to implement national program activities. In the course of such updates, the target indicators and funding volumes of national programs change, while the primary goals normally remain unchanged. A total of 1914 indicators were established for national programs in 2017, with 774 target values already achieved.

National programs are developed and updated taking into account the forecast for socio-economic development of the Russian Federation, industry-specific strategies, and budget constraints. Annual updates are submitted to the government by 1 April and coordinated with program implementation process owners prior to the drafting of the federal budget, i.e. roughly before the summer. An initiative-based approval system is in place to accelerate and optimise the program approval process. The procedure is implemented electronically via the national program's portal. All ministries and agencies, as well as concerned organisations, participate in the initiative-based approval.

Proposals to update national programs submitted as part of the initiative-based approval are sent for the review of the federal ministry or agency in charge of national program implementation. Following the review of incoming proposals, the ministry or agency decides to either accept or reject them. The ministry or agency must substantiate its decision to reject an initiative. The ministry or agency in charge of program implementation must submit even the rejected initiatives along with the national program to the Russian government and may be reviewed and supported at subsequent stages of the national program draft review.

Programs are also updated depending on how the budget is fulfilled. For example, spending for a number of programs in the social sector, as well as environmental protection, national security, and regional development, was scaled back in 2017 with consideration for changes in budget revenue. At the same time, spending increased for programs focusing on healthcare, education, law enforcement, and the manufacturing industry. Executive summaries of budget changes describe in detail the specific activities that necessitate changes in spending and the reasons for such changes. In this way, a connection is maintained between the budget and national programs.

National programs are supplemented by a program implementation plan for two or three years to come. It lists the milestones and timeframes for achieving them, the responsible officials, and the volume of financial resources allocated.

Every national program is accompanied by a financial and economic rationale and an assessment of the effectiveness of its implementation. The calculation of financial resources of the national program includes not just federal budget allocations but also subsidies from regional and local budgets and other sources. A forecast is made with respect to regional budget funds and extra-budgetary sources. For example, the environmental protection national program will receive 80% of the requisite funding from the federal budget, 13% from consolidated regional budgets, and 7% from private sources.

Implementation of national programs is subject to quarterly monitoring. The primary focus is on the achievement of milestones, information about funding volumes and government contracts awarded, and instances of failure to comply with timeframes or achieve milestones. The degree of achievement of milestones under national programs of the Russian Federation was estimated at about 88% in September 2017, calculated as a running total since the beginning of the year.

The Accounts Chamber of the Russian Federation, an independent agency tasked with monitoring budget performance, is actively involved in the process of evaluating the implementation of the budget and national programs.

A quarterly rating is published based on an evaluation of the timeliness with which milestones are achieved under each program. The ministries and agencies responsible for program implementation are ranked annually. This involves evaluating the number of activities completed and the amount spent on them.

Despite the considerable progress made in using the program-based approach, a multitude of problems remain unresolved. Specifically, approaches to evaluating unplanned expenditures as well as unforeseen results are yet to be developed. Even though program targets and objectives are considered when drafting the budget and are updated as part of the budget revision process, there have been instances where program outputs and outcomes remained virtually unchanged despite funding being considerably scaled back for specific national programs.

8.4 Project Management and Budgeting

The endeavour to make budget spending more focused on solving priority tasks resulted in the implementation of project management in the Russian Federation. The project management approach was first implemented in Russia on a large scale in 2005 with the approval of national priority projects in healthcare, education, housing, and agriculture. This experience cannot be considered a total success in terms of project management quality. The results within different aspects of these projects turned out to be mutually unbalanced. For example, a lot of hi-tech and costly medical equipment was procured as part of the 'healthcare' national project, while doctors were not properly trained to operate it (and necessary extra supplies and reserve parts were not included in the order). Some of the equipment remained underutilised. Weak control over spending resulted in instances of corruption and procurement of equipment at clearly overinflated prices. Misspending of funds was common. However, these factors failed to bring about a revision of projects in the face of rapidly growing oil and gas revenues.

When speaking of project management, it is worth mentioning the inaugural decrees of the Russian president (May 2012), which established the target indicators for various aspects of the economic and social policies for the following electoral period and defined the subsidy amounts for their achievement. The achievement of targets and objectives was essentially arranged using the PM approach and provided with budget allocations on a priority basis out of the federal and regional budgets. The implementation of decrees was monitored.

The use of the project management approach was expanded in 2016. A distinctive feature of the new phase of this approach was the creation of project offices that functioned as delivery units at various levels of executive government. The Strategic Development and Priority Projects Council under the president of the Russian Federation and the Project Office of the Russian Government were created at the national level. Priority projects are implemented at the national level in such areas as healthcare, education, mortgage lending and housing rental, housing infrastructure and urban environment, ecology, road safety and quality, integrated development of monotowns, small business and support of individual enterprise, control and oversight function reform, labour productivity, international cooperation and exports, and digital economy. A total of RUB 177 billion was allocated for their implementation in 2017. Federal budget subsidies amounting to RUB 100 billion per year have been allocated for 2018–2019.

Supervisors, managers, project committees, and functional clients are specified for every project. The priority project data sheet is drawn up, detailing the targets, indicators, and criteria of achievement, the list of national programs associated with the implementation of the priority project, a description of risks, an evaluation of the project budget, and information about process owners. A consolidated plan listing the milestones and activities is also developed. The project budget consists of subsidies from budgets at various levels (federal, regional, and municipal) and extra-budgetary funding. Project budget spending is distributed among the different aspects of project implementation. Priority project implementation is monitored, with an annual report prepared for every project.

In addition to priority national projects, ministries and agencies develop their own line projects. Unlike priority projects, line projects have a lower, sector-specific level. Project offices are established within ministries or agencies for project management. They are tasked with maintaining portfolios of line projects, drafting and monitoring compliance with implementation projects, and providing methodological, informational, and human resources for projects. Project offices are created not just at federal ministries and agencies but also at regional administrations.

The introduction of the project management approach called for a revision of the attitude to national programs that had in previous years served as the basis of program budgeting in the Russian Federation. In particular, this involved singling out the project and process aspects within national programs. The project aspect of national programs includes priority and line projects.

Development of national programs on the basis of the project management approach involves ranking the projects and other activities included in them in terms of their significance for achieving the ultimate objectives and outcomes. Such ranking is important for allocating budget subsidies among programs and changing funding during their implementation. It has been proposed that such ranking be carried out annually, as the significance of specific projects and activities during national program implementation may vary. The annual report on program implementation serves as a basis for decisions to reduce or increase funding for the program and its projects or to discontinue them ahead of schedule or to launch new projects or activities. If implemented, these innovations could more closely align the essence of budget planning with program and project budgeting.

8.5 Instruments of Direct Budgeting

In addition to the program and project approaches, direct budgeting instruments play an important role in Russia. Their role is to ensure that all public obligations of the state arising from the requirements of the laws are taken into account and to determine the qualitative and quantitative indicators of the activities of budget recipients.

The *Register of Spending Obligations* is compiled for this purpose. Such obligations arise out of laws, contracts, government resolutions, and ongoing programs or projects. Spending obligations are subdivided: providing public services, social security, budgetary investments, subsidies, inter-budgetary transfers, obligations under regional (international) agreements, and public debt servicing. Existing and newly assumed spending obligations are differentiated. Existing (i.e., accumulated) budget obligations normally account for up to 90% of planned budget spending, which is an indication of limited opportunities for structural changes.

The legal basis of each obligation (article of the law, government decision, etc.) is specified, as are the form of implementation of the obligation (subsidy, compensation, etc.), amount of expenditure, and category of recipients.

A number of methods are used in the planning of spending obligations. Formula budgeting (i.e., multiplying specific standardised costs by the population size [per capita]) is used to determine expenses for social benefits, compensations, stipends, and other social obligations of the government. The method of indexing the current subsidies (by the level of inflation or another established ratio) is used to calculate obligations involving payment for transportation, utility, telecom, and other services. Direct budgeting is used to calculate the amount of obligations under investment projects, regional (international) treaties and agreements, and servicing of the public debt of the Russian Federation.

Data from the *Register of Spending Obligations* are used to form the forward-looking financial plan of the Russian Federation and draft the federal budget. Some information about the *Register of Spending Obligations* is published on the website of the Russian Ministry of Finance (Minfin RF).

Along with the *Register of Spending Obligations*, the *Rationales for Budget Subsidies* are designed by federal ministries to calculate the amount of funding for spending obligations over a three-year period. The *Rationales for Budget Subsidies* describe outputs and outcomes, reflect the relationships between them and subsidies, offer an informative description of spending, and summarise the grand total of funds required.

Outputs are described using indicators of the volume and quality of services (e.g., the number of people who received medical aid, the number of beds in hospitals), the number of activities implemented (e.g., the number of audits and inspections, expert reviews, and so forth). When it comes to subsidies for social security benefits for the population, output indicators specify the number of beneficiaries (e.g., the number of citizens entitled to specific benefits, assistance, etc.). The planned budgetary investments are correlated with data on the industrial capacities being launched, the number of jobs created, and the anticipated dividend revenue. Data on spending for the implementation of national programs are accompanied by indicators of anticipated outcomes and outputs. For example, the indicator of 'public satisfaction with medical care' obtained through opinion polls is used to describe the achievement of the program goal to 'improve the quality and availability of medical care'.

The Russian Ministry of Finance assesses the quality of the *Rationales for Budget Subsidies* prepared by federal ministries. This assessment is an integral part of financial management quality monitoring and considers the availability of appropriate output and outcome indicators and their alignment with spending goals. Essentially, as the *Rationales for Budget Subsidies* is prepared, the Russian Ministry of Finance and other ministries engage in a dialogue that involves discussing the objectives and effectiveness of activities.

8.6 Performance-Based Budgeting in Budgetary Organisations

There are currently about 170,000 state and municipal organisations in Russia of federal, regional, and municipal subordination, the activities of which are subsidised from corresponding budgets. These organisations (budgetary organisations) are funded according to the 'state assignments', which are a form of public contracts containing performance indicators.

The state or municipal assignment includes the obligations of the organisation with respect to the capacity and quality of performance for which the organisation receives a specific amount of budget subsidies. The state assignment is defined for the term of approval of the budget, i.e. for up to three years. It contains indicators describing the quality and/or volume of services, the reporting requirements, and the procedure for controlling assignment completion. As a result, the traditional line-item budgeting previously used by such organisations in Russia has been replaced with a contract of sorts, which is based on per capita expenditures and targeted subsidies for specific output indicators, i.e. a kind of performance-informed budgeting or in some cases even formula budgeting.

State or municipal assignments are planned with the use of centrally compiled *Lists of State Services* and spending required for their implementation. The amount of a subsidy for a state assignment is planned so as to cover current expenditures and also provide funding for institutional development.

A particular state assignment contains a list of services provided by the organisation, a description of the consumers, and quantitative and qualitative characteristics of the services, and specifies permissible deviations from the required parameters. State or municipal assignments are currently used to fund education, healthcare, culture, science institutions, and other budgetary sectors. Performance of the state assignment is a condition for budget subsidy.

For example, for a typical Russian state university, a service called 'the implementation of educational programs' is established for a three-year period, and the areas and topics of research are part of that work. An indicator for the service is usually the number of students in various programs. The assignment for the work/research would contain qualitative characteristics of the expected results, numbers of publications, citation indices, etc.

The state assignment mechanism cannot fully resolve the problems inherent in relations between principals and agents or the problems of incomplete contracts. It is merely one of the ways to make the activities of public organisations results-oriented. In practice, it is impossible to fully guarantee the long-term stability of the planned indicators of state assignments as well as the corresponding subsidies, which undermines the incentives.

There is also the problem of the multitude of control indicators. For example, along with the state assignment, the volumes of commercial work and services can also be monitored by the overseeing ministry and documented in financial and business plans. Indicators pertaining to salary levels are also mandatory for organisations in the health and education sectors. As a result, organisations receive a multitude of mandatory or recommended target indicators that are not sufficiently harmonised, which complicates the process of budgeting and monitoring (Lavrov and Yastrebova 2017).

8.7 Lessons Learned

A fairly large number of PBB tools, ranging from presentational to direct budgeting, have been implemented in the Russian Federation over the past decade. This system retains internal contradictions, which are manifested in the absence of tangible progress when it comes to the effectiveness of budget spending. It is only fair to mention that international experiences do not demonstrate indisputable success with the implementation of PBB tools either. Obviously, the absence of quick results from the implementation of PBB tools is attributable not just to the incorrect or inconsistent application but also to more general problems.

One of the key objectives of PBB implementation is to achieve an optimum allocation of budget funds from the perspective of a balance of social interests. This requires introducing bidding and competitive procedures into the budgeting process, which would make it possible to identify and fund the priority programs and projects before others, taking into account the existing and newly assumed obligations. The use of outcome indicators in planning and monitoring budget performance, multi-year budgets, program budgeting, etc. serve as important preconditions for accomplishing this task. However, when all these mechanisms are provided by the executive branch of power, the outcome can be far from what is desired. Ministries and agencies prone to the 'maximising bureaucrat' effect focus on their own benefits, which can be far removed from public interests. It is therefore insufficient to apply only PBB mechanisms; the active and informed involvement of citizens and parliaments in the budgeting process is also called for. This can be specifically achieved by reducing the informational asymmetry between the government and the public when it comes to reviewing budgets, national programs, and projects. This issue is relevant for Russia across all levels of government. Otherwise, PBB tools will not serve to create the maximum possible social and economic benefits but will rather be used for bureaucratic bargaining between ministries and agencies as well as organisations associated with them. In the opinion of the Accounts Chamber of the Russian Federation, national programs are sometimes misaligned with the long-term goals of public socio-economic policy, and they are frequently implemented using an agency-focused approach.

The rationale behind budget decisions normally does not include analysis of the different scenarios of the behaviour of economic agents. Opportunities for cooperation, co-production, co-funding, public–private partnerships, i.e. contributions by various stakeholders to the achievement of common goals, are seldom evaluated.

The issue of stimulating effective spending of budget funds is equally relevant. Incentive mechanisms are either missing or extremely weak in the majority of PBB tools used in Russia. Chief executives of ministries and project officers should be both incentivised to spend their budgets effectively, achieving targets and performance indicators, and held more accountable for failing to do so.

Opportunities for saving budget funds, carrying over funds to the following year, or changing the spending structure are limited or non-existent. This is traditionally blamed on the risks of failing to meet the macroeconomic parameters of the budget and the resulting economic consequences. As a result, the problem known as 'use it or lose it' persists, while budget management comes down to enforcing the budget plan.

PBB should allow greater flexibility and factor in the risks associated with changes in the external environment, which are the rule rather than the exception in the Russian reality. However, in the existing practice, the formal accounting of risks is only practised at the program and project planning stage without any connection to the effects of such risks on the budget. This is currently a particularly important problem for Russia considering the volatility of the global energy market, sanctions, and continuing economic stagnation.

There are technical problems as well as systemic challenges, such as problems associated with the difficulty of finding objective and adequate indicators for quantifying outcomes, the degree of target achievement, and comparisons of alternative allocations of budget funds. Volumetric or weighted average indicators account for a considerable share of existing indicators, which cannot always be traced to any socially significant outcomes. This gives rise to the practice of 'working to meet the target indicator' that is the most convenient for bureaucrats responsible for its achievement.

The process of approving budget decisions becomes complicated under the conditions of applying PBB approaches because quantitative and qualitative parameters of performance need to be considered in addition to the traditional financial metrics. The expanding array of parameters considered in budget planning and the inadequate development of information technologies and big data complicate budget planning and revisions. Under such conditions, it is difficult to ensure manoeuvrability of budget management and achieve agile budgeting.

Increasing the effectiveness of budget spending is a task of paramount importance for the Russian government at this point. This can be achieved by continuing the PBB implementation process, making it comprehensive, and ensuring that all the process owners are motivated. Moreover, this is presently required in the face of the increasing budget constraints due to the shrinking revenues of the federal and regional budgets and the much tougher conditions for foreign borrowings and investments.

References

Desai, Raj M., and Anders Olofsgård. 2006. The Political Advantage of Soft Budget Constraints. *European Journal of Political Economy* 22 (2): 370–387. https://doi.org/10.1016/j.ejpoleco.2005.09.011.

Kornai, Janos, Eric Maskin, and Gerard Roland. 2003. Understanding the Soft Budget Constraint. *Journal of Economic Literature* 41(4): 1095–1136.

Lavrov, Aleksej, and Olga Yastrebova. 2017. *Reforma uchrejdenij budgetnoi sfery: predvaritelnij itogy i novie visovy.* Moscow: Izdatel'skij dom Vysshej shkoly ehkonomiki.

Ministry of Economic Development. n.d. *Portal Gosprogramm RF.* Received on 10 November 2017, from Portal Gosprogramm RF. https://programs.gov.ru/Portal/.

Ministry of Finance of the Russian Federation. n.d. *Principles for Good Governance of Public Finance.* Received on 7 November 2017, from Budget reform. http://old.minfin.ru/common/img/uploaded/library/no_date/2007/pfg-gopf_eng.pdf.

Ministerstvo finansov Rossii. n.d. *Reestr rashodnyh obyazatelstv.* Received on 10 November 2017, from Budgetnaya reforma. https://www.minfin.ru/ru/perfomance/reforms/budget/resoriented/registry/.

OECD. 2007. *Performance Budgeting in OECD Countries.* Paris: OECD Publishing.

Otkrytoe pravitelstvo. 2017. *Budget dlya grazhdan.* Received from Open.gov.ru: http://budget.open.gov.ru/.

Rasporyazhenie Pravitel'stva RF ot 17.11.2008 N 1663-r. red. ot 14.12.2009. *Ob utverzhdenii osnovnyh napravlenij deyatel'nosti Pravitel'stva RF na period do 2012 goda i perechnya proektov po ih realizacii.* Received on 30 April 2018, from Portal. http://www.consultant.ru/document/cons_doc_LAW_81994/.

Robinson, Marc. 2007. Performance Budgeting Models and Mechanisms. In *Performance Budgeting: Linking Funding and Results*, 1–18. Washington: International Monetary Fund.

Schick, Allen. 2014. The Metamorphoses of Performance Budgeting. *OECD Journal on Budgeting* 13 (2): 49–79.

CHAPTER 9

Performance-Based Program Budgeting in Ukraine (with a Focus on the Local Budget Level)

Nataliia Grynchuk

9.1 Introduction

In Ukraine, performance-based budgeting (PBB) and the comprehensive analysis and review of the efficiency and feasibility of expenditures by sectors, intended to increase transparency and accountability, is a component of the public finance management system, the development of which is ensured in accordance with the Governance Strategy of Public Finances approved by the Cabinet of Ministers of Ukraine for 2017–2021. The key strategy objectives include introducing an effective system of planning and assessing the execution of the national budget based on results, increasing the efficiency of public expenditures in the transition

N. Grynchuk (✉)
Regional Administration, Local Self-Government and Urban Management Department, National Academy for Public Administration under the President of Ukraine, Kyiv, Ukraine

M. S. de Vries et al. (eds.), *Performance-Based Budgeting in the Public Sector*, Governance and Public Management,
https://doi.org/10.1007/978-3-030-02077-4_9

from institutional maintenance to high-quality public service provision, supporting the budget decentralization process by ensuring a distinct distribution of relevant powers and resources, and ensuring local budget accountability.

All these directions have a common goal of achieving concrete, usually long-term, results that best meet the needs of society. Since these results should also be sufficiently objective, measurable, and predictable, a distinctive feature of such a budgeting method is a system for assessing the quality of the budgeted services and the efficiency of fiscal policies in general (see, e.g., Bouckaert and Halligan 2008; Moynihan 2008; Van Dooren et al. 2015; Stankus 2017; Zubenko 2017).

The first steps of introducing PBB in Ukraine were taken almost a decade ago. The Ministry of Finance of Ukraine order of 10 October 2010, no. 1147, 'On approval of the typical list of budgetary programs and performance indicators of their implementation for local budgets in the public administration' (as amended on 22 December 2010, no. 1608, and on 27 September 2012, no. 1035) approved the tasks and performance indicators that could be included in the 'public administration' program budget. These include indicators such as the number of received letters, appeals, applications, complaints, and adopted regulatory legal acts. The next step was the Ministry of Finance of Ukraine order of 30 November 2012, no. 1260, 'On amendments to the partial list of results of program budget performance indicators for local budgets for expenditures that are not considered when determining the volume of intergovernmental transfers'.

PBB is now applied in Ukraine at the level of the public budget and of some local budgets. To a certain extent, PBB makes it possible to track the efficiency and effectiveness of budget fund expenditures using information on performance indicators and other information contained in budget requests, program budget "passports", and completion reports on program budget "passports".

The goal of this chapter is to assess the application of PBB budgeting in Ukraine. The chapter highlights the problematic issues and confirms the complexity of the process at the local budget level, especially amalgamated local community budgets.

9.2 Current Developments of PBB on the Local Level in Ukraine

In 2017, a total of 998 local budgets in Ukraine had direct contact with the public budget (regional and district budgets, as well as budgets of cities of oblast subordinance and amalgamated local communities). In accordance with clause 18 of the Final and Transitional Provisions of the Budget Code of Ukraine, the mandatory application of PBB in their budget processes was ordered from 2017.

Other communities (about 10,000 city, village, and settlement budgets) were advised to apply PBB in their budget process by the decision of the relevant council. During the process of amalgamation, approximately 900–1000 amalgamated local communities are planned to be created between 2017 and 2020. It can be concluded that it will be essential to employ PBB into the budget processes of about 2000 local budgets by 2020 (Nemec and Grynchuk 2017).

In Ukraine, the typical general list of budgeted programs, including performance indicators, is approved: education, health care, social protection and social security, physical culture and sports, culture, social protection of families, children and young people. There is also a standard list of budgeted programs and performance indicators for local budgets in the field of state administration.

The standard lists for the budgeted programs include the purpose, objectives and performance indicators for each program. In the process of compiling the lists for the concrete municipality, the list of tasks and performance indicators can be specified and expanded. Although this approach can be somewhat formalized, the advantage is that it is able to provide a unified methodological basis for the implementation of PBB for local budgets, which is especially important in terms of delegated powers of local self-government bodies.

To create this standard list, Ukraine implemented a 'region specific' approach, prescribing detailed tables for each area. The structure of the table is as follows:

A. program title;
B. the volume of budget appropriations/budget allocations (including general funds and special purpose funds);
C. the grounds for the program budget implementation;
D. the purpose of the program budget;

E. the list of subprograms aimed at achieving the goal defined by the program budget "passport";
F. volumes of financing the program budget in the context of subprograms and tasks;
G. performance indicators of the program budget in the context of subprograms and tasks (indicators—cost, product, efficiency, quality indicators, units of measurement, sources of information, indicator values); only planned values are inserted, not benchmarks from previous years.

The number of performance indicators and their representation in groups of cost, product, efficiency and quality, is determined by the program budget specifics and should satisfy the requirements of its implementation. It is proposed that performance indicators should be applied that best reflect the achievement of the set goals, tasks and directions of using budget funds.

The performance indicators of the typical list for state administration tasks are oriented on the adoption, implementation, or elaboration of normative acts, orders, letters, appeals, and complaints in their total number. Such a formal approach only partly confirms the efficiency of expenditures in the field of 'public administration', as it does not cover the full set of tasks and functions performed by executive bodies of local self-government and does not allow the full monitoring of the program budget's execution.

The existing regulations do not provide comprehensive lists of indicators reflecting the implementation by local self-government bodies of the main functions assigned to them. For example, according to the Department of Social Policy of the Kyiv City Council, the product indicators are not only those that are included in the model list indicators, but also the amount of aid and compensation granted and paid, the number of subsidies/allowances allocated and paid, and the number of benefits granted and paid.

A very specific issue is the fact that, in accordance with the rules for drawing up program budget "passports" (Order of Ministry of Finance of Ukraine on 26 August 2014, no. 836), if changes are made to the local budget breakdown that leads to changes in the information and indicators approved in the "passports", the main administrators (chief controllers) of the budgetary funds shall submit updated program budget "passports" for approval to the local financial authority within two weeks.

However, changes in the breakdown of the local budget, the network, the staff profile, and the groups of institutions can occur repeatedly throughout the year. For example, in 2016 in the city of Mykolaiv alone, 1615 certificates were submitted on changes in the local budget breakdown. In each case, it was necessary to approve a new edition of the "passport". Considering the heavy workload associated with the approval of new versions of program budgets and the lack of an objective need to have such new versions for just a slight change in some indicator, such rules are inappropriate. The spending unit chief and administrators should have more flexibility to decide on the frequency and types of changes.

Changes to indicators can be caused not only by local needs and conditions, but also by the introduction of amendments in laws requiring an appropriate response and in the application of performance indicators. For example, the Law of Ukraine of 27 March 2014, no. 1166-VII 'On the Prevention of Financial Crisis and the Creation of Preconditions for Economic Growth in Ukraine' provided amendments to the Law of Ukraine of 21 December 1992, no. 2811-XII 'On State Aid to Families with Children': it determined that the childbirth allowance is paid in the amount of UAH 41280, regardless of the child's birth order. Previously, the size of the aid varied. Therefore, it became necessary to amend and reduce the number of performance indicators from six to two in the 'Childbirth Aid Subprogram' (in which the product indicator is the number of recipients of the monthly allowance at birth and the performance indicator is the average monthly allowance for a child's birth benefit).

Although the process of implementing PBB in selected cities and regions has been going on for many years, there are still factors that slow the process of obtaining positive results. These factors include constant changes in public policy priorities, reflecting changes in the government, foreign policy processes, etc., which negatively affect the processes in the formation of regional sectoral development strategies. As the chief administrator of budgetary funds does not have a coherent strategic planning system or sectoral strategic development plans, this leads to the results of PBB implementation being leveled out. Constant changes limit the opportunity to evaluate the efficiency of the use of budget resources.

Analyzing the overall situation with the implementation of PBB at the local budget level in Ukraine, one cannot ignore the fact that issues of control, especially public ones, remain unresolved. The current legislation (including the Budget Code and other regulatory sectoral acts) does not stipulate procedures for public control over the implementation of program budgets.

Another problem is the inadequacy of the software. Software is provided for information control and analysis of the expenditure and revenue parts of the local budget at all stages of the budget process by the local financial authorities. However, in the application of PBB, the automated information system for 'Local budgets at the city and district level' does not provide summary information on the state of expenditures in the industry as a whole, but only information broken down by budgetary programs. The lack of this function greatly complicates the workflow, and it takes a lot of extra time for financial institution employees to provide consolidated information and feedback to the control questions of the financial institutions of regional state administrations that need to be asked, mainly by the industry. We consider it expedient to introduce an automated system for exchanging the statistical data necessary for planning among executive authorities at all budget system levels.

Complexity, intricacy and an outdated normative framework do not help to establish effective budgeting. For example, an assessment of the effectiveness of the program budget is carried out according to the method specified in the Ministry of Finance of Ukraine letter of 19 September 2013 no. 31-05110-14-5/27486, and, at the same time, according to the procedure established by the Ministry of Finance of Ukraine order of 17 May 2011. This methodology uses a fundamentally different approach to assessing the effectiveness of program budgets.

During consultative trips by the author and the team to the amalgamated local communities, the employees of the financial and accounting structural subdivisions of the executive committees of local councils repeatedly mentioned the issues that arose during the introduction of PBB, in particular:

- lack of training of the relevant reformed local council personnel for the transition to PBB budgeting and lack of system training for amalgamated local communities;
- absence of a transition period from the time the amalgamated local communities were established and the implementation of PBB from

the first budget year. A striking example of this was the amalgamated local communities in which the first elections were held in December 2016. Despite the timely adoption of the joint budget in January–February 2017, these communities were in the period of forming executive bodies, and therefore there were no specialists to assume these powers. It is advisable for the established amalgamated local communities to provide a transition period of one or two years for the relevant executive body and budgetary institution specialists to be trained in implementing PBB;
- lack of subdivisions and specialists responsible for planning in general and for PBB in particular, leading to poor planning quality;
- lack of software for PBB budgeting in many amalgamated local communities;
- the overwhelming majority of amalgamated local communities have no sector managers of budgetary funds as legal entities, although they should be logically responsible for the programs and their implementation. Therefore, a whole range of PBB work is done by employees of the financial and accounting structural divisions of the executive bodies;
- weak link between regulatory acts on socioeconomic development planning and local budgets;
- low level of qualification of officials, of members/deputies of the amalgamated local community council, and of employees of the executive committee of the amalgamated local community council;
- unavailability of proper statistical information on amalgamated local communities;
- resistance to change by individual officials and institutions.

To provide a more detailed and focused picture of the current situation, we provide a case study focused on road and transport management in Kyiv.

9.3 PBB in Road and Transport Management in Kyiv: A Case Study

In the sphere of road and transport management, the capital of Ukraine is currently guided by the "Strategic Development Plan for Automobile Transport and Road Infrastructure until 2020", approved by the Cabinet of Ministers of Ukraine order no. 548 of 21 December 2015, the "Transport Strategy of Ukraine until 2020" approved by the Cabinet of Ministers of Ukraine decree no. 2174-r of 20 October 2010, the "Goal-oriented State Economic Program of Public Automotive Road Development for 2013-2018", approved by the Cabinet of Ministers of Ukraine decree no. 696 of 11 July 2013, and others. The State Agency of Motor Roads of Ukraine (Ukravtodor) released the revised draft of the decree of the Cabinet of Ministers of Ukraine "On the Approval of the Concept of the Goal-oriented State Economic Program for Public Automotive Road Development of National Importance for 2018-2022", considering the comments and proposals of the interested ministries. In addition, in light of implementing the areas of the "*Strategy* to Increase the L*evel of Road Safety in Ukraine until 2020*", the 'State Program for Increasing the Level of Road Safety in Ukraine *until 2020*' was approved. The state customer (the contracting authority) is the Ministry of Infrastructure.

However, the provisions of these legislative pieces generally do not address the development of individual territorial-administrative units or they bypass them indirectly. Consequently, the performance indicators of regional program budgets do not correlate with markers at the higher (state/national) level. At the same time, regional sector programs in the field of road and transport management are not currently available in Kyiv.

In terms of road transport network saturation levels, Kyiv is significantly inferior to most European capitals and major world cities. The density of the main street and road network in Kyiv is 2.13 km/sq km; streets and roads make up 2% of the city's territory. The intensity of traffic on the city bridges in the peak hours is double or triple their design capacity; most of the bridges were constructed in Soviet times (at which time, they fully met the road capacity requirements). However, current trends in urban development, population growth, and private passenger vehicles are exceeding the existing road capacity, and heavy traffic has become a routine phenomenon in the city streets, especially at peak times. In the existing traffic system, traffic jams regularly occur not only on main highways, but also on the small side streets that drivers try to use as bypass roads.

The road surface, as well as the overall operational condition of highways, requires a major upgrade. One of the most important issues is the limited budgetary resources for addressing the unsatisfactory technical conditions of more than 85% of the road surfaces, the terms of operation of which are currently exceeded. The extremely unsatisfactory technical conditions of the roadway surface are caused by: low volumes of regulated repair work, the level of which has recently amounted to only about 14% of the standard annual scope of work; unsatisfactory quality of road building materials and the possibility of outdated road construction machinery; frequent emergency closures of carriageways connected with the unsatisfactory technical conditions of engineering networks; uncontrolled movement of heavy vehicles along the city's road network; and the discrepancy between the previous norms of design loads for asphalt pavement with the existing loads of transport.

Due to the unsatisfactory technical conditions of the road network and of the technical means of road traffic organization, as well as the increased number of vehicles, the number of traffic accidents has increased.

Under financial constraints, the minimum action plan for executive authorities is generally defined as the maintenance of the existing roads throughout the year (sometimes only those that are most used). The actions that are performed, with minimal variations, are as follows:

- basic road works, including: patching and local restoration of sites with seriously damaged road pavement; repairing pavement cracks; technical maintenance of side drains and drainage systems, cleaning out debris and garbage; repairing or replacing road equipment that affects traffic safety—signs, fencing, etc.; repairing or replacing supporting walls in critical condition; controlling vegetation, as required by road safety requirements; and protecting against erosion;
- basic work on technical maintenance and reconstruction of bridges deemed necessary to ensure the constructive unity of the existing bridge and provision of a temporary bridge if the existing bridge has already reached a critical constructive state at the beginning of the analysis period.

It is obvious that this system is not satisfactory. Thus, the development of the Kyiv-based street and road network lags behind the real needs of the city, in terms of the low density of roads, the traffic congestion of the road network, and the unsatisfactory technical and operational condition of the road surfaces. In order to improve and organize the efficient functioning of the infrastructure of the city's road transport system and form an efficient street and road network that would be capable of reducing the time spent traveling from residence to work, improving the ecological state of the environment and the safety of transportation, works on the complex improvement of the city are carried out, in particular, measures to repair and maintain a street-road network as an object of city improvement.

9.4 Performance-Based Program Budget for Road and Transport Management in Kyiv

The formation of resource support, a list of tasks and activities assigned to the executive authorities in this area, and a system of performance indicators are carried out within the competence of the following program budgets:

1. *Program budget for 'Improvement of cities, villages, and settlements'*, the tasks of which were defined in 2017 as:
   a. provision of main repairs of transport infrastructure objects;
   b. provision of ongoing repairs of transport infrastructure objects;
   c. granting of maintenance of road facilities in the proper technical condition;
   d. statutory inspections of artificial structures;
   e. acquisition of municipal equipment;
   f. development of design and accounting documentation of objects on the city street and road network.
2. *Program budget for 'Activities and services not classified in other categories'*, the tasks of which are:
   a. ensuring the maintenance of traffic lights, traffic signs, and route guidance signs in appropriate conditions;
   b. equipment acquisition;
   c. ensuring the functioning of enterprises for improving traffic organization and safety.
3. *Program budget for 'Ensuring the functioning of industrial complexes (training centers or workshops) of public utility companies, district production associations and other enterprises, institutions and organizations of housing and public utilities'*, the tasks of which are defined as:

a. ensuring the functioning of the city's outdoor lighting networks;
b. major overhaul of outdoor lighting networks;
c. ensuring the renovation of the equipment and facilities of the public utility company 'Kyivmisksvitlo';
d. implementing the planning stage design of main repairs of facilities;
e. ensuring the performance of work on the overhaul of architectural and decorative lighting networks.

This list shows that one factor hindering the effectiveness of PBB implementation is the cumbersome structure of program budgets in the city's road transport sector. The situational formation of program budgets and budget tasks, in accordance with the current needs of certain budget periods, does not provide a clear understanding of what the ultimate goals are and disperses budget funds for the implementation of individual measures, rather than achieving the strategic goals of the chief administrator of budgetary funds.

The second problem is the fact that the system of performance indicators does not illustrate the results of the program budget execution, but merely records the statistical data. It does not enable the objective evaluation of the effectiveness of providing a budgetary service or of its qualitative social effects. Table 9.1 provides the list of indicators and targets used for the subprogram 'Ensuring proper technical conditions for the maintenance of road facilities' of the program '*Improvement and redevelopment of cities, villages, and settlements*' in 2017.

The results of the program-performance method in the budget process are not used for management decisions. There is no effective control over the program budget performance.

Our brief analysis of the existing system of one selected performance-based budget showed that PBB tools in the field of the functioning of the infrastructure of the city's road transport complex need to be improved. When forming a list of indicators, preference is given to such criteria as cost and product indicators. In the structure in which the cost indicators for the studied programs are currently used, these indicators only reflect the amount of expenditures for ensuring the fulfillment of the tasks. At the same time, the pricing factors (cost components) of the budget service (for example, road transport network, staff, necessary volumes of consumables, raw materials, machinery, and facilities) are not

Table 9.1 Performance-based budget for subprogram 'Ensuring proper technical conditions for the maintenance of road facilities' Kyiv

Indicator	*Unit of measurement*	*Source of information*	*Value*
Cost indicator			
Expenses for providing maintenance in the proper technical condition of objects of road facilities	UAH, in thousands	Decision	491,554.40
Product indicators			
The area of streets, bridges, overpasses (roads and sidewalks) scheduled for maintenance in the autumn-winter period	Square meters, in thousands	Operational programme	21,771.13
The area of streets, bridges, overpasses (roads and sidewalks) scheduled for maintenance in the spring-summer period	Square meters, in thousands	Operational programme	16,622.94
The number of draining pits (surface water drains) scheduled for maintenance	Unit	Operational programme	29,723.00
The number of observation pits scheduled for maintenance	Unit	Operational programme	13,787.00
The length of the barrier and pedestrian fencing scheduled for maintenance	Running meter (rm)	Operational programme	237,797.70
Efficiency (performance) indicators			
Average cost of maintenance of draining pits (surface water drains)	UAH/unit	Calculation	348,487.00
Average cost of maintenance of observation pits (surface water drains)	UAH/unit	Calculation	480,666.00
Average cost of maintenance of barrier and pedestrian fencing	UAH/rm	Calculation	39,232.00
Average cost of maintaining streets, bridges, and overpasses (roads and sidewalks) in the autumn-winter period	UAH/square meter	Calculation	10,594.00
Average cost of maintaining streets, bridges, and overpasses (roads and sidewalks) in the spring-summer period	UAH/square meter	Calculation	14,113.00

(continued)

Table 9.1 (continued)

Indicator	*Unit of measurement*	*Source of information*	*Value*
Quality indicator			
Dynamics of the cost of maintaining streets, bridges, overpasses (roads and sidewalks) in the autumn-winter period compared to last year	%	Calculation	118.74
Dynamics of the cost of maintaining streets, bridges, and overpasses (roads and sidewalks) in the spring-summer period compared to last year	%	Calculation	125.42
Dynamics of the number of draining pits (surface water drain) that were maintained in comparison with last year	%	Calculation	100.00
Dynamics of the number of observation pits (surface water drain) that were maintained in comparison with last year	%	Calculation	100.09
Dynamics of the length of the barrier and pedestrian fencing, which were maintained in comparison with last year	%	Calculation	100.47

Source Author, processed from the city website

highlighted in the structure of indicators, which makes it impossible to analyze the effectiveness of the use of material resources.

Indicators of costs sometimes replace the necessary indicators of the product. As visible in the selected program budgets in the sphere of the functioning of the city's road and transport complex, 'product indicators' are in reality generalized indicators of the network of road infrastructure objects. The methodological indicators of the product should characterize the results of the activities of the chief administrator of the relevant budgetary period within the program budget and may reflect the volume of output, services provided, or work performed, and the number of people who have been provided with public services. That is, the product indicator should specify the scope of actions that are to be carried out in the planned budget period with the network objects. This is not true for this subprogram.

Efficiency and quality indicators should be the most informative, considering both consumers of social services and the tools for providing these services. However, these indicators are very limited in the program budget "passports", because they do not disclose the degree of usefulness of implementing certain program activities, do not cover all types and consequences of budgetary services, and do not illustrate the state of consumer satisfaction with the budgetary service. Thus, the quality indicators of the clear majority of program activities are limited by the criteria for the dynamics of the cost and product indicators, not considering the compliance of the created products with the established industry standards and norms, namely the norms for the annual scope of works on current repairs of streets and roads, warranty service life of road surfaces, specialized equipment, standards of street illumination, etc.

The specific features of the formation of sectoral performance indicators in the road transport sector are a significant number of technical norms and standards that are factors of influence on the resource provision and the effectiveness of accomplishing the tasks set within program budgets. Such factors include a complex nomenclature of repair, construction, reconstruction, and other works, technical requirements for each of these types of work, the use of complex structured types of work, and a significant number of standards for the functioning of the road infrastructure that cannot be reduced to weighted average values. However, indicators at the program budget level should not contain technical characteristics, but should bear signs of high aggregation levels to characterize the generalized components of the formation of the cost of a budget service, namely, the network, the amount of raw materials planned for the budget period (costs), as well the regulated nomenclature of actions and the time necessary to ensure the implementation of the budget service or product, and the corresponding performance indicators—unit costs per unit of product and labor productivity indicators. In addition, quality indicators should characterize the state and level of goal achievement in the process of providing budget services; for example, ensuring the safety and security of all road users.

9.5 Conclusions

Our analysis shows that Ukraine faces many challenges in the process of implementing PBB at the local budget level. This is happening in a period of financial decentralization focusing on strengthening the responsibility of self-government bodies in spending budget funds, along with expanding their financial independence. The use of PBB was expected to increase the efficiency of using financial resources and ensure high-quality provision of services to communities, but at this stage it delivers more extra paperwork than real results.

Effective management activity in the decision-making process on the implementation of programs or individual program tasks, making changes or adjustments during the year, allocating or redistributing funds between tasks within the program is ensured using substantiated analytical information. This kind of information can be obtained only by monitoring and evaluating financial (budgetary) and socioeconomic indicators. Today, such an analysis does not involve reciprocal linking: independently from each other, reports on budget execution and ratings assessments of the activity of territorial administrations are based on the analysis of only certain socioeconomic indicators and do not provide comprehensive coverage of customer satisfaction with budget services. Thus, the task of detailing the performance indicators becomes urgent, the execution of which depends on a certain amount of budgetary resource support for program budgets. This requires improving approaches to the formation of performance indicators so that they reflect not the state of budget implementation, but the quality of service delivery and achievement of the set goal.

Effective performance and quality indicators are the most critical. However, the analysis showed that when generating standard lists, cost and product criteria are given priority. Even the proposed quality indicators need to be revised, as they are not fully able to assess the quality of public services provided within the program budget.

Too many indicators are used for subprograms—an optimal set would contain only core performance indicators that reflect the main service characteristics and outcomes.

The implementation of PBB in the budget process should not be limited exclusively to the procedures for drawing up program budgets "passports", revising their performance indicators, and changing the reporting on their implementation. Effective implementation requires presenting the results of using budgetary funds to direct customers of the budgeted services. Today, both the program budget "passports" and the reports on their execution are formally drawn up without a proper analysis of the reasons for underperformed or over fulfilled performance indicators, the implementation rates of past program budgets are not considered when establishing target performance indicators for the next year and forming budget requests. Drafting local budgets according to the program-target method is perceived on the ground as an additional burden on the chief administrator of budgetary funds, on the executive officer in charge of the program budget, and on employees of local financial bodies, increasing paperwork and escalating administrative expenses for reporting on budget execution. The attempt to 'adjust the results' to the expected goals without achieving significant changes in the effectiveness of using the budget can be a consequence of these conditions.

Additional obstacles to the successful implementation of the PBB method at the local budget level in Ukraine are connected with the existing framework, the absence of medium-term budget planning, the lack of a clear connection between strategic documents, targeted programs, and program budgets, and low levels of openness and transparency in the budget process, which makes it impossible for the public to monitor the program budget execution.

There is almost no link between PBB and strategic planning. Such a link would ensure the continuity of annual/mid-year budget planning and prevent possible deviations from the core goals. The detailed elaboration of indicators of the results and consequences of targeted, strategic documents at the program budget level would ensure the comparison of these indicators with the program budget objectives, facilitating the rapid adoption of necessary management decisions during the monitoring period.

Taking all this into account, a lot remains to be done for the successful implementation of PBB on the local level in Ukraine, especially developing a system of budget forecasting, establishing a system monitoring the effectiveness of public services (benchmarking), implementing measures to involve all stakeholders into PBB processes, and conducting professional training in modern methods of budgeting for specialists of local self-government bodies and particularly for the amalgamated local communities.

References

Bouckaert, Geert, and John Halligan. 2008. *Managing Performance: International Comparisons*. Oxon: Routledge.

Budgetary Codex Ukraine. 2010. Kyiv: Ukrainian Government (Відомості Верховної Ради України, 2010, № 50-51).

Moynihan, Donald P. 2008. *The Dynamics of Performance Management: Constructing Information and Reform*. Washington, DC: Georgetown University Press.

Nemec, Juraj, and Nataliia Grynchuk. 2017. *Performance Budgeting. The Teaching Material*. Bratislava: NISPAcee.

On Approval of the Typographical List of Budget Programs and Effective Indicators of Their Performance for Local Budgets in the Public Administration. 2010. Kyiv. Ukrainian Government (Наказ Міністерства фінансів України від 01.10.2010 р. № 1147 «Про затвердження Типового переліку бюджетних програм та результативних показників їх виконання для місцевих бюджетів у галузі "Державне управління").

Rules for Drawing Up Passports of Budget Programs of Local Budgets and Reports on Their Implementation. 2014. Kyiv: Ministry of Finance of Ukraine (Наказ Міністерства фінансів України від 26.08.2014 № 836 «Правила складання паспортів бюджетних програм місцевих бюджетів та звітів про їх виконання).

Stankus, Tetiana. 2017. *Performance-Based Budgeting in the Budget Process at the Level of Local Budgets* (Програмноцільовий метод у бюджетному процесі на рівні місцевих бюджетів). Kharkiv: Factor.

Strategy of Public Finance Reform 2017–2020. 2017. Kyiv: Ukrainian Government (Розпорядження Кабінету Міністрів України від 8 лютого 2017 р. № 142).

Van Dooren, Woulter, Geert Bouckaert, and John Halligan. 2015. *Performance Management in the Public Sector*, 2nd ed. London: Routledge.

Zubenko, Vyacheslav, ed. 2017. *Planning and Implementation of Local Budgets Based on the Performance-Based Budgeting Method*. Kyiv: NGO Institute for Budgetary and Socio-Economic Research.

CHAPTER 10

Performance-Based Program Budgeting in Slovakia: A Lost Opportunity (?)

Štefan Hronec

10.1 Introduction

The vision of joining the European Union caused the governments of Central and Eastern European countries to take reform steps. A puzzling issue for them was in particular the efficiency of public spending budgets. Slovakia was not an exception: various Slovak governments committed themselves in their program statements to taking steps to meet the budgetary goals. Slovakia, with support from the World Bank, made efforts to link inputs with outputs under the program budgeting concept, especially during its public finance reform in 2004. The aim was to allocate expenditures to individual programs created within the program structure, which, according to the Ministry of Finance of the Slovak Republic, is a logical, hierarchically ordered structure and is purposefully designed to set goals and objectives. The structure may include programs, sub-programs, and elements, as well as objectives

Š. Hronec (✉)
Department of Public Economic and Regional Development,
University of Matej Bel, Banská Bystrica, Slovakia
e-mail: stefan.hronec@umb.sk

M. S. de Vries et al. (eds.), *Performance-Based Budgeting in the Public Sector*, Governance and Public Management,
https://doi.org/10.1007/978-3-030-02077-4_10

and measurable indicators to evaluate the objectives of the program. (Methodical Instruction of the Ministry of Finance 2005).

Program budgeting was seen as a qualitative superstructure to the classical budget, and its introduction was intended to lead to an increase in the information value of budgets, as the goals and measurable indicators were set up to provide scope for monitoring and evaluating the fulfillment of objectives by the wider public as well. The tool was also intended to help elected representatives and public sector managers make more qualified decisions based on quality information in order to make the most efficient use of limited resources, to enhance the quality of public administration services provided to the public, and to improve communication with the public. Responsibility (and its documentation) for successful performances (i.e., achievement of goals) is essential (Bajusová 2013).

This management tool was expected to bring greater transparency, to link goals and public resources more visibly, to provide greater insight into the costs of service provision and the quality of service delivery, to increase the involvement of all departments in budgeting, which in turn would involve employees more closely in meeting strategic objectives, to identify the areas where most resources are placed and fail to produce desirable results (e.g., administration), and to identify the areas where more funds are needed.

Today, Slovakia implements this system of financial management at all levels of public administration. The first steps of its implementation began immediately after the establishment of the Slovak Republic as an experiment at the Slovak Ministry of Defence. Systematic program budgeting was brought to general attention particularly in connection with public finance management reform, which was a breakthrough in public finances under the conditions prevalent in Slovakia, as this project proposed concrete steps to increased efficiency, economy, and effectiveness, known as '3E'. The reform was approved in 2003 and had three areas: strengthening public finance transparency; enhancing strategic resource allocation planning and transitioning to budgeting for results (program budgeting); and establishing a stable medium-term fiscal framework (Bajusová 2013).

The aim of introducing program budgeting was 'to develop a budgetary system so as to be transparent to the public and to permit judgement of the purpose and resultant effect of resource spending and to increase the accountability of municipalities for expedient and effective spending'

(NKÚ Report 2011, p. 85). The extent to which this really happened is evaluated in the following text, using an example at the local self-government level; other segments of the public sector did not perform better.

10.2 The Opinions of Municipal Representatives About Performance-Based Program Budgeting in Slovakia—Primary Research

Within the research project *VEGA 1/0405/15—Program Budgeting as Part of the New Public Management*, we examined the process of compiling a program budget at the local government level in Slovakia. The primary research was conducted using a questionnaire. The secondary research focused on the system of compiling measurable indicators in order to compare the quality and content of the indicators of individual municipal budgets, and data were collected from municipal websites.

When examining the performance sections of the program budgets during the secondary research, we proceeded from the proposed program budget structure of the Ministry of Finance, which recommends splitting the program budget into 14 programs. We added two more programs covering housing issues and areas that could not be included under these programs in terms of the relevant classifications (COFOG). We examined the complexity of the measurable indicators as well as the standardization level in each size group.

The questionnaire survey was sent to 163 of the 2891 municipalities in Slovakia, and we received 163 answers. The questionnaire had 23 questions about the process and correlation of program budgeting. We examined the process of budgeting itself, the relationships of the various stakeholders in the budget process (the self-government, the mayor, chief administrator, municipality council, and any appropriate external target groups such as residents and legal entities), correlations to traditional budgetary systems, binding classifications, and—where appropriate—evaluation and monitoring systems.

Concerning the survey results regarding the creation, compilation, evaluation, and perception of program budgeting as a performance enhancer, the most positive responses were recorded for questions related to the alignment of program budgeting expenditures with applicable budget classifications, the linking of the results of monitoring and evaluating program budgeting with the final account, the systematic evaluating and monitoring, and the processing of the program budgeting by internal staff or by an external company. Almost 97.5% of the responding municipalities answered questions concerning the alignment of program budgeting with the budget classifications (7.2% of all the municipalities in the Slovak Republic). Of the respondents, 83.4% responded positively to linking the results with the final municipality account.

The least positive responses were recorded for questions focused on the relationship between the program budgeting process and the quality of the services provided, the participation in processing the annual budget, and the practical use of the results of the budget assessment in managing the provision of public services (positive or negative developments of the 3E indicators). The last area was focused on the legislative aspect of program budgeting. Only 33.7% of the responding self-governed municipalities had created separate local legislative standards (GIC) governing the program budgeting process, which is one of the basic conditions for successful implementation, according to Kubasta (2014). A low number of positive responses was also noted for the relationship between program budgeting and efficiency in the provision of public services. In general, municipalities are not aware of program budgeting as a tool that improves local government performance.

There was a comparatively high number of positive responses to the question focused on monitoring the comprehensive approach to self-government budgeting as a basic budget unit and its established organizations. In most cases, these are budget organizations set up within the framework of transferred and original competences in the fields of education or culture. Other organizations set up in the form of a non-profit organization or a business entity directly linked to the budget are not present. Expenditure on operations is shown as normal or as a capital transfer under the relevant COFOG classification (statistical classification of international standards). Local authorities responded positively (over 80%) to the question focused on taking into account the original and transferred competences in the budget process, defined by the appropriate source codes. The transferred competences, which include transferred state administration performance in the areas of the registrar, record keeping, construction, and basic education, are funded through regular transfer from the state budget. This source, in accordance with valid regulations, is referred to as KZ 111. Original competences such as the provision of preschool education and supplementary services within education (meals, free-time activities, art education, and children's school clubs), are financed from the municipality's own income and the regional self-government's KZ 41 (or KZ 43 or 46 as balances from previous years, or reserve funds). The approach of self-government in the event of transferred competences is more relaxed in terms of performance monitoring by means of measurable indicators. If the service is funded through a routine transfer and the funds are guaranteed, there is insufficient pressure to spend it efficiently. The indicators are then set as absolute outputs, without the possibility for comparisons between municipalities.

Four key questions were related to the perception of program budgeting as an efficiency enhancer. Two questions concerned the 3E monitoring and subsequent accounting in the management process. Of the surveyed municipalities, 93 monitor these indicators, but the results serve as a basis for further decision making in only 54 municipalities. Only 58 municipalities perceive program budgeting as a tool for increasing efficiency, and even fewer self-governments perceive it as a tool with an impact on the quality of the services provided. On the basis of these results, it can be stated that self-governments in the Slovak Republic lack internal motivation and belief in the positive effects of this budgetary method (similar research results were published by De Jong 2017). This lack of belief is exacerbated by insufficient staffing capacities.

10.3 How Performance-Based Program Budgets Are Really Constructed—Secondary Research

The secondary research focused on the abundance and types of measurable indicators of program budgeting. Program budgeting was examined using the same 163 municipalities that were the subject of the primary research. Among the examined municipalities, there was considerable variability in both the number and the types of monitored indicators. Most indicators were nominal, with no possible mutual comparison. Ratio indicators, which serve as a basis for comparison, for example, through benchmarking, were utilized only minimally in program budgeting. The following tablespresent the results of the analysis without taking into account the size or region of the local government (Table 10.1).

When comparing individual types of measurable indicators in absolute terms, the output indicators prevailed. The fewest indicators were set for *housing* and *social services*. The highest number was found for *planning, management, and control*. The *planning, management, and control* program was dominated by crazy indicators such as the number of meetings

Table 10.1 Representation of measurable output indicators according to programs

Output indicators	*Average*	*Municipalities with no indicators*	*% of municipalities with no indicators*	*Modus*	*Minimum value*	*Maximum value*
1. Planning, management, and control	1.180	34	20.860	1.000	0.000	5.000
2. Promotion and marketing	1.050	28	17.178	1.000	0.000	4.000
3. Internal services	1.130	19	11.656	1.000	0.000	4.000
4. Resident services	1.035	26	15.951	1.000	0.000	4.000
5. Security	0.919	44	27.301	0.833	0.000	4.000
6. Waste management	1.135	24	14.724	1.000	0.000	4.000
7. Culture	0.937	44	26.994	1.000	0.000	4.000
8. Transportation	0.908	50	30.982	0.500	0.000	4.000
9. Education	1.006	37	23.211	0.833	0.000	4.000
10. Sport	0.933	47	28.834	0.667	0.000	4.000
11. Roads	0.963	39	24.387	1.000	0.000	4.000
12. Living environment	1.018	32	19.632	1.000	0.000	4.000
13. Social services and healthcare	0.879	59	36.733	0.750	0.000	5.000
14. Administration	1.175	37	23.006	1.000	0.000	4.000
15. Housing	0.696	68	42.025	0.500	0.000	4.000
16. Civic facilities	1.460	12	7.362	1.000	0.000	4.000

Source Authors

held by the authorities, visits received, business trips undertaken, and contracts concluded by the municipality. These indicators predominantly reflect the consumption of the funds, not the benefits that should flow from their consumption. Increasing their value can be perceived as negative.

Simple output indicators were used in the *promotion and marketing* programs, predominantly monitoring the number of processed promotional materials, and in *resident services*, monitoring the number of operations executed. These indicators would be different for self-governments of different sizes. Performance monitoring problems were found with the programs with the highest volume of funds spent, namely *education* and *social services*. Most local governments only track the numbers of consumers in the target group, but not the impact that such public spending should entail. This is the result of a system of reallocating funds; the system is not oriented toward the impact but toward the output. The following table presents the application of impact indicators in local government (Table 10.2).

Outcome indicators reflect the positive effect of public spending. In the surveyed self-governments, these indicators were applied to a limited degree only in *civic facilities* programs, predominantly to express the degree of coverage by infrastructure networks or users of public projects, and in *planning, management, and control* programs, where the indicators focused on the success of the project. Ratio indicators that would, for example, monitor the volume of external resources earned per capita or the volume of surplus per capita as a result of good self-government are lacking.

Ratio indicators per capita were applied only to a minimum degree. Most of these indicators were for the *planning, management, and control* programs and for *civic facilities* programs. The number of such indicators reached a maximum value of 2. There is clearly space for the establishment of such indicators in the *planning, management, and control* and *waste management* programs (Table 10.3).

Ratio indicators per unit of performance were minimally applied by the municipalities. Almost none of the municipalities applied such indicators in most programs. Most indicators were found within the *administration* and *culture* programs (Table 10.4).

Ratio indicators in Slovak municipalities do not create prerequisites for monitoring performance or for the mutual comparability of self-government performance.

Table 10.2 Representation of measurable impact indicators according to programs

Impact indicators	*Average*	*Municipalities with no indicators*	*% of municipalities with no indicators*	*Modus*	*Minimum value*	*Maximum value*
1. Planning, management, and control	0.350	114	69.940	0.200	0.000	5.000
2. Promotion and marketing	0.310	116	71.166	0.000	0.000	2.000
3. Internal services	0.330	119	73.006	0.000	0.000	2.000
4. Resident services	0.199	132	81.332	0.000	0.000	2.000
5. Security	0.234	128	78.732	0.000	0.000	3.000
6. Waste management	0.288	121	74.438	0.000	0.000	3.000
7. Culture	0.237	127	78.119	0.000	0.000	2.000
8. Transportation	0.209	130	79.755	0.000	0.000	2.000
9. Education	0.204	132	81.391	0.000	0.000	2.000
10. Sport	0.155	140	86.094	0.000	0.000	3.000
11. Roads	0.224	129	79.141	0.000	0.000	2.000
12. Living environment	0.233	127	77.914	0.000	0.000	2.000
13. Social services and health care	0.183	137	84.126	0.000	0.000	3.000
14. Administration	0.411	107	65.951	0.500	0.000	2.000
15. Housing	0.117	145	88.957	0.000	0.000	2.000
16. Civic facilities	0.520	89	54.601	0.000	0.000	3.000

Source Authors

Table 10.3 Representation of ratio indicators per capita according to programs

Ratio indicators per capita	*Average*	*Municipalities with no indicators*	*% of municipalities with no indicators*	*Modus*	*Minimum value*	*Maximum value*
1. Planning, management, and control	0.060	153	94.230	0.000	0.000	2.000
2. Promotion and marketing	0.01	162	99.591	0.000	0.000	1.000
3. Internal services	0.000	163	100.000	0.000	0.000	0.000
4. Resident services	0.015	160	98.510	0.000	0.000	1.000
5. Security	0.003	162	99.591	0.000	0.000	1.000
6. Waste management	0.022	159	97.751	0.000	0.000	1.000
7. Culture	0.020	159	97.955	0.000	0.000	1.000
8. Transportation	0.000	163	100.000	0.000	0.000	0.000
9. Education	0.011	161	98.773	0.000	0.000	1.000
10. Sport	0.004	162	99.591	0.000	0.000	1.000
11. Roads	0.011	161	98.773	0.000	0.000	1.000
12. Living environment	0.046	155	95.399	0.000	0.000	1.000
13. Social services and health care	0.014	160	98.598	0.000	0.000	1.000
14. Administration	0.098	147	90.184	0.000	0.000	1.000
15. Housing	0.003	162	99.591	0.000	0.000	1.000
16. Civic facilities	0.090	149	91.411	0.000	0.000	1.000

Source Authors

Table 10.4 Representation of ratio indicators per performance unit according to programs

Ratio indicators per performance unit	*Average*	*Municipalities with no indicators*	*% of municipalities with no indicators*	*Modus*	*Minimum value*	*Maximum value*
1. Planning, management, and control	0.050	155	95.340	0.000	0.000	2.000
2. Promotion and marketing	0.010	161	98.773	0.000	0.000	1.000
3. Internal services	0.010	161	98.773	0.000	0.000	1.000
4. Resident services	0.014	160	98.598	0.000	0.000	1.000
5. Security	0.003	162	99.591	0.000	0.000	1.000
6. Waste management	0.031	158	96.933	0.000	0.000	1.000
7. Culture	0.051	154	94.888	0.000	0.000	1.000
8. Transportation	0.000	163	100.000	0.000	0.000	0.000
9. Education	0.015	160	98.598	0.000	0.000	1.000
10. Sport	0.004	162	99.591	0.000	0.000	1.000
11. Roads	0.011	161	98.773	0.000	0.000	1.000
12. Living environment	0.046	155	95.399	0.000	0.000	1.000
13. Social services and health care	0.012	161	98.773	0.000	0.000	1.000
14. Administration	0.086	149	91.411	0.000	0.000	1.000
15. Housing	0.000	163	100.000	0.000	0.000	0.000
16. Civic amenities	0.020	160	98.598	0.000	0.000	1.000

Source Authors

The largest number of these indicators was recorded under the *planning, management, and control* program. In other cases, the maximum value of the set indicator was 1. The most represented number for all the programs was 0. There are mainly reserves in the use of program budgeting as a tool for monitoring and improving performance.

10.4 Conclusion

Based on the analysis of the status of program budgeting within self-government as reflected in the research sample, it can be said that no conditions have been created for the use of the program budgeting as a performance enhancer. There are more findings within our research supporting this statement, although this slightly contradicts the generally positive responses regarding program budgeting from municipal representatives.

Among the examined municipalities, there was considerable variability in both the numbers and in the types of monitored indicators. Most indicators were nominal, reflecting the number of applications or actions executed, without any possibility for mutual comparison. Ratio indicators serving as a basis for comparison (for example through benchmarking) are rare in program budgeting. If the same nature of public services are provided, a certain standard in their provision should be achieved. Otherwise, monitoring such indicators can reveal either the over-equipped or under-equipped capacity of self-government.

Self-governments do not attach much value to the real monitoring of performance outcomes. If we look at the stated targets, it is clear that many were inserted to fill space and are not connected with reality.

The correct selection of indicators is also a problem. For example, some municipalities monitor the number of kilometers driven or the number of journeys made. Indicators that have no real link to global municipal performance are frequently measured, such as the number of council meetings. The most common types of monitored indicators in education are the number of pupils, children enrolled in kindergarten, extra-curricular activities, meals provided, etc. These indicators may be useful for individual municipalities, but they do not have any meaning for mutual comparison in terms of performance.

The basic source of the dysfunctionality of program budgeting is the administrative and professional complexity of the program budgeting system. In human terms, one factor can be the staffing capacity of local authorities. The experiences of other countries show that it is necessary to build capacities that are able to manage and implement the entire performance-based budgeting process. In addition to the broad agenda that stems from their original and conveyed competences, the targeted use of this performance-enhancing instrument makes it especially difficult for professional staff to learn. Financial department employees often lack the appropriate university education, having only vocational economic certifications obtained through a secondary vocational education, and are therefore unable to apply these practices in the practical exercise of economic activities. The human resources in self-government in charge of program budgeting are mostly specialized in routine accounting operations and are not able to handle a more demanding assessment of the effectiveness of public funds spent in relation to performance indicators.

In terms of administration, the methodological guidelines and the rules set by the Ministry of Finance did not establish a binding and comparable (according to the size of the self-government) set of indicators. This has led to considerable heterogeneity in the evaluation of self-government performance and the impossibility of evaluation in relation to self-government. Moreover, the guidelines lead to the filling of excessive (and oftentimes artificial) numbers of tables with indicators and targets. For example, the performance-based budget of a medium size city of 30,000 inhabitants might have over 100 pages of tables filled in with 'some' data (see Bajusová 2013).

The administrative burden is also a result of the obligatory regular processing of two monitoring reports and one evaluation report. Additionally, the program budget is combined with the traditional budget, with no option to choose only one of them. In many cases, these budgets are not interlinked in terms of classifications, and therefore do not fulfill a complementary function, but they make the budgetary process less clear.

References

Bajusová, Daniela. 2013. *Programové Rozpočtovanie V Kontexte New Public Management*. Ekonomická univerzita v Bratislave Národohospodárska Fakulta, 138.

De Jong, Maarten. 2017. Poland. In *Toward Next-Generation Performance Budgeting Lessons from the Experiences of Seven Reforming Countries*, ed. Donald Moynihan and Ivor Beazley, 111–123. World Bank Group.

Kubasta, Celeste. 2014. *Investing in Results: Using Performance Data to Inform State Budgeting—State Experiences & Lessons Learned*. National Association of State Budget Officers.

Methodical Instruction of the Ministry of Finance (Metodické pokyny Ministerstva financií Slovenskej republiky). 2005. *Interaktívny rozpočtový portál rozpočet.sk*. [cit. 6 May 2013]. Available at http://www.rozpocet.sk/app/homepage/rozpocetVCislach/dokumenty/7/.

NKÚ SR. 2011. Záverečná práva o výsledku kontroly implementácie programového rozpočtovania v rozpočtovom procese miest a obcí. In *Spravodajca* 1/2011. [online]. NKÚ SR 2011 [cit. 10 March 2013]. s. 81–87. Avaliable at http://www.nku.gov.sk/documents/10157/164413/Spravodajca+%C4%8D.+1_2011.

CHAPTER 11

The Development of Performance-Based Budgeting in Slovenia

Maja Klun

11.1 Introduction

Various terms for the concept of performance-based budgeting (PBB) are used in the literature, as noted by Mauro et al. (2016). Slovenian legislative documents use the term 'programming budget' or the term defined by the law, i.e. *special part of the budget.* The literature focused on PBB emphasises that the concept provides a better foundation for the future economic situation and fiscal policy (e.g. Krievins 2007; Pollitt 2001; Hou et al. 2011; Aristigueta and Justice 2006; Schick 2014; Sicilia and Steccolini 2017; Mauro et al. 2016). The main idea of PBB is to enable policymakers to communicate properly with their voters and other stakeholders. Decisions about the allocation of public funds to various programs, about implementation activities, and about the desired target values for the implementation of certain programs provide better insight into the allocation than ranking public expenditures solely on the basis

M. Klun (✉)
Faculty of Administration, University of Ljubljana,
Ljubljana, Slovenia
e-mail: Maja.Klun@fu.uni-lj.si

M. S. de Vries et al. (eds.), *Performance-Based Budgeting in the Public Sector*, Governance and Public Management,
https://doi.org/10.1007/978-3-030-02077-4_11

of economic classification. The PBB concept is considered as a tool to improve the efficiency and effectiveness of public services and a factor of greater transparency and accountability in the use of public money. Nevertheless, in most countries, the correlations between the allocated funds and the results of consumption, as well as the problems of excessive measurement or too many indicators, remain to be resolved (e.g. Joyce 1993; Wang 2008; OECD 2007; Sterck and Scheers 2006; Sterck 2007; Bleyen et al. 2017).

In their review of the literature, Anessi-Pessina et al. (2016) note that PBB was launched in Europe with the introduction of new public management, although the concept itself is much older. In times of crisis and savings, the budgetary process has been upgraded by emphasising other elements of a sound budgetary process, such as public participation in budget preparation and inter-organisational cooperation. Upon reviewing 60 papers on PBB, Mauro et al. (2016) noted that there is no common concept and that the concepts used differ even within the country, depending on the decision-making level. Based on the examined studies, PBB has the greatest impact on organisational factors and factors related to the responsibility and effectiveness of program implementation. The presented review of PBB development in Slovenia shows that Slovenia faces similar problems and experiences to other countries.

11.2 The Slovenian Experience with Performance-Based Budgeting

Slovenia has passed through several development stages of the budgeting process. First, after gaining independence in 1990–1992, the government began adopting the concept of an integrated budget. In the same period, the level of public debt was defined. A second period, from 1993–1999, was more comprehensive. The economic classification of revenues and expenditures was determined, budget execution rules were defined, and charts of accounts for public expenditure were introduced. The Court of Auditors was established and external control was determined. The most important period for PBB was after 1999, when Slovenia began to adapt its budget system to EU rules. The adoption of the Public Finance Act (Official Gazette of the Republic of Slovenia, no. 79/1999; official Slovenian abbreviation: ZJF), which entered into force in the 2000 budget year, provided Slovenia with a program classification. Slovenian legislation used the terms 'result-oriented budgeting' and 'performance budgeting'.

The legislature lays down three components of the budget—namely, the general and special parts of the budget and the development program plan. The general part of the budget shows the classical economic classification of the budget revenue and expenditure. The development program plan shows investments for a five-year period by budget users. The most important part of the budget for PBB is the 'special part of the budget'. The special part contains the program classification of the budget and the institutional classification. This shows the expenditures of individual budget users according to specific areas, now referred to as the expenditure policy. Each budget user is obliged to submit a financial plan justification, which provides important additional data on the use of budget money, as it does not merely involve data on the purpose of use. According to the law (ZJF, Art 16), the justification should also include:

- a presentation of objectives, strategies, and programs in an individual area;
- legislative and other bases for the anticipated strategies and programs;
- the coordination of objectives, strategies, and programs with long-term development planning documents and budget memoranda;
- starting points and indicators on which calculations and assessments of required funds are based and the expected value of the indicators after the budget year; and
- other clarifications that enable an understanding of the proposed strategies and programs.

These elements of explanation of financial plans indicate a move towards PBB, since there is a need to define objectives, programs, and indicators and to report on the results achieved. These are the basic characteristics of PBB. Officially, PBB was introduced in Slovenia in 2000, when the first relevant documents of the state budget were prepared for the 2001 budget year. For local budgets, the first use of PBB elements was set for 2006.

11.2.1 The First Ten Years of Performance-Based Budgeting in Slovenia

The law on public finance itself was not enough to introduce PBB at a glance. Several implementing regulations and necessary explanatory documents followed after the law. For example, decrees on procedures for preparing the national budget were frequently amended with increasingly detailed definitions of the tasks of the budget-spending units in implementing PBB. All further decrees increased the result-measuring requirements beyond those of the ZJF, i.e. the explanation of a financial plan draft had to include the following mandatory elements: physical, financial, and descriptive indicators to measure the set objectives, as well as the starting points and indicators on which the calculations and assessments of the required funds are based. The financial plans, therefore, present the proposed work program and the annual implementation plan.

The appropriate legal basis for the introduction of PBB in Slovenia was presented in 1999, with the enforcement of the legislation in 2000. In addition to the legislation itself, relevant documents related to the reporting on eligible use were adopted: instructions on the preparation of a final account for the national and municipal budgets, methodology for preparing reports on the achievement of objectives, and the results of direct and indirect budget-spending units. However, all these bases were insufficient to fully establish the concept in practice.

In its audit report on financial statements and the implementation of the state budget for 2001 and 2003, the Court of Auditors found that ministries were still not reporting with sufficient objectivity and transparency. In 2003, the situation had somewhat improved; however, the Court of Auditors still stated as its main reservation the inappropriate definition of financial plans, which did not contain sufficiently clear definitions of the objectives and anticipated results for an individual program in relation to the initial state in the field the program was intended to affect. Appropriate operational criteria and indicators with anticipated values were not defined for individual programs, and this prevented an assessment of an individual program's success following implementation. Since the budget planning itself was deficient, the reporting was not focused on program results and outputs. The Court of Auditors stated that the situation remained similar in an audit in 2004. The audit report on the final accounts for the 2005 budget provided a detailed analysis of the initial state. According to the findings, five ministries had improved their planning compared to 2004; however, the average score for objective setting was still just 1.5 (maximum 5). The lowest score was for objective measurability (1.1); the scores for the level of explanation for requested budget funds (1.3) and reporting on outputs (1.5) were also low (Audit Report on Final Account of the Slovenian 2005 and 2006

Budget). Furthermore, the established issue of the failure to set objectives, to outline the indicators and the initial and anticipated values, and to define actions was noted as a significant finding. The structuring of the ministry subprograms was extremely diverse. Some were too complex and varied to allow overall objectives and hence indicators to be defined. Some subprograms were cost accounts that were therefore unsuitable for setting objectives and indicators (e.g. salaries).

In June 2005, the Ministry of Finance adopted the development strategy of internal public finance controls for the 2005–2008 period, due to the aforementioned recommendations and findings of the Court of Auditors and the actual situation in the development of PBB in Slovenia. The main goal of the strategy was that by 2008, all the ministries would include PBB as a basic budgeting element, and thus clearly define the long-term objectives and the desired effects of public expenditure. In doing so, they were to use clearly defined objectives and indicators that would enable evaluating the achievement of the desired effects. By 2008, most direct budget users were to have set measurable performance indicators for public expenditure. A special group of experts was formed in order to realise and actually implement the strategy. The group of experts was composed of representatives of the Ministry of Finance (mainly administrators of individual expenditure areas), a representative of the Institute of Macroeconomic Analysis and Development (IMAD), representatives of the Court of Auditors, a representative of the Faculty of Administration of the University of Ljubljana, and an IMF representative. The main tasks were as follows:

- to analyse the current situation;
- to prepare detailed instructions and expert bases for the PBB-compliant planning of financial plan drafts;
- to prepare appropriate training and to offer daily expert assistance in introducing the concept into the ministries; and
- to report on the work performed.

The group initially met in June 2005. One of its first actions was to prepare new instructions on the formation of financial plan drafts for budget-spending units. The instructions included detailed explanations of the relevant terminology (output, result, input, objective, indicator, outcome, etc.) and appropriate instructions for the formation of objectives and indicators, together with practical examples. After the instructions had been drawn up, training workshops were organised for the Ministry of Finance employees who were responsible for individual direct budget-spending units. Later, training was carried out for representatives with budget responsibilities from each ministry. Members of the group also offered individual consultations for selected/pilot ministries (the Ministry of Agriculture, Forestry and Food, the Ministry of Education and Sport, the Ministry of the Environment and Spatial Planning, and the Ministry of Labour, Family and Social Affairs).

At the group's proposal, in 2006 all ministries were required to re-evaluate the relevance of program qualifications and the classification of budget items in individual subprograms and to prepare draft documents on the separation or combination and restructuring of subprograms to enable the definition of measurable, standardised objectives and indicators. Items within the subprograms had to be harmonised with actions or measures to achieve the objectives as effectively as possible, while items whose influence on the subprogram's function was difficult to assess were to be excluded. The expert group offered individual consultations at select ministries in the formation of some subprograms and their combination into rational groupings. General items were also defined as special subprograms. The expert group had to conclude its work in early 2007, due to the change in government. Individual consultation and training had not yet been expanded to every ministry, so not every ministry had restructured its subprograms and analyses of the set objectives and indicators. The group did not focus particular attention on reporting on outputs at the selected ministries, only suggested that ministries should follow the financial plan explanation as the basis for reporting, and that the report structure should match the one established in the proposal. During its brief period of operation (one budget cycle), the group did not succeed in developing mechanisms to link results and fund allocation, since most of its time was devoted to training and restructuring budget items for individual budget-spending units (Andoljšek et al. 2007). The Court of Auditors found in later audit reports that the greatest progress had been achieved in the group's selected ministries. The instructions for preparing financial plan proposals were later partially integrated into the annual budget.

In 2007, after the elections and the establishment of a new government, the Ministry of Finance formed a new, smaller working group that was still to follow the strategy set up in 2005. The group was again composed of an IMF representative, a representative of the Faculty of

Economics of the University of Ljubljana, representatives of the Ministry of Finance, and a representative of the Ministry of Transport. The mandate of this group quickly ended, as the group operated for only one year. The assigned tasks of this working group were (Čok et al. 2008):

- to review the work to date in Slovenia in the PBB field;
- to identify programs within the test ministries where PBB could be introduced (the Ministry of Finance, Ministry of Transport, and Ministry of Education and Sport were selected); and
- to produce a case study of parallel PBB for the Tax Administration of the Republic of Slovenia, the Roads Directorate and the *Primary Education* program within the Ministry of Education and Sport. This involved bodies within the selected ministries.

The final report of the working group included some interesting conclusions. Within the case study on the appropriate performance assessment of bodies within the ministries, it was established that introducing PBB to, for example, the Tax Administration would require the proposal of a functional structure for programs that in general did not match the organisational structure at that time. Another important finding of the group was that the information system related to the budget process did not provide adequate support in the preparation of the budget, in the automated monitoring of functional expenditure, or in evaluating and monitoring indicators. In relation to the body within the Ministry of Transport (the Roads Directorate), the group noted that several measures should be implemented in order to adequately and accurately measure the set objectives with relevant indicators, inter alia, the appropriate aggregation of data, the establishment of a database, and an appropriate analytical system. Despite this, a new method of disclosure would make monitoring outputs simpler and make the functioning of the administration itself more efficient. The group did not carry out parallel PBB at the Ministry of Education and Sport.

The report makes clear that the second group faced similar problems to the first, since one of the problems in implementing PBB lies in the overburdening of the staff in budget-spending units, where there are not enough individuals employed to carry out planning, reporting, and monitoring, but require various employees to perform this work alongside their other ongoing duties. The group concluded its work with findings that generally matched those of the previous group (Čok et al. 2008):

- the consistent implementation of PBB requires a commitment from the entire Slovenian government, and one ministry will need to be appointed to lead the project;
- the PBB concept entails a radical transformation in the understanding and implementation of the budgeting process and its implementation will last for several years;
- organisational changes will be required for a series of budget-spending users;
- specific funds must be linked to investment in information support; and
- it would be rational to engage external experts in the project.

In 2008, the Ministry of Finance co-financed the project within the framework of targeted research projects aimed at creating a better PBB environment. Within the framework of the research, a survey was carried out among the administrators of the subprograms in individual ministries on whether the administrators prepare or participate in the preparation of long-term and short-term objectives of budgetary expenditure and in setting the target values of the selected indicators. Of the administrators for various subprograms in various eligible use areas who were surveyed, 27% responded to the questionnaire. The answers showed that 85% of the administrators took part in preparing long-term objectives and target values, either independently or as part of a working group; 87% participated in setting short-term objectives. During the research period, 3–5 objectives were defined within the subprograms; however, most administrators thought that there should be between 6 and 10 objectives. The majority of respondents considered that the objectives were well-defined (the average rate was 4.4, on a scale of 1–5); the adequacy of the indicators was rated slightly lower (3.8). Nevertheless, some administrators felt that the subprograms were too comprehensive. Most of the time, one person was in charge of one subprogram, while in some cases certain administrators covered several subprograms (Aristovnik et al. 2010). The conclusions of the research also produced some other interesting findings related to the introduction of PBB in Slovenia (Aristovnik et al. 2010):

- certain budget users did not yet provide adequate explanations of financial plans because objectives were not set and there were no indicators and/or target values;
- plans for use were far too focused on economic classifications rather than on program financing;

- budget users inadequately report on the measurable achievements of program implementation;
- budget users do not display performance information comparatively; consequently, their effectiveness and efficiency cannot be assessed; and
- education and training for program administrators was inadequate.

The first ten years of PBB in Slovenia did not produce everything that was expected, and it was clearly necessary to take further steps to put the system into practice.

11.2.2 Reform Processes After 2010

The next wave of changes in PBB development occurred in the 2010–2012 period. Until this period, the programming budget was more focused on institutional budget users, who distributed the funds for programming purposes to 24 areas of use, which were further divided into major programs, subprograms, and activities. With the 2010 reform, the government wanted to make a move towards a program allocation of funds in such a way that the purposes of use would first be defined and the institutional classification would be subordinate to the purposes. After the reform, the 'areas' of use were renamed 'policies'. Each policy has set objectives that budget users abide by in their spending. In the context of the reform, a reduction in the number of purposes was foreseen: the initial proposal was to create 12 use policies. This change was met with resentment from the budget users, who warned that some purposes of use were being disregarded. The resentment primarily concerned the positioning of institutional users, who saw a threat in connection with their operation and even existence. The expert public also criticised the 12-policy structure by pointing out that it would be hard to aggregate them into 10 purposes of use according to the Classification of the Functions of the Government (COFOG). In the end, 16 policies were defined in the 2016 budget only; for all subsequent years, 24 policies (purposes) of use have been used again.

An important measure of the reform process was the upgrading of the information system of the Ministry of Finance for the preparation of the budget in 2011. The upgrade was carried out in such a way that budget users had to enter objectives, indicators, indicator values, and target values into individual frameworks. An appropriate code was assigned to each objective and indicator, enabling later analytical approaches. The change in the information system led to the establishment of a single scheme in the explanation of the budget users' financial plans, which is used by all budget users. An example of an objective, indicator, and its values can be derived from the indicator 'Labour productivity (GDP in Purchasing Power Standards [PPS]) per employed person (EU28 = 100)'. The indicator is defined as the objective under code 6849 (increase in economic competitiveness), and the measurement unit (MU) is determined (namely, the index) with the base year 2013 and the index value 79.30. Thus, the target value for 2018, for example, is 81.70.

Information support thus eliminated one of the weaknesses identified by experts and research from previous years, i.e. that many budget users do not set objectives and indicators or that they are not clearly defined. With a defined display scheme, all the budget users were required to lay out the basic information. This was the starting point for rethinking budget spending in terms of goals that should be achieved. Without this navigation table, most budget users were unable to write explanations, set goals, and define indicators; for example, the Ministry of Culture determined in an earlier phase that their main goal is to exist. This change promoted defining goals and indicators in connection to selected policies as an important starting point in developing PBB.

Despite this improvement, there are still certain problems connected to the implementation of PBB in Slovenia. In its 2014 review, the IMF concluded that the budget documents submitted to the National Assembly must give the complete picture of public finances—the general government sector and all its components. Budgetary process reforms focused mainly on the state budget, but not on other public finances budgets, such as local budgets, the pension insurance fund budget, and the health insurance fund budget. Similarly to the IMF, the Slovenian Evaluation Society, in their 2015 consultation, noted that the program structure that would allow the evaluation of program performance was not yet established at the level of the local government. Furthermore, the representatives of the Court of Auditors pointed out that some systemic conditions for the implementation of program management in 2015 had not been met. Inter alia, they drew attention to inadequate legislation, the lack of strategic and development frameworks, the non-inclusion of all units of the general government sector in program management, and inadequate state accounting that fails to offer support to program accounting. According to the Court of Auditors' findings, many other shortcomings arise from the audit reports on the budget (Evaluators Society 2015):

- there is no direct link between the strategic documents and budget planning;
- subprograms are too non-homogenous in content (linked to objectives that are too general)—a 'bottom-up' approach;
- objectives (with exceptions) are inadequate at all levels;
- sufficient financial transparency, comparability, and traceability are not ensured in the financial plans;
- methodological explanations (calculation methods, data acquisition resources, and the like) for calculating performance indicators are not defined;
- the organisational scheme of the ministries is not sufficiently consistent with the functional and program structure of the financial plans;
- when the same subprogram was managed and implemented by several ministries, no joint analyses of the effects of the subprogram were prepared; and
- reports on the achieved objectives and results do not take into account all the criteria for good reporting; therefore, the effectiveness of the subprograms cannot be evaluated on this basis.

The current government, which, in the framework of its public administration development strategy until 2020, recorded the objective of 'strengthening public finances by setting up an appropriate top-down budget planning and establishing a programming budget at the level of the state' (Government of the Republic of Slovenia 2015), also recognises the majority of the identified shortcomings. Within the explanation of this objective, the government notes that wider reasons for poor PBB implementation in Slovenia lie in poorly defined state measures and related general government expenditure, since the content aspect is often subordinate to the financial aspect. Within the framework of the set objective, it strives to link the strategic plans and priorities of the government with the preparation of the state budget, setting up comprehensive policies that will involve the local level as well as the state level. Consequently, the planning of the allocation of public funds to the programs is to be determined over a multiannual period in accordance with the policy objectives they were designed for. In addition, the information system is expected to be upgraded in such a way that other budget users are gradually involved, and indirect budget users also gradually adopt programming budgets. A new reporting system and a detailed evaluation of individual programs are to be developed and the process of consolidating budgets for reporting purposes is to be automated. It is interesting that the process of change includes staff training for determining the performance indicators that would be included in the budget preparation process. In its document, the government also recognised that there are several risks that could prevent the achievement of the set objectives; these risks are seen primarily in the lack of awareness of the need to measure performance and efficiency, in monitoring the implementation of measures, and in the lack of vision of individual ministries with the strategic objectives of the government. Regardless of all the set measures, the target value of the set objective indicates a modest implementation, since the envisaged target value is only determined for more than five institutions that fully implement the set goal.

11.3 Performance-Based Budgeting in Slovenia in Numbers

As mentioned earlier, the budgetary expenditure structure has been divided into 24 purposes (policies) of use since the introduction of PBB in Slovenia, with the exception of 2012. Although the purposes have changed slightly in the past, they remained relatively the same; however, the objectives and indicators have changed. Objectives and indicators were rarely defined in the first few years, but with the introduction of a supportive information mechanism, the transparency of the objectives and indicators is now clearer. In 2017, Slovenia had 1457 indicators in the framework of the adopted programming budget; on average, this involves app. 60 indicators per policy; however, the range is considerable. The lowest number of indicators is in the framework of the ‘pension security’ policy (two indicators—but the policy accounts for app. 8% of public expenditures), and the highest in the framework of the ‘internal affairs and security’ policy (136 indicators—this policy spends less than 3% of public expenditures). On average, three indicators are set for each objective. Within the policy framework, several general objectives are set—on average up to five. There are several specific objectives within the framework of programs and subprograms.

The number of indicators per policy is not directly connected to the budget expenditure per policy. According to the adopted budget, in the last three years, Slovenia has devoted the largest share of state budget expenditures to the policy of 'public debt transactions and cash resource management', allocating almost one-third of all public expenditure to it. There are three other policies, namely 'education and sport', 'pension security', and 'social protection' that together require the same amount of expenditure as the above-indicated policy. Less than 1% of the total public expenditure of the state budget is spent on six policies, while other policies require between 1 and 6% of all public expenditure. A more detailed allocation of funds by policies is shown in Table 11.1.

Table 11.1 The structure of budget spending according to policies (%)

Policy	*2015*	*2016*	*2017*
Spatial Planning and Housing Activity	0.22	0.20	0.25
Political System	0.45	0.41	0.47
Intervention Programmes and Obligations	0.60	1.25	0.56
Health Care	0.86	0.56	0.65
Local Government	0.96	1.13	0.87
Sources of Energy and Energy Efficiency	0.93	0.76	0.92
General Public Services and Joint Administrative Services	0.94	1.02	1.16
External Policy and International Development Cooperation	0.82	2.43	1.25
Culture and Civil Society	1.45	1.21	1.35
Economic and Public Financial Policy	1.49	1.32	1.49
Environmental Protection and Environmental Infrastructure	3.62	1.30	1.50
Science and Information Society	1.68	1.73	1.96
Justice	1.94	1.92	2.28
Labour Market and Working Conditions	2.59	2.43	2.49
Defence and Protection	2.78	2.43	2.67
Internal Affairs and Security	2.67	2.62	2.82
Agriculture, Forestry, Fishery, and Food	3.20	3.01	3.17
Payments to the European Union	3.51	2.90	3.27
Enterprise and Competitiveness	2.76	4.68	3.76
Traffic and Transport Infrastructure	6.99	4.32	5.43
Social Security	8.03	7.35	7.91
Pension Security	11.87	9.58	10.77
Education and Sport	12.40	10.94	12.31
Public Debt Transactions and Cash Resource Management	27.24	34.48	30.73
Total (EUR billion)	12.82	14.20	12.35

Source Ministry of Finance of the Republic of Slovenia (2017)

As an example, the 'traffic and transport infrastructure' policy includes three general goals (support of economic development, efficient mobility and safe transport of humans and goods, and decrease of CO_2 emissions); it is divided into six programs, which are divided into subprograms. Each subprogram has its own specific goals. Within this policy, the program 'road transport and infrastructure' has three goals and three subprograms (management and maintenance of state roads, investments and road building, and development of highway and road network) with additional specific goals and indicators. An example of one subprogram is presented in Table 11.2. The value is defined for the whole subprogram.

As this example shows, specific goals represent some kind of work plan and indicators present the extent of the plan. For defined specific goals, it is determined which general goal in the policy is followed. In the selected case, all specific goals follow the general goal *efficient mobility and safe transport of humans and goods.* Despite this, it is difficult to evaluate the effectiveness of money spending on this basis. For the general public, it is just information about work planned and done; it is not possible to evaluate whether it is efficient or effective. At the same time, the results are not used in consideration of the future financing of the subprogram.

Table 11.2 Presentation of defined goals and indicators for the 'Road Transport and Infrastructure' program inside the selected policy

Name of the subprogramme	*Defined goals*	*Indicators*	*Expected value in 2017 (%)*	*Value*
Management and maintenance of state roads	Maintenance of state roads network	Regular maintenance and winter maintenance	65	84.1 million EUR
	Traffic monitoring, automatic calculation of traffic	Share of roads with automatic calculation of traffic	59	
	Maintaining a list of road equipment, periodic road evaluation	Updated list of road equipment	8	
		Road evaluation according to MSI method	50	
	Achieving an optimal level of regulation in the construction of public roads	Timely issued permits and consents	95	

Source Ministry of Finance (2017)

11.4 Conclusion

As various other studies have shown, we can state that the PBB concept in Slovenia has been developing for quite a long time. However, even after such a long time, it is still difficult to say that program budgets link the allocated funds with results. In considering PBB, a great deal of emphasis is still focused on changing comprehension and the need to improve program planning. Nevertheless, each central budget user should report on achieving the goals and the value of indicators defined in the financial plan after the end of the budget year. As noted, there are no direct connections between results and financial resources for the next budget years. Despite that, the budget users are under the Court of Auditor's inspection, which reports about the effectiveness as well as the efficiency of budget spending. Therefore, performance measurement is indirectly under evaluation.

Schick (2014) effectively identified the problems of introducing the PBB concept into practice; these problems also apply to the practice in Slovenia. According to Schick (2014), the main obstacles are: rigidity of budgets, political pressures, and insistence on gradual change. The rigidity of the budget is shown in the 'fixed use', which is determined by various laws and treaties and past decisions. According to some estimates, more than 90% of the Slovenian budget is fixed. According to the OECD estimate, more than 75% of the fixed budget expenditure prevents program-based allocation based on results—as the results are 'pre-defined'.

Political decision-making on allocation rarely focuses on the predicted results, as other criteria for allocation predominate, and it is usually not desirable to deal with one's own prosperity. In decision-making, policy focuses more on economic classification than on program expenditure planning.

Although Slovenia prepares bi-annual budgets, the budgetary process itself is still too short to enable serious analyses of the measurement of results and their effects and the necessity of certain activities. Decision-making is largely based on past needs and rarely on the need to implement set programs. This is not indicative of the positive use of the PBB concept in the coming years; even the last development strategy implies a gradual transition and improvement in the implementation of program planning for public expenditure. In view of all this, we can conclude that major shifts, in particular, more extensive reforms, are required in

Slovenia in order to be able to talk about the actual implementation of the adopted PBB concept. Although the beginnings were promising and it was possible to apply the good practices of other countries that have already examined and improved their approaches, it is clear that the development of real PBB in Slovenia will be slow. With the exception of the unification of the preparation of financial plan justification through the information system and by templates prepared by the Ministry of Finance, it is not possible to talk about progress from the introduction of the concept to the present. To summarise—tables are filled on a central level, but a real program performance approach is still in the future.

References

Andoljšek, Žiga et al. 2007. *Zaključno poročilo o delu skupine za uvajanje k rezultatom usmerjenega proračuna*. Internal Material.

Anessi-Pessina, Eugenio, Carmela Barbera, Mariafrancesca Sicilia, and Ileana Steccolini. 2016. Public Sector Budgeting: A European Review of Accounting and Public Management Journals. *Accounting, Auditing & Accountability Journal* 29 (3): 491–519. https://doi.org/10.1108/aaaj-11-2013-1532.

Aristigueta, Maria, and Jonathan Justice. 2006. The Status of Performance Budgeting: Introduction. *Public Performance & Management Review* 30 (1): 7–13. https://doi.org/10.2753/pmr1530-9576300100.

Aristovnik, Aleksander, Janez Šušteršič, Stanka Setnikar-Cankar, Maja Klun, Matjaž Novak, Primož Pevcin et al. 2010. *Vzpostavitev sistemov merjenja učinkovitosti in uspšenosti javnega sektorja v Sloveniji na mikro in makro nivoju. Končno poročilo raziskave*. Ljubljana in Koper: Fakulteta za upravo in Fakulteta za Management.

Bleyen, Pieter, Daniel Klimovský, Geert Bouckaert, and Christoph Reichard. 2017. Linking Budgeting to Results? Evidence About Performance Budgets in European Municipalities Based on a Comparative Analytical Model. *Public Management Review* 19 (7): 932–953. https://doi.org/10.1080/14719037.2016.1243837.

Čok, Mitja et al. 2008. *Poročilo o delu skupine za načrtovanje proračuna na osnovi doseženih rezultatov* (Report on Work of the Group Responsible for Planning the Budget Based on Achieved Results). Internal Material.

Društvo evalvatorjev (The Slovenian Evaluation Society). 2015. Revidiranje programske uspešnosti. Retrieved 16 August 2017 from https://www.sdeval.si/en/39-objave/objave/586-revidiranje-programske-uspesnosti.

Hou, Yilin, Robin S. Lunsford, Katy C. Sides, and Kelsey A. Jones. 2011. State Performance-Based Budgeting in Boom and Bust Years: An Analytical

Framework and Survey of the States. *Public Administration Review* 71 (3): 370–388. https://doi.org/10.1111/j.1540-6210.2011.02357.x.

Joyce, Philip G. 1993. Using Performance Measures for Federal Budgeting: Proposals and Prospects. *Public Budgeting & Finance* 13 (4): 3–17. https://doi.org/10.1111/1540-5850.00987.

Krievins, Mārtiņš. 2007. Performance-Based Management Reforms: Good Practices and New Challenges. Paper Presented at Conference on Good Governance and Public Administration Reform.

Mauro, Sara Giovanna, Lino Cinquini, and Giuseppe Grossi. 2016. Insights into Performance-Based Budgeting in the Public Sector: A Literature Review and a Research Agenda. *Public Management Review* 19 (7): 911–931. https://doi.org/10.1080/14719037.2016.1243810.

OECD. (2007). *Performance Budgeting in OECD Countries.* Paris: OECD Publishing.

Pollitt, Christopher. 2001. Integrating Financial and Performance Management. *OECD Journal on Budgeting* 1 (2): 7–37.

Računsko sodišče (The Court of Auditors). 2005. *Revizijsko porocilo o predlogu zaključnega računa proračuna Republike Slovenije za leto 2005.* Ljubljana: Računsko sodišče.

Schick, Allen. 2014. The Metamorphoses of Performance Budgeting. *OECD Journal on Budgeting* 13 (2): 49–79. https://doi.org/10.1787/budget-13-5jz2jw9szgs8.

Sicilia, Mariafrancesca, and Ileana Steccolini. 2017. Public Budgeting in Search for an Identity: State of the Art and Future Challenges. *Public Management Review* 19 (7): 905–910. https://doi.org/10.1080/14719037.2016.1243809.

Sterck, Miekatrien. 2007. The Impact of Performance Budgeting on the Role of the Legislature: A Four-Country Study. *International Review of Administrative Sciences* 73 (2): 189–203. https://doi.org/10.1177/0020852307077960.

Sterck, Miekatrien, and Bram Scheers. 2006. Trends in Performance Budgeting in Seven OECD Countries. *Public Performance & Management Review* 30 (1): 47–72. https://doi.org/10.2753/pmr1530-9576300103.

Vlada Republike Slovenije (Government of the Republic of Slovenia). 2015. *Javna uprava 2020, Strategija razvoja javne uprave 2015–2020.* Ljubljana: Ministrstvo za javno upravo. Dostopno na (16 avgust 2017). http://www.mju.gov.si/fileadmin/mju.gov.si/pageuploads/JAVNA_UPRAVA/Kakovost/Strategija_razvoja_SLO_final_web.pdf.

Wang, XiaoHu. 2008. Convincing Legislators with Performance Measures. *International Journal of Public Administration* 31 (6): 654–667. https://doi.org/10.1080/01900690701641232.

Zakon o javnih financah (ZJF). *OGRS*, No. 79/1999 on 30 September 1999.

CHAPTER 12

Performance-Based Financing of Kindergartens: Bulgaria

Nadezhda Bobcheva

12.1 Introduction

Education is a human right. It is one of the most powerful drivers for development, raising incomes and promoting economic growth. Education is central to most development strategies, because no country has ever succeeded in the long term without sustained investment in human capital. For many governments, education is among the top priorities, and government spending on it is high. Beyond the political goodwill behind educational expenditures, there is mounting scientific evidence of short-term and long-term economic benefits of early childhood education. Financing early childhood education, however, remains a challenge. In an era of budget deficits and a high degree of scrutiny over government spending, better educational management is needed to efficiently and effectively use public funds.

The goal of this chapter is to evaluate the system of performance-based financing of kindergartens in Bulgaria. The state allocates large

N. Bobcheva (✉)
Municipal Council of Silistra, Silistra, Bulgaria
e-mail: nbobcheva@mail.bg

M. S. de Vries et al. (eds.), *Performance-Based Budgeting in the Public Sector*, Governance and Public Management,
https://doi.org/10.1007/978-3-030-02077-4_12

sums of money for this level of preschool education, and these resources are distributed to municipalities on the basis of a formula. Does this system motivate improvements in quality?

12.2 National Background

Preschool education in Bulgaria has two levels—nurseries for children through the age of three (usually from 10 months to 3 years old) and kindergartens for children from 3 to 6 years of age or to the age when they enter primary school. The nurseries are under the jurisdiction of the Ministry of Health and are not considered part of the education system. Kindergartens are under the jurisdiction of the Ministry of Education and Science. Nursery attendance is voluntary, and fees are charged by public and private providers. Recent legal amendments, such as the new Preschool and School Education Act (PSEA) that entered into force on August 1, 2016, provide for two years of compulsory preschool education, which applies to all 5 and 6-year-olds. These two years of mandatory preschool education may be attended either at kindergarten or in preparatory groups at primary schools.

General government expenditure on education in Bulgaria is among the lowest in the EU. In 2014, it accounted for 4.1% of GDP (below the EU average of 4.9%) and for 9.7% of total general government expenditure (Ministry of Finance). While the system is underfunded at all levels, authorities estimate that—in relative terms—spending on education will decrease as a result of measures to increase the transparency and efficiency of spending and to optimize the school system network. According to the 2016–2019 Convergence Program of the Republic of Bulgaria, education expenditure is projected to decrease to 3.2% of GDP in 2019 and to 8.7% of total public spending (Ministry of Finance).

In the 2015/2016 school year in Bulgaria there were 2002 kindergartens, in which 232,000 children are enrolled, of which almost 52% were boys (data in this part from the National Statistical Institute). There are state, municipal, and private kindergartens. The state kindergartens are regarded as being of national importance and therefore are directly funded by central authorities, including the Ministry of Education and Science and other ministries and bodies. Those kindergartens have a special purpose. The municipal kindergartens may be opened, transformed, or closed by order of the mayor of the municipality following a decision of the Municipal Council. Private kindergartens have to operate in accordance with the legislation and have to meet state standards. The number of licensed private kindergartens continues to increase, but they remain an option for only some parents, because of the high tuition levels. Private kindergartens were not regularly subsidized by any level of public administration before 2017. In the 2015/2016 school year, there were 92 private kindergartens in Bulgaria, and 3333 children, or 1.4% of all pupils, were enrolled in them. This situation may change; one provision of the new PSEA was that as of 2017, private kindergartens and schools are entitled to receive public funds. The budget allocations will be set by the budgets of the municipalities in which they are seated, the number of students enrolled, and the state subsidy. Private kindergartens and schools will have to present regular financial reports. Control over spending will be implemented by the municipal administration and the Regional Education Authority.

The main types of kindergartens are all-day, half-day, or weekly. Children are predominantly enrolled in all-day kindergartens—in the observed school years, the percentage of all-day students was above 90%. There is a dual rationale for this: the support of maternal employment and the promotion of child development. Parents get support in bringing up the child, and the preschool education provides a combination of education, play, and care. Comprehensive care for preschool children involves meals, rest and sleep, and various educational programs.

The coverage of children in kindergartens estimated by the group net enrollment rate decreased for three consecutive years, from 83.6% in 2013/2014 to 82.9% in 2014/2015 and to 81% in 2015/2016. The main reasons for the decrease are high unemployment rates and the economic difficulties encountered by many families, limiting the ability to pay fees and willingness to enroll. Following that, the increasing number of economic migrants is also a factor. The national average number of children in a kindergarten was 116; the number was significantly larger in urban areas (156) than in rural areas (57). Kindergarten groups each had an average of 23 children: 24 in urban areas and 19 in rural areas (National Statistical Institute).

Parents or guardians are free to choose which kindergarten their child attends. Students are enrolled after filing an application form and being ranked according to various criteria. While preschool education was not a requirement until recently, there are impressive facilities available, sufficient to enroll the entire child population in all-day kindergartens. However, these facilities are unevenly distributed across the country.

Over the last several years, there has been a shortage of available places in kindergartens in large Bulgarian cities.

The national curriculum for preschool institutions is based upon an appreciation of individual differences in development and learning, as well as on an appreciation of the child's integrative and balanced development. The objectives, contents, and activities are designed separately for the first and second age groups of children. For the sake of better transparency, they are divided into various fields; however, the suggested curricula extend over the stringent limits of a single field and are placed into the context of the children's everyday life in a kindergarten. The following subject fields are included in kindergarten activities: physical exercise, language, art, society, nature, study, and mathematics. Interdisciplinary activities such as ethics, health care, safety, and traffic education are incorporated into all those fields. Kindergartens can offer programs of different length. The day-program includes education, childcare, and meals. It lasts from 6 to 9 hours and can take place in the morning, in the afternoon, throughout the day, or in turns.

12.3 Financing Preschool Education in Bulgaria

Preschool education in Bulgaria is financed by a mix of central government funding, funds from local governments, and parents. Other sources of funding, such as donations and contributions from private companies and government entities, are also allowed.

Parents pay fees for using municipal kindergartens to the extent determined by the Municipal Council in compliance with the Local Taxes and Fees Act. The council decides whether there should be a fee as well as the fee rate. The Council can lower or even exempt certain categories from paying fees, such as low-income families, families with twins, and families with many children. Parents are often excused from paying tuition fees, but they still pay a monthly sum for food. Parents also pay for extracurricular activities, such as dance and music classes.

In Bulgaria, there is a public debate regarding the municipal fees for using kindergartens ('Fee for attendance at kindergartens and other social services'). The debate is focused on whether municipalities could charge parents for compulsory education and, subsequently, the amount that local authorities have to contribute. Indeed, financing preschool education has been a challenge for poor municipalities and the issue of how effectively and efficiently public funds (both state and municipal) are spent is increasingly important. It is important to note that contributions from the national budget are fixed. Kindergarten directors are in charge of the day-to-day financial management; their activities are overseen by the municipal financial department. In this way, achieving efficiency and effectiveness in preschool education financing rests with Bulgarian local governments.

The new PSEA introduced two additional local fees: the 'fee for raising and upbringing activities in compulsory preschool education' to be used by the kindergarten or the school beyond the activities financed by the state and the 'fee for general support activities within the meaning of the PSEA that are not financed from the state budget and that are carried out by personality development support centers'. Both fees could be introduced after January 1, 2017, following the decision of the municipal council. The decision of whether to introduce such fees and at what rates rests with the local council.

Municipalities use very different approaches to set fees connected with preschool education. Because of this, the annual amount collected ranges significantly (Sofia excluded)—from 702 leva in Kovachevtsi (less than 2 leva per capita) to 4,252,496 leva in Varna (slightly more than 8 leva per capita). The amount collected varies even among municipalities from the same population group. For example, in municipalities from 50,000 to 75,000 inhabitants, the total amount collected ranges from 191,075 leva in Silistra to 700,603 leva in Kurdzhali (data by NAMRB for 2015).

12.4 Allocation of Central Government Grant Using a Performance Formula

In order to increase efficiency and effectiveness, a 'student voucher' system was introduced in Bulgaria for kindergartens and schools and was implemented to allocate central grants. For preschool education, the state contribution is planned and estimated according to the number of children the kindergarten has for a fiscal year—N(c). For every child enrolled, the kindergartens receive a fixed amount of money from the state budget. This fixed amount is in accordance with the unified expenditure standard (UES). The standard is set for a fiscal year, so adjustments are made in kindergarten budgets according to standards that can change because the school year (from September to June) actually spans two fiscal years. The quality of education provided is not an issue in the UES. The amount is the same for every child regardless of achievement.

This UES is different for different types of groups in kindergartens—it differs for children enrolled as all-day or half-day students, for children of different ages—for 2–4 years old or for 5–6 years old, and for different municipality sizes (there are four UES levels and four municipal categories). The main principle applied in preschool financing is the 'money follows the child' concept. The UES is expected to cover the main costs of the school—staff salaries, overhead expenses, and building maintenance (except capital improvements), all of which are financed by the national budget. The municipality is formally mainly responsible for capital expenses.

The UES provides an option for local governments to modify the formula for financing kindergartens in order to meet local needs and preferences. Usually, the formula looks like this: FF = MFC + SFC (FF—funds allocated, MFC—major formula components, SFC—supplementary formula components). Supplementary formula components could be funds provided for 'conditionally fixed' costs, for reserve funds, and for children with special educational needs, for inclusive education, for meals, or for something else at the discretion of the local government.

This approach to financing preschool education should make kindergartens closely dependent on the number of enrolled children, as this number determines the majority (or all) of their budget. The implementation of this type of financing for kindergartens was expected to create a kindergarten education market in Bulgaria, to ensure that kindergartens would reform from the inside out, use the funding in more efficient and effective ways by providing better educational services, and compete on that market to attract children with the quality of education they provide; i.e. better quality = more children willing to enroll in a certain kindergarten = more money flowing into the kindergarten budget. However, these expectations were not fulfilled. We document this using the case of the Silistra Municipality.

12.5 The Case of the Silistra Municipality

Located on the banks of the Danube River and bordered by Romania to the north, the municipality of Silistra occupies a territory of 516 sq. km. It is comprised of the city of Silistra and 18 villages. The city is a medium size for Bulgaria, and it is a major city in its district. The total municipal population was 47,723 inhabitants in 2016.

In the 2015/2016 school year, 1347 children were enrolled in kindergartens, divided into 49 groups. The total number of available places was 1358: the system was operating at full capacity. Thus far, the preschool education infrastructure has been able to accommodate all children living in the municipality. The municipality of Silistra operates nine kindergartens—six in the town of Silistra and three in rural areas. Some kindergartens in smaller villages are branches of those in larger ones. For example, the kindergarten in the village of Babuk is a branch of the one in Kalipetrovo. The kindergartens in the villages of Yordanovo and Bradvari are affiliated with the kindergarten in the village of Ishirkovo. The kindergarten in the Delenki neighborhood of the village of Aydemir also has a branch. Such combined structures are the result of merging kindergartens. Some years ago, all 16 branches were independent kindergartens. With the introduction of delegated budgets and the diminishing numbers of children, mergers became the best solution for keeping the system in operation.

The municipality of Silistra collects 'kindergarten fees'. These fees are levied in accordance with the local by-law adopted by the Municipal Council of Silistra; however, the fees for kindergarten attendance are not set at a cost recovery level and they are below the national average. In all the years observed, the share of fees for kindergarten attendance was 1% of the total municipal revenues (local fee revenues are rather limited in Silistra—between 5 and 8% of total revenues; the national average is 9%). One reason is that the municipality of Silistra stopped collecting the fees from children in the compulsory preparatory groups at kindergartens in 2014.

The central government subsidy covers app. 75% of municipal kindergarten expenditures in Silistra; the rest is provided by the municipal budget (as indicated, direct private contributions at this level are marginal). App. 15% of the total municipal expenditure on education is spent on preschool education. Related local fees cover only app. 50% of municipal contributions—preschool education is cross-subsidized on the level of app. 50% from other municipal revenues. The legal expectation, as stated above, is that state should cover running costs and the municipality should cover capital costs; in reality, the municipal budget's contributions to an individual kindergarten also cover large parts of the running costs, such as maintenance and heating.

Municipal kindergartens are not legal bodies with independent budgets—their costs are part of the municipal budget. Because their operation is not financially independent and kindergartens are a sensitive local social service, Silistra does not re-allocate resources to kindergartens on the basis of any formula; it simply covers the costs (using supplementary formula components to do this). There is no direct link between the quality of kindergarten management and the 'subsidy'. Better management just means less cost to the municipal budget. The annual costs per child vary significantly among different kindergartens within the municipality of Silistra. In 2015, the annual allowance per child in local kindergartens ranged from 462 leva up to 1760 leva.

12.6 Conclusions

The 2007 education reform in Bulgaria introduced a formula for funding kindergartens. The expectations were typical—the creation of a 'quasi market' with a positive impact on performance. However, nothing like this happened. Available data on the costs and financing of preschool education in Bulgaria reveal that there is no direct link between kindergarten performance and the allocation of funds, especially because of the system by which money is used on the local level. Municipalities do not reward better-performing kindergartens and do not punish less performing units—they simply guarantee full cost coverage for all of them.

The central formula is transparent, but it has some limitations. For example, the present division of municipalities into four categories has proven to be far from optimal, because the municipalities in one group are not homogeneous, and meanwhile very similar municipalities may receive different levels of grant. The formula is also insufficiently predictable, as the UES levels can change every year.

In these conditions, the theoretical expectation that formula-based financing in education can create quasi-competition and motivate better performance remains a poor theory.

References

Ministry of Education and Science. 2016. *Data from the Section on Preschool and School Delegated Budgets*. Accessed 7 April 2017. http://www.mon.bg/?go=page&pageId=9&subpageId=66.

Ministry of Finance. 2016. *General Public Finance Data*. Accessed 7 April 2017. www.minfin.bg.

Municipality of Silistra. *Data on Preschool Education and on Municipal Costs and Expenditures*. Accessed 3 April 2017. http://www.silistra.bg.

NAMRB National Association of Municipalities in the Republic of Bulgaria. 2015. *Database on Local Finance*. Accessed 7 April 2017. http://www.namrb.obuchi-se.org/norway/bg-bg/%D0%BD%D0%B0%D1%87%D0%B0%D0%BB%D0%BE.aspx.

National Statistical Institute. 2016. *Data on Kindergartens (Pre-primary Education)*. Accessed 18 April 2017. http://www.nsi.bg/en/content/4792/kindergartens-pre-primary-education.

CHAPTER 13

Performance Based Funding of Universities: Czech Republic and Slovakia

Peter Pisár, Miroslav Šipikal, Robert Jahoda and David Špaček

13.1 Introduction

Higher education funding in the world is mostly multi-source, both in terms of type of funds and content itself, which is funded under it. In terms of funds, the largest share of public resources comes from public sector (Pruvot et al. 2015). An important question thus becomes the way in which these public funds are reallocated between individual

P. Pisár (✉)
Department of Finance and Accounting, Faculty of Economics,
Matej Bel University, Banská Bystrica, Slovakia
e-mail: peter.pisar@umb.sk

M. Šipikal
Department of Public Administration and Regional Development,
Faculty of National Economy, University of Economics, Bratislava, Slovakia
e-mail: miroslav.sipikal@euba.sk

M. S. de Vries et al. (eds.), *Performance-Based Budgeting in the Public Sector*, Governance and Public Management,
https://doi.org/10.1007/978-3-030-02077-4_13

higher education institutions. There are several ways of redistribution in the world, with three of which are most often used—financing through performance or historical indicators, project funding and funding through negotiation of individual contracts with universities. Performance-based funding is specifically enhanced in support of research and development.

Despite the growing use of performance-based funding, one of the missing knowledge is the empirically confirmed impact of this funding in education systems, especially under conditions other than in developed countries. Less developed systems may tend to look for ways to respond to increased demands other than by enhancing and improving the quality of science itself, and the introduction of performance-based funding alone can potentially not bring the desired effects. Some existing studies from these countries have already shown that, in addition to a possible increase in publications, this also causes negative effects, such as a large differences in publishing between research areas, an increase in number of publications in predatory journals, or the preference of quantity instead of quality (Good et al. 2015; Pajić 2015). Research of this type of funding within these systems is very important also due to fact that even universities in the developed countries also respond and adapt their activities to suit the system as much as possible (Agasisti and Haelermans 2016).

In this chapter, we will look at the experience of performance-based funding for universities in the case of the Slovak Republic and the Czech Republic. Both countries are not belonging to the world leaders in research and their schools do not occupy high places in world rankings (Kwiek 2012). In both countries significant elements of performance-based financing were introduced about ten years ago, so it is possible to compare the changes that it caused. The part on Slovakia is more comprehensive and includes more details about the system. Because the Czech conditions are almost identical, in this part we only highlight extra issues connected with pervasive effects of performance financing of research at the university level.

R. Jahoda · D. Špaček
Department of Public Economics, Faculty of Economics and Administration, Masaryk University, Brno, Czech Republic
e-mail: jahoda@econ.muni.cz

D. Špaček
e-mail: david.spacek@econ.muni.cz

13.2 Performance-Based Funding of Research in the Higher Education in Slovakia

Higher education institutions in Slovakia are publicly funded in a number of ways, primarily funding two key activities—education and research. Funding for education is primarily based on the number of students, and the components of the performance funding of this part of the budget are applied to a small extent, In recent years, the employability of students measured by their unemployment rate, which may be seen as a funding element, has also been taken into account. On the contrary, in the case of research, the main part of the funding is based on performance indicators, so we will further deal with this area of financing.

Research in the Slovak Republic is currently funded by four basic ways—the Ministry of Education, Science and Research of the Slovak Republic (hereinafter referred to as the Ministry of Education SR) subsidies based on performance-based indicators, project funding through national and international grant schemes, EU resources from structural funds and entrepreneurial activities or private sector financing.

Performance-based public financing of higher education has started in Slovakia with the beginning of this century, when the first method of calculating subsidies for universities was published by Ministry of Education. At the beginning, major percentage from all of the funding was primarily based on the number of university students. This changed significantly during the years—student based funding currently accounts for approximately a comparable share of total funding as performance-based research funding of universities. The introduction of this funding was mainly aimed at enhancing the performance and quality of higher education, when nearly a third of the population is studying abroad, especially in the Czech Republic (Fischer and Lipovská 2015) and research activities of universities were very limited.

At present, the key sources of funding for research in terms of volume are the resources allocated by the Ministry of Education SR allocated under subprogramme 077012. This subprogramme has fixed financial allocations for each year, so all available funds in this chapter are allocated on the base of formula (as the total sum is capped, explosion of received "points" means only decreased value of one point). Several performance indicators are defined within this program, mainly indicators related to publication and project activities of universities. At present, the following parameters are applied for funding research:

a. the results of the evaluation of the quality of the research activities of the higher education institution according to the last comprehensive accreditation (weight 0.43);
b. the share of higher education institution in the amount of funds received in last two years for research activities within the framework of foreign grant schemes (weight 0.10);
c. the share of higher education institution in the volume of funds (current transfers) acquired in last two years in research activities from public administration bodies (excluding state programs) (weight 0.09);
d. the share of higher education institution in the volume of funds (current transfers) acquired in last two years in research activities from entities other than public administrations and foreign entities (excluding grant schemes) (weight 0.03);
e. the share of higher education institution on the average number of postgraduate students in the daily form of doctoral study after the dissertation examination in calendar year before examination (weight 0.10);
f. the share of the higher education institution in publishing activity using scales for scientific, research or artistic activities (weight 0.225); and
g. the share of the higher education institution in artistic creation according to point system (weight 0.025).

From this, we can see that performance-based financing of research is mainly aimed at gaining grants and publishing. The publication activity then evaluates a large number of different outputs, with an emphasis on journals registered in SCOPUS and Web of Science databases. The use of performance-based funding delivered number of changes in university outputs. In the next section, we will analyze the most crucial ones.

13.2.1 The Increase of the Scientific Outputs of Universities

A good indicator of the volume of research output is considered to be scientific publications (Moed et al. 2002; Hicks 2012), so in this case we will compare the volume of scientific articles in the web of science and Scopus database between 2007 and 2016, four years before and five years after the change in the method of financing.

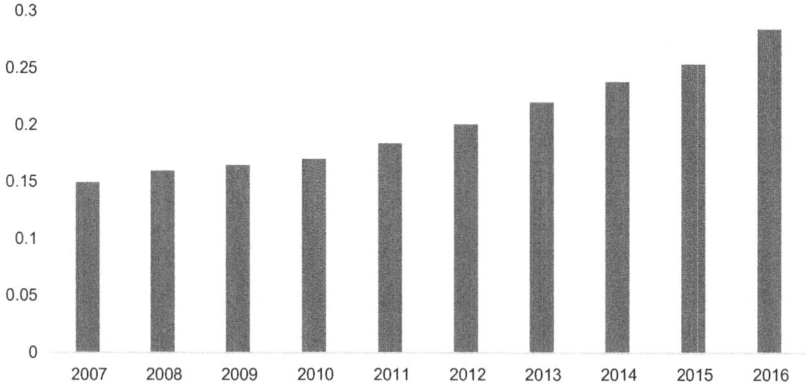

Fig. 13.1 The average number of articles published in the WoS database by teachers of Slovak public universities (*Source* Pisár and Šipikal 2017)

During this period, publishing activity has increased significantly in Slovakia. In 2016, the total volume of published articles in the WoS database was nearly twice as high as in 2007. This difference is roughly the same as the one per university teacher, as shown in Fig. 13.1. The same trend can be seen in articles written in the SCOPUS database.

However, this increase should be brought into context of the overall increase in publication outputs. To compare the performance change, we can take the neighboring country of Austria. There is a different funding system based on individual university negotiations with the Ministry of Education and the budget being allocated on the basis of the social needs of the state and the functions expected from the university (Pruvot et al. 2015). Here, the opposite trend came, when before 2013, performance indicators still determined the financing. When we look at changes within Austria, we can see a significant increase in publishing activity for that period, which is even faster than in the case of the Slovak Republic. In absolute figures, these differences are even greater as the total volume of publishing activity in Austria is 2.8 times higher. As a result, the overall publishing activity in both countries is very comparable, despite the introduction of performance funding in Slovakia. More important than performance funding, the issue of supporting appropriate research specialization and top-class researchers appears to be more important.

If we summarize the performance change in the number of publications, performance funding has led to an increase in the number of them after its introduction. However, if we look at the whole system in more detail, we can identify some of the key factors that point to adapting to the university's research system other ways than by direct increasing the volume and quality of scientific research.

13.2.2 Changes of Performance Within Different Groups

In the previous section, we could see that there has been a significant increase in the number of publications after implementing performance-based funding. However, if we look in more detail on where this increase occurred, we can note that the growth in the number of publications was recorded mainly by universities with initially worse publication results. More detailed figures are shown in Table 13.1. Before the changes in funding, more than 90% of the publications in the SCOPUS database came from 50% of the top-performing universities, up to 55% of which were from two of the most important Slovak universities (Comenius University and Slovak Technical University). What is interesting, the share of more efficient universities in the total volume of publishing activity measured by the Ministry of Education SR methodology, which is used to allocate performance subsidies, developed differently. The top performers share has increased over the years. The third column

Table 13.1 Development of % shares of different groups of universities

	2007	*2009*	*2011*	*2013*	*2015*
TOP2—SCOPUS	55.27	55.58	50.35	43.85	42.51
TOP2	35.80	33.03	36.09	37.29	37.76
TOP2 funds	36.95	35.45	35.34	35.06	36.08
TOP20%—SCOPUS	78.60	77.90	73.92	66.77	65.48
TOP20%	48.83	46.87	51.71	53.48	57.19
TOP20% funds	51.54	51.39	51.60	51.38	52.44
TOP50%—SCOPUS	91.39	90.65	90.21	86.80	85.03
TOP50%	62.17	60.97	64.48	67.46	71.42
TOP50% funds	72.40	71.11	71.55	71.45	72.94

Source Own processing based on data from SCOPUS and Ministry of Education SR, TOP 2—share of performance of two TOP universities in Slovakia (UK and STU), TOP20% and TOP50%—share on performance of 20% or 50% publicly most active universities in Slovakia, SCOPUS—share on number of articles in SCOPUSE, Funds—share on subsidy from Ministry of Education SR of the table is the development of the total amount of subsidies granted from the Ministry of Education of the Slovak Republic, including the non-performance based financing, and this share has virtually no change between the groups in Table 13.1.

This development suggests that the introduction of performance-based funding has significantly increased publications in higher quality journals in the initially less publicly active universities, probably due to the activation of top-class teachers in those schools who are able to do, only in other oriented system were not push to do that. The second reason may be the effort of less-performing universities to look for other ways of increase of publications, what we will talk about later in predatory journals. On the contrary, at the best universities, they have probably only focused on higher quality journals, but the introduction of performance-based funding has led to the spread of these research and the publication of partial or less substantial research results. However, at the university level, the change in funding system surprisingly did not lead to another distribution of financial resources.

13.2.3 Creation of Own Publication Platforms

One possible way how to increase the number of publication is to create your own publishing platforms. In terms of performance financing in the SR, the emphasis is placed on the publications registered in the SCOPUS and Web of Science databases. It should be noted here that these databases record journals that have to meet certain conditions, but they work on a commercial basis and their role is not primarily to guard the quality of these journals. As a result, the number of journals in the region of Central and Eastern Europe almost tripled over the period (Pajić 2015). For example, the number of journals registered in Web of Science or Scopus in economics has risen from 4 in 2000 to 17 in 2015 (Grancay et al. 2017). If we then compare these increases, the publication level after the introduction higher share of performance-based funding has virtually not increased. A large part of this increase is in journals published by universities themselves, which is unusual in Western Europe. These often support each other, to increase their impact factor (Teodorescu and Andrei 2014).

Universities are trying to improve performance not only by own journals. A good example of this is the publication of monographs. Given that monographs issued by the universities themselves and it is often just a question of paying for editions, monographs dominate in publication activity compare of impact journals, which is again the phenomenon of Central and Eastern European countries. In particular, it is also seen in foreign monographs, which are considered to be the highest category and have twice the weight of their home monographs. Universities simply publish significantly more monographs abroad, although they are in the Slovak language and therefore have the character of a domestic monograph. For example, in 2014 and 2015, out of 465 foreign monographs, 148 were in Slovak (about a third), which did not differ in qualitative terms from the half-rated domestic monograph. The authors thus just adapted their activity to the criteria and published the domestic monographs they had published at home abroad.

13.2.4 Increase in the Number of Publications in Predatory Journals

It was not only universities, but also publishers, who have reacted on introduction of funding based on number of publications. They created journals registered in Scopus and Web of Science databases and such journals allow publishing (with financial participation) lower quality or even bellow elementary quality papers (Srholec and Machacek 2017). This type of journals is used to be referred to as "predatory". According to Machacek and Srholec (2017) in 2004 the Scopus database published about 2000 papers in predatory type journals (approx. 0.1%), this figure increased in 2015 to app. 60,000 papers (approx. 3%).

Such types of publications were practically of no interest in the absence of performance-based financing, and publication in them was more of a coincidence than a targeted intention, so there were almost no publications from the Slovak universities until the year 2009. The situation has changed since implementation of performance-based funding and led to rapid increase in number of publications in these journals. This increase can be seen in Fig. 13.2.

Figure 13.2 shows estimates of the number of these publications based on two databases. The first column is based on a database compiled by the Ministry of Education of the SR. In 2016, these journals were identified, based on an increase in publications in these journals as a means of obtaining funds. In the first step, the Ministry of Education of the Slovak Republic did a comparatively narrow list of only 11 journals, which were labeled as predatory and thus not included in the system for funding distribution. Other authors (for example, Grancay et al. 2017),

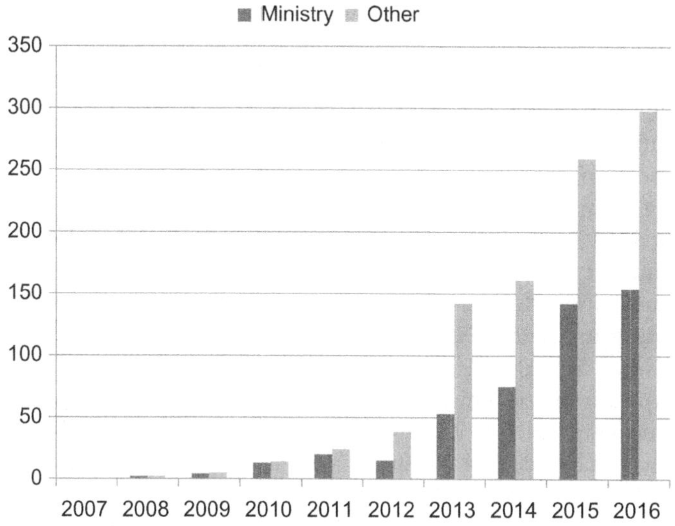

Fig. 13.2 Number of publications in predatory journals (*Source* Own construction)

who have studied this issue, have introduced a wider range of these journals. Based on them, we have expanded our original list by six other journals with predatory journals signs. If we also count their outcomes, the amount of publications in predatory journals has almost doubled, as can be seen in Fig. 13.2 as well (second column). In both cases, we see a rising trend, showing gradual adaptation to the need to publish articles in those databases and to find ways to make it easier. If we take 2011 as the basis, since then, these numbers have increased several fold and considerably faster than in the case of all publications in the SCOPUS database. Overall, their share on total publications has changed from 1.5% in 2011 to around 5% in 2016. As the international comparisons show (Machacek and Srholec 2017), the Slovak Republic achieves the second worst results from the OECD countries, though still less as developing countries. This increase is also partially eliminated by the fact that, in recent years, databases have also taken steps to reassess the inclusion of some journals that have subsequently been expelled from databases (e.g. The *Mediterranean Journal of Social Sciences*), so they could not produce further predatory articles. An even larger range of such outputs can be seen among journals that are not included in the SCOPUS database and are therefore not subject to at least some degree of quality control.

The use of the above-mentioned methods is connected with several important facts. The first reason is the fact that all registered journals in these databases had the same weight for the allocation financial resources in the performance-based system until 2016. Only in 2017, the impact factor of these journals began to apply for the first time. The journals were divided into six categories according to the impact factor and higher impact factor gains more resources for the university. The system encouraged individual employees to publish the highest possible number of outputs, regardless of their quality. Indications of such behavior can be seen, for example, on data on the average impact of journals in which the Slovak scientists published in the field of economics, apart from journals within the Central and Eastern Europe journals. Until this system has changed, this average impact factor of these journals has been improving from 0.365 in 2000, from 0.479 in 2005 to 1.137 in 2010, and after the introduction of performance funding, this average has fallen to 0.817 in 2014 (Grancay et al. 2017). As an example of the University of Economics, we can see how the evaluation of the outputs of the conferences changed in the transformation from Ministry funding to individual researcher. Prior to performance funding, conferences serve as first step to the article in the reviewed journal. Performance-based financing has introduced financial reward also for the conferences themselves, but does not distinguish between different conferences and their financial value is the same. However, the University of Economics has approved in their internal evaluation system that conferences, which result as the proceedings registered in the WoS database, has much higher volume than other conferences. In Table 13.2 we can see how this has led to the adaptation of researchers' own activities.

Table 13.2 Participation of EU staff at conferences

	2010	*2011*	*2012*	*2013*	*2014*	*2015*
Conferences total	1449	1128	1225	1313	1128	999
Conferences with proceedings in WoS	91	63	126	162	317	343
Share of WoS conferences	6.28	5.59	10.29	12.34	28.10	34.33

Source Own calculations

The share of attendance at conferences that have had a proceeding registered in WoS has increased rapidly, but with the overall decrease in attendance at conferences. From budget point of view, this step has had a negative effect on funding. At the same time, it has restricted participation at conferences that do not have a direct record, which is usually the best conferences that still understand the conference only as a means of getting comments and the publication itself is done in the form of a scientific article. These examples show that scientists are also greatly adapting their outputs to set rules, and misallocating performance indicators to an individual greatly impacts on the performance and efficiency of a performance-based funding system.

The second was the very late and inconsistent allocation of financial resources, including the methodology by which the funds were allocated. According to the valid methodology for allocating resources for universities in the Slovak Republic, funding is always only 1 year ahead. Methodology often not clear at the beginning of the year, and the budgets of universities are usually approved only in March of the given year. The methodology of the calculation has often partially changed on an annual basis, and the change occurred at the time when the activities for which the finances were allocated were implemented. The system works in such a way that, according to the methodology in 2016, funding for universities is allocated for the year 2017, but taking into account activities from years 2014 and 2015. This leads to a very short period of time when schools are forced to perform, which may lead to problems of good management of universities (Pruvot et al. 2015).

Third, for the performance-based financing policy itself, it is important to correctly set the ratios between the different outputs—weights. If such funding has to lead to excellent research, the top performance (publications) should be evaluated above the standard, otherwise universities will try to replace it with a larger number of less important publications. In Slovakia, this system is set up to support to a certain extent this substitution. This is given by a short lead time for assessing outputs as well as a very complicated system for categorizing publishing outputs when there are more than 50 different categories.

Fourth, the way universities transfer these performance requirements to the scientists themselves is also important (Abramo et al. 2011). Given that the criteria for budget calculations and the performance-based funding system are not known in advance, universities face internal pressure to create within universities systems that are set to the detriment of higher quality but focused on volume and short-term results. Since the labor laws that do not allow for retrospective performance assessment, universities have to create their own ways of transferring performance to the scientists themselves.

13.3 Performance-Based Funding of Research in the Higher Education in the Czech Republic: Selected Issues

Because the Czech system is almost similar to the Slovak situation, we only very briefly characterize the Czech system of research and development evaluation (nicknamed as "RIV" according to the Czech abbreviation for the Register of Results Information), which was used for financing of publication outputs till 2017. After this short part, we highlight extra pervasive effects, connected with "RIV" system, issues not mentioned (or indirectly mentioned) in the Slovak part of this chapter.

The "RIV" system has undergone a major transformation over the last 13 years. The system was originally designed only for the purpose of evaluating the number of research results of individual organizations, but over time it has become an important instrument of the performance component of higher education funding. The evaluation system has allocated a number of "RIV points" to each publication output. Selected details on development of the evaluation system are described in Table 13.3.

Since its inception, the system has suffered from a number of imperfections that originated from its very nature—will to quantify scientific outcomes using bibliometrics and statistical methods. Regular changes to evaluation methodology created significant financial instability (ex-post. With application to the results of the research that have already been submitted to the system). Among the negative aspects we can also mention the way in which the national methods of evaluation were transposed into internal university systems. Based on numerous interviews with representatives of Czech universities we can mention the following hot issues.

1. There has been a change in the wage system for academics based on their success in collecting "RIV points" or even adjusting the criteria for qualification progress of academics.

Table 13.3 Selected facts of the research outcomes system evolution in the Czech Republic

Year	*Number of pages—main document (all documents)*	*Value of selected outputs (points) Czech/English*		
		Book	*Article in WoS*	*Proceedings*
2004–2005	6	1	0.5/2	
2006	36	5/20	5+[a]	1/4
2007	29	12.5–50	10+[a]	0.1–0.4
2008	25	20–40	5–145[a]	8 (WoS)
2009	28	20–40	10–305[a]	8 (WoS)
2010	45	Similar to 2009 methodology. Some changes in local journal evaluation not in WoS or Scopus and new research outputs assessed (applied research outputs)		
2011	46			
2012	50			
2013–2016	60	4–120	10–305[a]	8–60 (WoS)
2017+	57 (130)	New system combining quantitative and qualitative approach		

Source Government of the CR (2004–2017)
Note [a]Formula included the impact factor of the journal and the median impact factor or the position (ordered by IF) among other journals from similar area

2. Universities have periodically evaluated changes to the methodology with respect to the weighting of the publication outputs.
3. Some universities held seminars where academics familiarized themselves with changes to the evaluation system and drew attention to publishing channels that bring more "RIV points".

In this environment, it is not surprising that in some faculties the main goal of academics was not to produce the best possible research, but rather an attempt to produce outputs that would be in line with the short-term interests of their universities.

The extra implementation problem of "RIV" was evaluation of books and book chapters. As the previous table showed, between 2006 and 2012 the book as a research output, brought a significant number of "RIV points". At the same time, this type of research output was fairly easy to produce (the book must have at least 50 pages of text, the review process was rather pretended, the cost of publishing is negligible). In this situation, the publication of monographs has become a very widespread way of collecting "RIV points". Some universities have gone rather too far in motivating their staff to regularly publish their outputs as a book.

There were cases when two books differed by less than 30%. Another example of perverse behavior was the systematic publication of diploma theses at the cost of the university and their subsequent records as a scientific book. The system has come so far that some academics managed to issue dozens of scientific monographs in the period under review. The response came after 2013. The regulator started to assess the quality of monographs, resulting in a heavy burden on external referees. Each referee had dozens of books a year to evaluate.

"RIV" in its before 2017 form was the tool motivating for quantity, not quality, especially in social sciences. The results can be documented—majority of papers by Czech authors in journals indexed in databases like WoS or Scopus was published in local journals, and the number of papers in conference proceedings registered in such databases rocketed. Machacek and Srholec (2017, p. 6) argue: "The results show that there are several times more locally oriented journals published in the Czech Republic and Slovakia, as well as in the other former Eastern Bloc EU countries, than in comparable advanced countries. Roughly half the authors contributing to Czech journals are based in the Czech Republic and another tenth in Slovakia. The publishing of national, or at best regional, indexed journals appears to be an Eastern European phenomenon. Some of the journals published in the Czech Republic or Slovakia are just as good as respected international journals, however, a clear majority of them have only provincial status".

From this point of view we may speak not only about predatory journals (see Slovak part), but also "predatory" scientific conferences (see also Slovak data). Such conferences can be organized in attractive places and produce conference proceedings (with 300–400 EUR fee per paper) including hundreds of papers of very disputable quality, but indexed in WoS, Scopus or similar databases.

Because of many implementation problems RIV system was abolished form 2017, but its scores will be used for financing of universities and research institutions for more than five following years (the argument for this is the need to protect necessary stability of financial flows). With respect to this fact, the schools using manipulations to earn large numbers of RIV points would benefit from such unfair practices also in short-term future.

However, the preparation of the new system is still not finished. One idea is to use the impact of articles (measured by Article Influence Score—AIS indicator) as the core weight factor may just create new pervasive effects—artificial focus on journals with high AIS, without taking into the account audience needs and reality of high AIS (many journals started to increase their impact by manipulations with references—for example they include into the system of the review criteria also the number of references to previous articles in a journal). Moreover, the fact that book publications may, but must not, be also prestigious is not solved by such system at all.

13.3.1 Selected Pervasive Effects from "RIV" in Data

The Slovak part indicates that universities may try to create own publication platforms. The existing analyzes in the Czech Republic clearly describe concrete forms and approaches. Machacek and Srholec (2017, p. 4) for example speak about "samizdat" journals and even name some of them. They identified 13 journals registered in Scopus and issued by Czech universities with more than 33% of articles written by own university staff. The journal Scientia Agriculturae Bohemica, published by the Czech Agricultural University in Prague is the "top" with more than 80% of papers by authors from this institution (p. 31).

Another journal directly mentioned by these authors (p. 32) is Acta Universitatis Agriculturae et Silviculturae Mendelianae Brunensis, indexed in Scopus from 2007. This journal published during the period 2013–2016 in total 968 (!) articles. From this 56% of articles was published by authors from Mendel University, 89% of authors are from the Czech Republic and 10% form Slovakia. One author from Mendel University managed to publish during the above mentioned period 34 articles in this journal, 15 from them in 2016.

The impact of such practices on the total number of WoS points is critical. Authors of this chapter calculated it using existing older RIV points data sets—Table 13.4. The data show that for example in 2012 (most critical year), the university "earned" 65.4% of total RIV points by publishing in its own journal.

The specific form of publication platform is so-called "citation circles" (Teodorescu and Andrei 2014), very much connected with the above mentioned "predatory conferences" proceedings. Such practices are well visible via the tools included in WoS or Scopus databases, but this does not prevent today from their use (example might be the conference paper of disputable quality written by Czech authors in WoS registered conference proceedings, quoted by other Czech authors—many times

Table 13.4 RIV points of Mendel University 2008–2012

Category of publication	*2008*	*2009*	*2010*	*2011*	*2012*	*Total*
	Points	*Points*	*Points*	*Points*	*Points*	*Points*
Books	431,153	221,935	192,742	622,661	132,535	1,601,026
Conferences	1615	43,683	49,010	174,737	48,370	317,415
WoS journals	79,624	381,925	121,970	102,303	134,959	819,781
Scopus journals	450,554	548,363	776,355	972,436	901,460	3,649,168
"Approved" Czech journals	127,741	159,187	217,968	245,281	63,547	813,742
Other journals	12,969	0	0	0	0	12,959
Total	1,103,646	1,355,093	1,357,063	2,117,418	1,280,871	7,214,091

Source Authors' calculations from RIV

from the same department—in other WoS conference proceedings paper one or two years later).

13.4 Conclusions

The introduction of performance-based financing in the Czech Republic and Slovakia has brought about a number of visible changes in the functioning of higher education, particularly in the field of universities research output. The general positive fact is that in recent years there has been a significant increase in the publishing activity of universities in both countries. Nevertheless, this increase is comparable to increase of performance in other countries, e.g. neighboring country Austria.

On the other hand, compared to the developed countries pervasive effects are much more visible (Auranen and Nieminen 2010). These effects are visible in different forms, like, efforts to create own publication platforms, publishing in predatory journals, creating citation circles, establishing "samizdat" journals, all related to the substitution of quality by quantity. The tendency to prefer easier ways to achieve the necessary outputs and to ensure higher education funding and personal growth, rather than the path of concentration on improvement in quality, is very visible. The positive issue is the fact that these negative and unfair practices are subject of more and more frequent criticism by local authors and already also areas of first "cleaning" actions by university management, especially in the Czech Republic.

Acknowledgements "This work was supported by the Slovak Research and Development Agency under the contract No. APVV-14-0512" and by Czech Research Grant Agency GACR project "Performance Management in Public Administration: Theory and Practice in the Czech Republic and Other CEE Countries", ID (CEP) GA16-13119S.

References

Abramo, Giovanni, Tindaro Cicero, and Ciriaco Andrea D'Angelo. 2011. The Dangers of Performance-Based Research Funding in Non-Competitive Higher Education Systems. *Scientometrics* 87 (3): 641–654. https://doi.org/10.1007/s11192-011-0355-4.

Agasisti, Tommaso, and Carla Haelermans. 2016. Comparing Efficiency of Public Universities Among European Countries: Different Incentives Lead to Different Performances. *Higher Education Quarterly* 70 (1): 81–104. https://doi.org/10.1111/hequ.12066.

Auranen, Otto, and Mika Nieminen. 2010. University Research Funding and Publication Performance—An International Comparison. *Research Policy* 39 (6): 822–834.

Fischer, Jakub, and Hana Lipovská. 2015. Brain Drain-Brain Gain: Slovak Students at Czech Universities. *Journal on Efficiency and Responsibility in Education and Science* 8 (3): 54–59. https://doi.org/10.7160/eriesj.2015.080301.

Good, Barbara, Niki Vermeulen, Brigitte Tiefenthaler, and Erik Arnold. 2015. Counting Quality? The Czech Performance-Based Research Funding System. *Research Evaluation* 24 (2): 91–105. https://doi.org/10.1093/reseval/rvu035.

Grancay, Martin, Jolita Veinhardt, and Ērika Sumilo. 2017. Publish or Perish: How Central and Eastern European Economists Have Dealt with the Ever-Increasing Academic Publishing Requirements 2000–2015. *Scientometrics* 111 (3): 1813–1837.

Hicks, Diana. 2012. Performance-Based University Research Funding Systems. *Research Policy* 41 (2): 251–261. https://doi.org/10.1016/j.respol.2011.09.007.

Kwiek, Marek. 2012. Universities and Knowledge Production in Central Europe. *European Educational Research Journal* 11 (1): 111–126. https://doi.org/10.2304/eerj.2012.11.1.111.

Machacek, Vít, and Martin Srholec. 2017. *Mistni casopisy.* Praha: IDEA.

Moed, Henk F., Marc Luwel, and A.J. Nederhof. 2002. Towards Research Performance in the Humanities. *Library Trends.* 50 (3): 498–520.

Pajić, Dejan. 2015. Globalization of the Social Sciences in Eastern Europe: Genuine Breakthrough or a Slippery Slope of the Research Evaluation

Practice? *Scientometrics* 102 (3): 2131–2150. https://doi.org/10.1007/s11192-014-1510-5.

Pisár, Peter, and Miroslav Šipikal. 2017. Negative Effects of Performance Based Funding of Universities: The Case of Slovakia. *NISPAcee Journal of Public Administration and Policy* 10 (2). https://doi.org/10.1515/nispa-2017-0017.

Pruvot, Enora Bennetot, Anna-Lena Claeys-Kulik, and Thomas Estermann. 2015. Strategies for Efficient Funding of Universities in Europe. In *The European Higher Education Area*, 153–168. Springer International Publishing. https://doi.org/10.1007/978-3-319-20877-0_11.

Srholec, Martin, and Vít Machacek. 2017. *Predatorske casopisy ve Scopusu*. Praha: IDEA.

Teodorescu, Daniel, and Tudorel Andrei. 2014. An Examination of 'Citation Circles' for Social Sciences Journals in Eastern European Countries. *Scientometrics* 99 (2): 209–231. https://doi.org/10.1007/s11192-013-1210-6. Data from Web Pages of the Czech and Slovak Ministries for Education.

PART IV

Conclusion

CHAPTER 14

Effectuating Performance-Based Budgeting Takes Time

Juraj Nemec and Michiel S. de Vries

14.1 Introduction

The switch to performance-based budgeting, seen as a more transparent method of allocating public resources (Allen and Tommasi 2001), is recommended by many international organizations and donors because traditional budgeting shows where the money was spent, but it does not give any idea as to the results of this spending. Performance-based budgeting is expected to address this gap, informing all stakeholders on what a public body is trying to achieve by answering questions like 'What is to be achieved from allocated resources?' and 'What do citizens receive in exchange for their money?' Performance-based budgeting is expected

J. Nemec (✉)
Department of Public Economics, Faculty of Economics and Administration, Masaryk University, Brno, Czech Republic
e-mail: juraj.nemec@umb.sk

M. S. de Vries
Department of Public Administration and Institute of Management Research, Radboud University Nijmegen, Nijmegen, The Netherlands
e-mail: m.devries@fm.ru.nl

M. S. de Vries et al. (eds.), *Performance-Based Budgeting in the Public Sector*, Governance and Public Management,
https://doi.org/10.1007/978-3-030-02077-4_14

to shift the focus from inputs to outputs and/or outcomes, from 'How much money do I get?' to 'What should I achieve to obtain this money?' Performance-based budgeting presents (in theory) important advantages—it is expected to improve the planning of service supply, to help to combat corruption via increased transparency, to serve as a 'bridge' between a public body and all relevant stakeholders, to increase management efficiency, to improve audit and control processes, and to help to reorganize expenditure programs (OECD 2014).

However, these positive expectations have not been fully met in practice because of the implementation problems indicated in this book. The later chapters show that many countries still struggle to create budgets in such a way that the taxpayers get value for their money and that the budget is not only spent as agreed, but that it is reflected in performance, that is, in the achievement of targets, whether these targets are outputs or outcomes.

This book provides examples of experiences from different countries with various forms of performance-based budgeting. It delivers important lessons, valid for any group of countries and any sociopolitical situation, thanks to the varied sample. The chapters in the first part of the book assess the situation in a number of selected developed countries. The US chapter deals both with the history and with the concrete case of the use of performance-based budgeting at the university level. The second part of the book deals with the experiences of selected developing/transitional states, and the last part deals with direct performance-based budgeting—performance-based financing.

All the chapters document that performance-based budgeting is alive, but its implementation problems may grow if the implementation capacity is insufficient, as is mainly—but not exclusively—the case in less-developed countries. The book confirms that many factors affect performance-based budgeting or performance reform issues in the budgetary process, with different weights given to different conditions.

Based on a review of 61 journals published between 2002 and 2011, Lu et al. (2015) identified the 27 key factors that affect the success of performance-based budgeting and the integration of performance information into the budgetary process. Overall, the top three factors affecting the use of performance in budgeting were 'Quality of Measurement,' 'Political Support,' and 'Executive Leadership Support.' The chapters of this book indicate that these findings were realistic, but the weights of the factors may differ, depending on the level of development of the country, and perhaps two factors need to be added: patience and forethought. As various chapters in this book show, patience is necessary because it takes time after the introduction of performance-based budgeting for the targets to be achieved. The longer performance-based budgeting is practiced, the more visible the positive effects are. This is partly also the case because performance-based-budgeting is full of pitfalls, unanticipated effects, and unexpected reactions from agencies that point to the reality of perversity effects, futility effects, and jeopardy effects. These effects can often only be countered after they have emerged, making it even more necessary to be patient about achieving the expected results.

14.2 Performance-Based Budgeting in the Developed World

The chapters in the first part of this book analyze the situation in developed countries, beginning with a chapter reflecting on US historical experience and current reality. Aziza Zemrani first briefly describes the history of performance-based budgeting in the USA, showing that the 'modern' history of this instrument is now more than 100 years old. The 1912 US Commission on Economy and Efficiency report recommended a performance-type approach to budgeting and was a core source for significant reforms in budgeting during this period in the country. The time for serious rational budgeting in the US government started after the 1950s. The Planning, Programming, and Budgeting System (PPBS) approach was adopted for the entire federal government during the Johnson administration (however, despite its comprehensiveness and rationality, this PPBS scheme operated only for a short period). Despite the often-disappointing results of the performance-based budgeting efforts of the 1950s and the PPBS experiments of the 1960s, reformers continued to advocate its use, and in the 1990s the Clinton administration showed renewed attention to performance measurement. Zemrani summarizes the academic arguments on why early performance-based budgeting schemes failed (or at least did not deliver expected outcomes)—arguments that are fully in line with the core factors found by Lu et al. (2015), mentioned above.

The second part of the US chapter evaluates the varying effects of performance-based budgeting in higher education. Zemrani points out that it takes time for performance-based budgeting to achieve its aims and that the effects depend on the nature of the funded organization and its ability to adapt to the system. By distinguishing three categories of higher education—doctoral and research universities, master's colleges, and baccalaureate and other institutions—and by categorizing states based on the number of years that such performance-based budgeting has been in practice, Zemrani determines the varying effects of performance-based budgeting on efficiency as measured by the ratio between enrolment and degrees awarded. The outcomes indicate the time needed for performance-based budgeting systems to become effective. The longer such systems are in use, the more impact they seem to have. Hence, one of her conclusions is that the implementation of performance-based budgeting requires consistent efforts and is time-consuming. Furthermore, the effects are dependent on the extent to which an agency is limited in adapting its expenditure levels; the doctoral and research universities are more able to adapt and the baccalaureate and other institutions are much less able.

In Chapter 3, Roberta Ryan and Joseph Drew examined the case of New South Wales, Australia, which introduced performance monitoring for all councils in 2014 (Australia is one of the forerunners in performance-based budgeting). The focus of their chapter is on the core precondition for successful performance-based budgeting: effective performance monitoring. They show that this is the most difficult issue connected with performance-based budgeting, as gaming and other unanticipated outcomes are a real possibility and cannot be ignored. They show the limited success of previous schemes and discuss how the New South Wales system tries to address the many dilemmas that occur in performance monitoring. This refers, among others, to the utility of the system for end-users; to the degree to which indicators for performance are representative for the performance of a system as a whole; to frequent calls for increasing the number of indicators, while that approach might diminish its usefulness; to the need to incorporate contextual mediators and environmental constraint; and to the possibilities to detect unreliability in the data and to remove misleading metrics, which appear as a consequence of the jeopardy effects.

In Chapter 4, Ed Vosselman and Tjerk Budding give an historical overview of the developments in performance-based budgeting at the local and national level in the Netherlands. The process started there in the 1970s and it gradually developed into the system that is currently in use. At the start, neither local nor national projects proved successful: the resulting insights were not considered useful in daily practice. New attempts to connect political and economic dimensions seem to be more successful. This is another example of how much time and effort are needed to create a system that can be trusted, provides the needed information, and thus increases transparency. The authors mention the barriers to be overcome, especially concerning problems of definition and measurability and the necessary cooperation of middle management to obtain both data and information useful for making decisions. At the local level, it was difficult to compare costs and performances between municipalities. Enabling these comparisons involves changing laws and changing the questions to be answered by the agencies and departments in presenting their performance. One important contemporary tool for such a connection is performance-based budgeting: forecasting and target setting for the performance of governmental organizations and their parts. The authors point out that performance-based budgeting involves translating activities and resource consumption into numbers and relating to the demand for governance and control from a distance. This is not a simple linear and straightforward process; it involves the work of many people, including managers, controllers, and auditors. Instead of aiming for the optimal solution and total control, the authors indicate that trust in what others are doing is also important, especially since an organization cannot be totally controlled from the outside.

In Chapter 5, Christoph Reichard and Nicole Küchler-Stahn evaluate the situation of performance-based budgeting at the local level in three German-speaking countries: Germany, Austria, and Switzerland. They conclude that there are indications that performance-based budgeting systems emerged reluctantly and hesitantly, but with growing performance-based budgeting experience, the usefulness of performance-based budgeting for municipal steering is being more positively assessed, especially by politicians involved in budgeting. Switzerland has had the longest experience with such budgeting and the system is most accepted by elected politicians there. It is not surprising that their main recommendation is that governments need time, as well as sufficient capacities, a performance culture, and a clear focus to enable adequate and useful performance measurement and the identification of a limited number of meaningful and reliable targets and indicators.

Sara Giovanna Mauro describes in Chapter 6 how performance-based budgeting was introduced in Italy as an element of performance management and the subsequent reforms. This chapter provides insights into performance-based budgeting in Italy in central government institutions (ministries) and explains how the reform has been interpreted and how it has been implemented over the last several years. It addresses the impact of new theories in public administration in legislation that tend to adapt to the proponents of performance-based budgeting and to neglect the challenges involved. The legislation led to managerial and organizational reforms including internal controls and budget offices at the central level, at first aiming at performance-based budgeting by revising the process and mechanisms of public spending in Italy, all of which resulted in the production of an abundance of performance information. It remained difficult to push the system further as Mauro concludes that the budgeting was linked to strategic objectives but not to the operational goals and their achievement. She mentions the limited ability of public organizations to measure and manage their performance and connect this to public budgeting. Nonetheless some serious side-effects are visible, such as the feeling of additional bureaucratic obligations and the demotivation among the staff as a consequence of increasing constraints in their autonomy and flexibility (perversity effects).

- The sample selected should be fully representative for the developed world—and clearly documents what is stated in the introduction to this book—that in 'standard' conditions;
- performance-based budgeting is complicated because measuring performance is a typical 'wicked problem';
- introducing performance should be a simultaneous top-down and bottom-up process, as both political will and consensus and organizational leadership support (as well as employee acceptance) are necessary;
- developed countries also have to cope with important implementation problems when introducing performance-based budgeting schemes;
- well implemented schemes may deliver positive effects; and
- the size and scope of the use of performance-based budgeting in the developed world differs.

14.3 Performance-Based Budgeting in Transitional Countries

The examples of performance-based budgeting in transitional countries come mainly from the Central and Eastern European (CEE) region. As indicated in the preface, this was, at least partly, an intentional selection. This region is in the process of possibly the most complicated systemic change in human history—it is changing its former centrally planned and centrally organized system (called socialism) to different forms of a new socioeconomic order. The basis for all the changes is the free market system, but the nuances significantly differ. Some CEE countries (Bulgaria, the Czech Republic, Slovakia, and Slovenia in our book) are already European Union (EU) members and formally accepted all the rules valid for modern market-based democratic societies. Other countries from the region (Ukraine in our book) are still at the early stages of the EU accession process. Yet others have decided to try their own path, something like a state-regulated market economy—developmental state trajectory (Russia). Because of this unique situation, the CEE region is a real 'social' laboratory and the lessons learned from its conditions can have worldwide importance and provide valid arguments for all less-developed countries. Only one non-CEE country is included in the sample, South Africa, and its experiences demonstrate that 'will' is a core precondition for implementing effective (or at least partly effective) performance-based budgeting schemes in transitional conditions.

In Chapter 7, Govender and Reddy address the fact that African countries are the 'new kids on the block' in performance-based budgeting, especially in sectors that are directed toward poverty reduction. In South Africa, performance-based budgeting is even required by the 1994 constitution and in the subsequent legislation. Both because municipalities themselves saw the need to perform better and because the central government induced them to do so, this resulted in significant budget reforms, in the development of a Performance Information Handbook tool in 2012, and in further standardization later. Despite some problems, the South African government sees this development as predominantly positive and as something to be proud of. It says so even though the side effects, as addressed in the introductory chapter, are also visible in South Africa, e.g. improperly defined projects, unreliable data, lack of integration of performance to budget information, the impossibility to allocate budgets to operational projects, the difficulty in monitoring actual spending, and limited budget transparency. Nonetheless, an increasingly strong alignment emerges between budgets allocated and performances as measured with monitoring by Performance Monitoring and Evaluation Units.

Addressing the European transition countries, in Chapter 8 Andrey Klimenko describes how performance-based budgeting has evolved in Russia through a top-down process, how it is embedded in performance management, and how performance is linked to budgeting. He describes the breadth of performance management and the plans undertaken from 2017 onward. He writes, 'A fairly large number of performance-based budgeting tools, ranging from presentational to direct budgeting, have been implemented in the Russian Federation over the past decade.' It is a reflection of national priorities being translated into priority projects in almost every policy area. Klimenko addresses the advantages thereof as envisaged in Russia and the organizational and managerial reforms involved, but also notes the issues involved in finding 'objective and adequate indicators for quantifying outcomes' and the complications involved in 'applying performance-based budgeting approaches because quantitative and qualitative parameters of performance need to be considered in addition to the traditional financial metrics.' Nonetheless, it seems that Russia has endorsed and is increasingly implementing the ideas behind direct performance-based budgeting.

What happens when the capacity, focus, and proper analysis of the reasons for the underperformance or over-fulfillment of performance indicators are absent is described by Nataliia Grynchuk in Chapter 9, when she presents the current situation in the country and a concrete case study on the budgeting of road and transport management in Kyiv, Ukraine. This chapter points out that it is not the introduction of performance-based budgeting as such that improves performance, but that it is all a question of 'how.' How such a system is introduced, whether it is only based on the analysis of certain socioeconomic indicators or provides comprehensive coverage of customer satisfaction with budget services, what kind of indicators are prioritized, and how many indicators are used determines whether the system results in just an increase in administrative burdens or a real improvement in public services.

Stefan Hronec comes to a similar conclusion in Chapter 10 when describing the introduction of performance-based budgeting in Slovakia. Despite high expectations, the results are disappointing. Expectations were about increasing transparency, establishing a visible link between goals and public resources, providing greater insight into the costs of service provision and the quality of service delivery, increasing the involvement of all departments in budgeting which in turn would involve employees more closely in meeting the strategic objectives, and identifying areas where most resources are placed and do not produce desired results. Stakeholders were, however, disappointed in the relationship between the budgeting process and the quality of the services provided, their participation in processing the annual budget, the practical use of the budget assessment in managing the provision of public services, and the effects on efficiency in the provision of public services. In Slovakia, municipalities seem unaware of program budgeting as a tool that improves local government performance. The authors say this is demonstrated by the deficient indicators in use. Mostly the performance indicators are nominal instead of ratios, dominated by simple output measures and lacking outcome indicators.

A more optimistic perspective, though far from perfect, is described by Maja Klun in Chapter 11. In Slovenia, a law was needed to further performance-based budgeting on the central level (performance-based budgeting has not yet been introduced on the municipal level in Slovenia). This law was passed in 2000; it stipulated that public budgets should be justified by having the funded agency or program present its objectives, strategies, and programs in an individual area, including how to coordinate these with long-term planning and budget memoranda and providing the starting points and indicators upon which the calculations and assessments of required funds are based and the expected value of the indicators after the budget year. The financial plans present the proposed work program and the annual implementation plan. A court of auditors revealed every year whether progress was made and assessed the organizational difficulties encountered as well as whether the information was sufficient to prepare budgets. After almost eight years, recommendations were made for improving performance-based budgeting. The difficulties did not result in abandoning the idea but in adding recommendations for making it start to work. These recommendations involved making one ministry the lead ministry, asking for complete commitment, inviting outside experts, implementing reform where necessary, and increasing the budget for information gathering and assessment. Although the dilemmas remained and the system was far from perfect, solutions were sought through upgrading and standardizing the information system, training staff, and extending the budgeting process to biannual budgets. Even after these changes, it remained problematic to link performance to the budget. Despite all the institutional measures taken by the Slovenian government to improve the system, Klun is skeptical about the progress made.

All these examples clearly document how difficult it is to implement effective performance-based schemes in less-developed countries (Slovakia and Slovenia are formally already part of the group of developed countries, but such 'location' is based mainly on GDP levels and not government performance). In cases of top-down and bottom-up support, the implementation capacity limits progress and chances for actual results; this is true for South Africa and maybe partly Russia and Slovenia. In a top-down (and formal) approach, as in Slovakia and Ukraine, there is no chance to implement effective performance-based financing schemes without any international support. It seems that it was mainly the World Bank that provided these countries with knowledge and templates. However, because the schemes are implemented as a 'must' for central governments and were not required on the local or organizational levels (also because of the limited implementation capacity mentioned above), the introduction of performance-based budgeting ends at the formal filling in of hundreds of tables that do not serve anyone (futility effect).

14.4 Performance-Based Financing

Two examples of problems connected with introducing direct performance-based budgeting and performance-based financing schemes are also included in the book. Both come from the CEE region, where performance-based budgeting was expected to replace the 'socialist' subjective allocation of resources from the central to the executive level. The idea is great in theory—using formulas to allocate resources to public organizations should deliver financial predictability, transparency, and objectivity—but does not work always well in practice.

Nadezhda Bobcheva describes kindergartens in Bulgaria in Chapter 12. The central government uses performance indicators for subsidizing them, and even does so in a formula-based way. However, local governments just transfer the money to the agencies using a need-based approach. In this situation, performance-based budgeting does not make much sense as a motivational tool. When municipalities do not reward better-performing kindergartens and do not punish lower-performing units, simply guaranteeing full cost coverage for all, the performance-based budgeting system loses its potential impact on the performance of kindergartens.

The example shows the importance of coherent aims between governmental layers when the budgeting is layered in intergovernmental arrangements. In such cases, it is advisable for the different spheres to have comparable ideas about the use of performance information in their budgeting.

In Chapter 13, Peter Pisar, Miroslav Sipikal, David Špaček, and Robert Jahoda describe the experiences with performance-based funding for universities in the Slovak Republic and the Czech Republic. They conclude that such performance-based budgeting—based on, for instance, the number of scholarly publications, did indeed result in an increased number of publications authored by Slovak and/or Czech researchers in higher quality journals. Although this outcome can only be judged as positive, it also had a 'perversity effect' in that less-performing universities looked for other ways to increase their number of publications, specifically in predatory journals and by creating their own publishing platforms, as seen in editing new journals and publishing monographs using their own university press. This perversity effect of performance-based budgeting based on research output is shown by the authors as reflected in the number of publications in predatory journals, which increased enormously after the introduction of this type of budgeting, while the impact factor of the publications fell. Their conclusion is that 'in some faculties the main goal of academics was not to produce the best possible research, but rather to produce outputs that would be in line with the short-term interests of their universities.' Thus, the system is far from perfect, as perversity 'effects are visible in different forms, including efforts to create personal publication platforms, publishing in predatory journals, creating citation circles, and establishing "samizdat" journals, all related to the replacement of quality with quantity.'

This chapter shows that the introduction of direct performance-based budgeting should not be taken lightly. All the side effects suggested in the public administration literature emerged in this case, and in general when a system is not properly thought through. The Czech and Slovak authorities have two options: abandon the system or adapt and improve it in order to remove such effects. The first alternative is not very good, as it might mean a return to the 'socialist' subjective allocation of funding, where the amount of allocated state subsidies is linked to patronage and not results. Choosing the second option involves an incremental process in which the remuneration of low-quality research diminishes and only high-quality publications are rewarded. This is again reflective of the fact that it takes time to establish a system in which the objectives are achieved and side effects are minimized.

14.5 Conclusions

Many dilemmas and imperfections can and do emerge in the practice of performance-based budgeting, but it is clear that none of the governments of the countries described in this book is willing to abandon the idea of performance-based budgeting. Rather, they install additional laws and regulations, audit offices to impose performance-based budgeting and to monitor whether the information is valid and reliable, and consider what can be done to make the system work.

Perhaps the incremental approach, from the introduction of a performance-based budgeting that has all three side effects, namely perversity, futility, and jeopardy effects, to a system that gradually removes these effects, is the only way to accomplish adequate performance-based budgeting—budgeting that in the end does achieve its goals of value for money, value for many, transparency, and more rational decision-making instead of political decision-making when it comes to budgeting. Perhaps the agents who are asked to provide information about their performance need the escapes—in the literature referred to as perversity and jeopardy—in order to go along with the introduction of performance-based budgeting. Perhaps the only possible next step is to expand the measurement of performance to the extent of a futility effect. Perhaps those two initial steps with all their side effects are a necessary precondition to improving the system, to changing laws, and to convincing the stakeholders that different indicators and targets are in order, that society is not served by those perverse reactions to performance measurement, and to getting support for optimizing the system. In that sense, the noted frontrunners have had their share of side effects and are in the stages of optimizing, whereas the laggard countries still face those side effects and have to go through that phase. To ask them to immediately introduce a performance-based budgeting system, without the agencies having the possibility to escape, might result in completely different side effects and even a choice to abandon the system of performance-based budgeting.

If this analysis is correct, the critics are right in saying that performance-based budgeting has negative side effects. They are, however, mistaken, if their analysis stops at that point. The side effects might well need to emerge if the system is to be improved. The specifics of the public sector, in which totally different institutions, habits, and mores exist than in the private sector, might well require such a phased approach. One has to experience the drawbacks of a system in order to optimize it even though a final optimization may be impossible.

Therefore, amidst all the theoretical cynicism surrounding the subject, there is hope at the end of the tunnel. Perhaps in the end there will be a lack of opportunities for further advancement, but the idea is too important to abandon it before the issues are addressed. The study of public administration is not based on cynicism, but on critical analytical analysis. This means that we are aware of the hurdles, but that we do all we can to overcome those hurdles, and to provide stakeholders with the tools to overcome these hurdles. Governments experimenting with performance-based budgeting that ignore the obstacles on the way cannot improve the system. When governments face these obstacles, it is the beginning of the path toward optimizing the system. Perhaps the system will never be perfect, but one should at least observe how different countries deal with the dilemmas and paradoxes before announcing to the world that it would be better to return to the classic budgeting methods. To make such an announcement would be to risk acting like the Chinese emperor mentioned in the introduction.

References

Allen, Richard, and Tommasi Daniel, eds. 2001. *Managing Public Expenditure. A Reference Book for Transition Countries*. Paris: OECD Publishing.

Lu, Elaine Yi, Zachary Mohr, and Alfred Tat-Kei Ho. 2015. Taking Stock: Assessing and Improving Performance Budgeting Theory and Practice. *Public Performance & Management Review* 38 (3): 426–458. https://doi.org/10.1080/15309576.2015.1006470.

OECD. 2014. *Budgeting Practices and Procedures in OECD Countries*. Paris: OECD Publishing.

Index

M. S. de Vries et al. (eds.), *Performance-Based Budgeting in the Public Sector*, Governance and Public Management,
https://doi.org/10.1007/978-3-030-02077-4

The manufacturer's authorised representative in the EU is Springer Nature Customer Service Centre GmbH, Europaplatz 3, 69115 Heidelberg, Germany. If you have any concerns regarding our products, please contact ProductSafety@springernature.com

Printed and bound by CPI Group (UK) Ltd, Croydon, CR0 4YY
30/09/2026
02225442-0012